The Spectacular Theatre of
Frank Joseph Galati

Related Titles

American Theatre Ensembles Volume 1
Edited by Mike Vanden Heuvel
ISBN: 978-1-3500-5154-6

Great North American Stage Directors Volumes 1-4
Edited by James Peck
ISBN: 978-1-3500-4569-9

Great North American Stage Directors Volumes 5-6
Edited by James Peck
ISBN: 978-1-3500-4602-3

Ivo van Hove: From Shakespeare to David Bowie
Edited by Susan Bennett and Sonia Massai
ISBN: 978-1-3500-3154-8

Steppenwolf Theatre Company of Chicago: In Their Own Words
John Mayer
ISBN: 978-1-4742-3945-5

The Spectacular Theatre of Frank Joseph Galati

Reshaping American Theatre in Chicago, Illinois

methuen | drama
LONDON · NEW YORK · OXFORD · NEW DELHI · SYDNEY

METHUEN DRAMA
Bloomsbury Publishing Plc
50 Bedford Square, London, WC1B 3DP, UK
1385 Broadway, New York, NY 10018, USA
29 Earlsfort Terrace, Dublin 2, Ireland

BLOOMSBURY, METHUEN DRAMA and the Methuen Drama logo are
trademarks of Bloomsbury Publishing Plc

First published in Great Britain 2022
This paperback edition published 2024

Copyright © Julie Jackson, 2022, 2024

Julie Jackson has asserted her right under the Copyright, Designs and Patents Act,
1988, to be identified as Author of this work.

For legal purposes the Acknowledgments and Disclaimers
on pp. x–xi constitute an extension of this copyright page.

Cover design: Ben Anslow
Cover image: *She Always Said, Pablo* (1987), Goodman Theatre production (Photo © Mary Griswold)

All rights reserved. No part of this publication may be reproduced or transmitted
in any form or by any means, electronic or mechanical, including photocopying,
recording, or any information storage or retrieval system, without prior permission
in writing from the publishers.

Bloomsbury Publishing Plc does not have any control over, or responsibility for,
any third-party websites referred to or in this book. All internet addresses given
in this book were correct at the time of going to press. The author and publisher
regret any inconvenience caused if addresses have changed or sites have ceased
to exist, but can accept no responsibility for any such changes.

A catalogue record for this book is available from the British Library.

Library of Congress Cataloging-in-Publication Data

Names: Jackson, Julie, 1948- author.
Title: The spectacular theatre of Frank Joseph Galati: reshaping American
theatre in Chicago, Illinois / Julie Jackson.
Description: London; New York: Methuen Drama, 2022. |
Includes bibliographical references and index. | Summary: "Frank Galati has been
a prominent American artist since the 1980s and continues to create new and innovative work for the theatre.
This book focuses on the Chicago years (1969-1996), and offers theatre historians, patrons, scholars, and
students a unique source of primary information about a pivotal figure in a significant era of American theatre.
It features exclusive interviews with Galati, selections from his unpublished notes and
speeches, the observations of colleagues on his rehearsal process, and in-depth case studies of productions written,
conceived, and directed by Galati, including The Grapes of Wrath (1988-90)"– Provided by publisher.
Identifiers: LCCN 2021060132 (print) | LCCN 2021060133 (ebook) | ISBN 9781350286214 (hardback) |
ISBN 9781350286252 (paperback) | ISBN 9781350286221 (epub) | ISBN 9781350286238 (ebook)
Subjects: LCSH: Galati, Frank. | Galati, Frank–Criticism and interpretation. | Northwestern University
(Evanston, Ill.)–Faculty–Biography. | Theatrical producers and directors–United States–Biography. | Dramatists,
American–20th century–Biography. | Theater–Production and direction–Illinois–Chicago–History–20th century.
Classification: LCC PN2287.G344 J33 2022 (print) |
LCC PN2287.G344 (ebook) | DDC 792.02/33092 [B]–dc23/eng/20220331
LC record available at https://lccn.loc.gov/2021060132
LC ebook record available at https://lccn.loc.gov/2021060133

ISBN: HB: 978-1-3502-8621-4
PB: 978-1-3502-8625-2
ePDF: 978-1-3502-8623-8
eBook: 978-1-3502-8622-1

Typeset by RefineCatch Limited, Bungay, Suffolk

To find out more about our authors and books visit www.bloomsbury.com
and sign up for our newsletters.

Dedication

In memory of absent friends and colleagues who helped make Chicago off-Loop theatre the best profession in the world.

Tommy Biscotto 1947–1984
J Pat Miller 1945–1985
David Emmons 1952–1986
James O'Reilly 1927–1990
Michael Merritt 1945–1992
Larry Sloan 1960–1995
John Paoletti 1944–1996
Michael Maggio 1951–2000
Glenna Syse 1928–2001
Marji Bank 1923–2006
Ralph Lane 1928 –2006
Fred Solari 1951–2006
Paul Sills 1927–2008
Bernie Sahlins 1922–2013
Bob Sickinger 1927–2013

Joyce Sloan 1927–2013
Sheldon Patinkin 1935–2014
Meshach Taylor 1947–2014
Roberta Custer 1944–2015
Fred Katz, 1935–2015
Richard Fire 1945–2015
Tom Towles 1950–2015
Glenne Hedley 1955–2017
Martha Lavey 1957–2017
John Mahoney 1940–2018
Malcolm Ewen 1975–2019
Rev. James Shiflett 1930–2019
Stuart Gordon 1947–2020
Bradley Mott 1956–2020
Jack Wallace 1933–2020
Bill Norris 1946–2021

Johnny Mohrlein 1947–2021
Richard Christiansen 1931-2022

Contents

List of Illustrations	viii
Acknowledgments	x
Disclaimers	xii
Author's Preface	xiii
Introduction: A Pivotal Figure in a Stagestruck Town, 1969–1996	1

Part 1   The Rise of Off-Loop Theatre: Frank Galati and the Chicago Style

Introduction to Part 1	15
1 Theatre Chicago Style: Second to None	19
2 One Who was Working: 1969–1986	41
3 The Hottest Theatre Artist in Chicago	65

Part 2   Staging Stein and Steinbeck: Two Case Studies

Introduction to Part 2	91
4 A Cubist Dramaturgy: *She Always Said, Pablo*	95
5 The Telling Not the Tale: *The Grapes of Wrath*	118

Part 3   Backstage Process and Onstage Themes: Maternal Projects

Introduction to Part 3	145
6 Rehearsing Ensemble: Working All Together All the Time	149
7 Mise-en-scène as Activism: Galati's Dangerous Women	172

Epilogue	199
Bibliography	203
Index	207

Illustrations

1. Writer and director Frank Galati speaks of the making of *Knoxville* at Asolo Repertory Theatre in February 2019. *Sarasota Herald-Tribune.* Staff photo / Dan Wagner — 10
2. Barbara Robertson center, Maria Racossa far right. Woodscock Music Festival production of *Strider*, 1981. Courtesy of the photographer. Photo by Lisa Howe-Ebright — 58
3. BJ Jones (seated) and Jo Lauck. *Division Street*, New Broadway Theatre, 1981. Courtesy of BJ Jones. Photo by Mary Griswold — 60
4. Martha Lavy, Steppenwolf Theatre production of *Aunt Dan and Lemon*, 1987. Courtesy of the photographer. Photo by Lisa Howe-Ebright — 75
5. Margi Bank, Goodman Theatre production of *She Always Said, Pablo,* 1987. Courtesy of the photographer. Photo by Mary Griswold — 107
6. Left to right: Marji Bank, Larry Russo, Carman Pelton, and Susan Nussbaum. Goodman Theatre production of *She Always Said, Pablo*, 1987. Courtesy of the photographer. Photo by Mary Griswold — 114
7. From Ludwig Wittgenstein's *Philosophical Investigations* (1953) — 119
8. Left to right: Gary Sinise, Jim True, and Jeff Perry. Steppenwolf Theatre production of *The Grapes of Wrath*, 1990. Courtesy of the Steppenwolf Theatre Company. Photo by Paul Cunningham — 129
9. Troupe members of the Steppenwolf Theatre Company performing a stage adaptation of John Steinbeck's *The Grapes of Wrath* at the Royal George Theatre. Photo by Steve Kagan/Getty Images — 133
10. Glenne Headly, 1987. Courtesy of the Headly Estate — 175
11. Larry Russo and Susan Nussbaum, Goodman Theatre of *She Always Said, Pablo*, 1987. Courtesy of the photographer. Photo by Mary Griswold — 178
12. Gary Sinise and Lois Smith, Steppenwolf Theatre production of *The Grapes of Wrath*, 1990. Photo by Paul Cunningham — 179

13 Left to right: Martha Lavey, Linda Emond, Sally Murphy,
and John Hutton in the Goodman Theatre production of
The Winter's Tale, 1990. Courtesy of Virgil Johnson.
Photo by Steve Leonard   183
14 Cherry Jones, Goodman Theatre production of *The Good
Person of Setzuan,* 1992. Courtesy of the Goodman Theatre.
Photo by Charles Osgood   187
15 Poster for the Roundabout Theatre production of
The Glass Menagerie, 1994. Courtesy of the artist, Scott McKowen   190

Acknowledgments

It took a village to write this book. There would be nothing to say without the insight and generosity of the theatre patrons, artists, and producers who granted me their time in formal interviews and informal conversation, including Lynn Aherns, Tom Alino, Peter Amster, Stafford Arima, Mary Badger, Cheryl Lynn Bruce, Kevin Chamberlin, Jim Corti, Paul Edwards, Sara Freeman, Mary Griswold, Wendall Harrington, Mark Jacoby, Virgil Johnson, BJ Jones, Mary Elizabeth Burke Kennedy, Linda Kimbrough, Ruth Landis, Martha Lavey, Michael Maggio, Marin Mazzie, Michael Merritt, John Mohrlein, Susan Nussbaum, Sheldon Patinkin, Bill Pullinsi, Rondi Reed, Ann Reinking, Kevin Rigdon, Barbara Robertson, Larry Russo, Norma Saldivar, Steve Scott, Lois Smith, and Jessica Thebus. I am indebted to the brilliant journalists and arts reporters who are quoted in this book, particularly Richard Christiansen (*Chicago Tribune*), Glenna Syse (*Chicago Sun Times*), Hedy Weiss (*Chicago Sun Times*), Jonathan Abarbanel (*Windy City Times*), and Bill Williams (*Chicago Reader*). Numerous friends and readers have helped save me from myself, particularly Sally Banes, Franny Clarkson, Bryan Conger, Rachel Kraft, Keith Cushman, Sara Freeman, Jim Lane, Marti Lyons, and Sheldon Patinkin.

I am indebted to the brilliant and generous photographers who allowed me to include their work: Paul Cunningham, Mary Griswold, Lisa Howe-Ebright, Charles Osbourn, and Dan Rest. Special thanks to the artist Scott McKowen for permission to use his stunning poster for *The Glass Menagerie* and for providing the high-resolution scan included in this book. In the midst of a pandemic, Denise Schneider (Goodman Theatre) and Madeline Long (Steppenwolf Theatre) took the time to locate rare and invaluable production photos for me. Many thanks to Sarah Zimmerman and the staff at the Chicago Public Library, Harold Washington Center Special Collections for their remarkable work in preserving the history of Chicago Theatre and to the staff of the Northwestern University, McCormick Library of Special Collections for their help with Galati's personal archives. Many thanks to Tere Zimmerman and her son Evan for their tech wizardry and to my editors at Methuen Drama, Ella Wilson and Lara Bateman.

And, of course, Frank. This book is as much by Frank Galati as about him. He allowed me untold hours of stimulating conversation, personal interviews, and fabulous stories as well as unfettered access to his extensive private archives. I was invited into his classroom at Northwestern University and given access to the cast, rehearsal period, and previews of three major Chicago productions: *Morning Star* by Sylvia Regan, Steppenwolf Theatre,1999; *Valparaiso* by Don DeLillo, Steppenwolf Theatre 2000; the Kander and Ebb musical *The Visit*, Goodman Theatre, September 2001. Frank made it possible for me to see multiple previews and performances of his Chicago and New York productions between 1999 and 2005. It was a blast.

Last but far from least, I want to acknowledge my students at Columbia College, Indiana University Northwest, and Marshall University. If they learned half as much from me as I learned from them, I was a good teacher.

Sections in Chapters 1–5 expand and extend research published in my 2017 *Theatre History Studies* article "Not Just Rock 'n' Roll: Chicago Theatre, 1984–1990" (volume 36: pp. 75–111) and my 2005 *Theatre Topics* article "Theatrical Space and Place in the Presentational Aesthetic of Director Frank Galati" (volume 15, Number 2, pp. 131–148).

Additional information about the creative team and staff for the productions mentioned in this book and additional production photos are available at spectaculartheatre.net.

Disclaimers

Unless otherwise noted, undocumented quotations attributed to Frank Galati are taken from a series of conversations and interviews conducted with the author between 1999 and 2006.

Undocumented quotations attributed to Galati's colleagues and collaborators are taken from conversations and personal interviews conducted between 1999 and 2018.

Punctuation and emphasis in quotations taken from Galati's speech manuscripts appear as written in the original document.

Unless otherwise indicated, stage right and stage left refer to the point of view from the audience.

Every effort has been made to identify and credit the photographer and source of the images that appear in this book.

The author and publisher gratefully acknowledge the permission granted to reproduce the copyright material in this book.

Every effort has been made to trace copyright holders and to obtain their permission for the use of copyright material. However, if any have been inadvertently overlooked, the publishers will be pleased, if notified of any omissions, to make the necessary arrangement at the first opportunity.

The third party copyrighted material displayed in the pages of this book are done so on the basis of "fair dealing for the purposes of criticism and review" or "fair use for the purposes of teaching, criticism, scholarship or research" only in accordance with international copyright laws, and is not intended to infringe upon the ownership rights of the original owners.

Author's Preface

In 1968 Norman D. Dietz published a slim volume entitled *Fables & Vaudevilles & Plays: Theatre More or Less at Random*. Dietz is now in his nineties and a renowned narrator of recorded books but in the late 1960s, he was a young man with a passionate belief in the healing power of theatre. "When we play together," he wrote in his introduction,

> what we are really doing is celebrating. We are making holy whoopee about what it means, as we see it, to be human, to be alive together in a world full of strangers ... And in our celebrating, we are, almost inadvertently, providing, for ourselves and for one another, that occasion for community, which is the theatre's chief, if infrequent, contribution to the common life of man.[1]

Dietz's ebullient declaration was appropriate to the times and to the Chicago theatre scene where I first met and worked with Frank Galati. The theatre artists and artisans who found their way to the Windy City in the 1970s were making a different sort of theatre there, not avant-garde or politically motivated but a theatre with explosive energy and palpable immediacy, a very theatrical theatre as Frank would say—a theatre that could only be theatre.

Chicago theatre was conceived in those early days as an irreverent, immediate, and exuberant event intended to generate enough interest and income to make a living for its makers—failing that, enough to pull another show together. Nobody with any sense expected to make it big. In those days, there was no big to make, not in Chicago. Nonetheless, the first wave of freshly minted midwestern MFA's flocked to Chicago in untold numbers. Our expectations were defined by the idealism, ensemble experience, and make-do budgets of fledging academic theatre programs. Day jobs were plentiful, the press was enthusiastic, and friends were already there or on their way. We were children of the sixties who, like Dietz, had a raucously good time providing occasions for community in abandoned storefronts, neighborhood bars, church basements, and a former bowling alley. If we weren't actually making holy whoopee, it was surely the next best thing.

In 1976, Frank was a professor of literature in the Department of Speech at Northwestern University and already celebrated in the city as a gifted actor and rising stage director. I was an untried and unknown MFA but Dennis Zacek, artistic director of the Victory Gardens Theatre, took a chance and hired me to design costumes for *June Moon*, a Depression Era comedy by George S. Kaufman and Ring Lardner. My budget for 20 period costumes was $200.00. I scored a pair of vintage socks with clocks from a thrift store bin for actor John Mohrlein and gave him a borrowed pair of elasticated sock garters to hold them up. Mohrlein, an actor who never let a good "bit" go unbitten, planted his foot on the seat of a downstage chair in the first act and pulled up his pant leg to fiddle with the garter as he pondered a problem. The audience loved it. He was one of the co-producers of Novel Ventures, a new independent production company Frank was involved with and Frank came to see John in the Victory Gardens show. The following week, I was hired to design costumes for his adaptation of Stanley Elkin's comic masterpiece *The Dick Gibson Show*, the first Novel Ventures production.

Dick Gibson was a breakthrough for both of us. Elkin had been skeptical about the project but he came to see the show and loved it. Later, some people in Hollywood optioned his novel, *The Living End* and asked him to write the screenplay. "Stanley didn't want to," explained Frank, "but he'd just seen our show and he recommended me." That would be the first of many commissioned screenplays for Frank. After *Dick Gibson* opened, I found steady design work in the Chicago area and never had to show my portfolio again. The following year, Sheldon Patinkin hired me as a Resident Artist and instructor in the theatre program at Columbia College, a private fine and performing arts school in the Chicago Loop. The school didn't pay well but the job included comprehensive health insurance and Sheldon encouraged us to accept freelance work whenever it was available. I was among the many composers, stage managers, actors, designers, and directors who were able to establish freelance careers in the city because of the small but reliable salary and all-important benefits provided by Columbia College.

In those days, Chicago was truly an exciting and perhaps a unique place to be a theatre maker or theatregoer. I got in the habit of watching and listening to the audience and during intermission, I'd talk to complete strangers about what they thought and how they felt about the show. No one ever refused to talk to me or even seemed put out by my approach. I also formed a lifelong habit of watching myself watch theatre and took mental snapshots of moments that moved me, often not knowing why I was moved. Many of these "snapshots" appear in this book.

By my reckoning, theatre does not exist in the absence of an audience and we, the audience, know when theatre makers understand that we are in fact, what it's all about. The scrappy productions mounted in Chicago during the mid-1970s often missed or overreached the mark but even so, the audience applauded with enthusiasm and returned for more because they felt valued by performers who engaged, assaulted, confronted, comforted, and confounded them in the shared space of the theatre—none more so than Frank Galati. Every time he walked on the stage as an actor and later, when he directed a company onto the stage, he loved the audience with his entire being and the audience loved him right back. Even when they didn't like or understand what he was doing, even when he made them flinch or frown or roll their eyes—but especially when he made them laugh—they loved him.

I left Chicago in 1996 to complete a PhD in theatre and drama at the University of Wisconsin-Madison. As a graduate student and later as a professor, I felt once again that it was possible to make holy whoopie about what it is to be alive together in a world full of strangers. My dissertation advisor, the inimitable Sally Banes, urged me to write about Frank and the Chicago style of the 1980s and I thank her for it. But for a very long time, I didn't know how to write what I most wanted to write about. How do you write about loving the audience? In Frank's theatrical world, collaboration is more important than ownership, process is valued over product, awareness over commentary, presence over imitation, and revelation over edification. In the waning years of the twentieth century, I was not sure how or to whom an account, much less my critique of collaboration, awareness, presence, process, and revelation in the theatre would be useful.

The contemporary theorists and philosophers as well as the brilliant historians and critics I read or worked with in graduate school opened a new world for me. Nonetheless, it was my students, one generation after another at Indiana University Northwest and then at Marshall University, who validated my interests, not by what they did or said but by who they are and what they value. Over the past twenty years, undergraduates—no matter what we try to teach them—are increasingly more interested in what a play can do or be in the world than what it is when nobody's at home. Until recently, undergraduate analysis of cause-and-effect linkage was unlikely to consider performance as an action with real-world consequences. But in 2019, a chemistry major submitted a performance critique that traced the arc of her own thoughts and emotions scene by scene as she watched a university production of *The Curious Incident of The Dog in the Night-Time*. Her essay began, "What I will remember most about this production is that I was there." She got an A. A few years ago, I watched a faculty member use the phrase "I didn't believe you" in the critique of a high school student's scene work. The young Appalachian woman on stage was clearly confused and said, "Of course not. That would be silly." When her critic was silent—apparently struck dumb—she explained without a trace of irony, "I was acting." It seemed to me that in all innocence, she had said something profound.

Recent generations of theatre majors are increasingly impatient with conventional casting, wary of aesthetic partitions, and keenly aware of bias and assumed privilege embedded in a text. Those in search of fame and fortune seek it elsewhere. Those who stay value work that allows them a sense of community, agency, and responsibility. They are too often disappointed. Nonetheless, in these students I see a paradigm shift in how we think about and enjoy the arts and perhaps, how theatre will be made in the twenty-first century. I also see a remarkable kinship between recent generations and Frank Galati. Maybe I'm seeing what I want or hope to see. Nonetheless, I believe that anyone who loves the theatre for what it is and what it could be is indebted to and will find validation in the joy, intelligence, and commitment that infuse his life's work: the telling of tales in a room full of strangers.

Julie Jackson
August 2021

Note

1   Norman D. Dietz, *Fables & Vaudevilles & Plays; Theatre More or Less at Random* (Richmond, VA: John Knox Press, 1968), a ii.

Introduction: A Pivotal Figure in a Stagestruck Town, 1969–1996

Unlike the iconic Chicago hotdog (celery salt, tomato slice, and piccalilli required) and gooey inch-thick pizza, Chicago theatre is a moving target—consistently vibrant, perpetually evolving, and irrepressibly eclectic. However, between 1969 and 1996, historic and economic forces coalesced in a distinct style of theatrical production in Chicago, Illinois. There were a great many iterations of the Chicago style in that era but Frank Galati's boundless energy, artistic inclinations, and physical presence—his personal qualities, values, and convictions—touched them all. Galati is one of Chicago's own, born, raised, and educated in the city's environs. If he wasn't already in Chicago in 1969, he would have very likely found his way there. But if he hadn't, Chicago theatre would have taken on a very different aspect and trajectory. In 1993, Daniel Selznick wrote, "Greeting him in an Evanston coffee shop, it is hard to believe that this tall, bearish, unassuming man is a pivotal figure in the evolution of theater in any stage-struck town."[1] Between 1969 and 1996, Galati was engaged at every level of the evolution and dissemination of the influential theatrical style that emerged in Chicago during that era, a style he helped shape even as he was shaped by it. He was, without a doubt, a pivotal figure in that stage-struck town.

By 1989, Chicago was widely perceived as ground zero for the next generation of significant innovation in American theatre. By the end of the twentieth century, the hallmarks of the Chicago style had surfaced in or been assimilated by not-for-profit and university theatres across the United States. By the second decade of the twenty-first century, theatre patrons were as likely to encounter ensemble driven, frankly theatrical audience-oriented storytelling on Broadway (*Natasha, Pierre, and the Great Comet of 1812*, 2012) as in Chicago and just as likely to encounter the conventions of twentieth-century realism at the Steppenwolf Theatre (*Between Riverside and Crazy*, 2016). Nonetheless, what Chicago-based theatre makers offered their audience in the last quarter of the twentieth century was not so much a new kind of theatre as a new kind of experience in the theatre. They were not and did not claim to be ahead of their time. They were, however, very much of their time, perhaps more so than any other American theatre center of the period.

Frank Galati is an extraordinarily prolific American theatre director, author, actor, and educator. Since 1972, he has worked in palatial auditoriums and storefront theaters, in prestigious American opera houses, universities and museums, on and off Broadway, and at major regional institutions on large stages and small. He has adapted non-dramatic literature for the stage, television, and Hollywood filmmakers. In 1972, he accepted a tenure track position in oral interpretation at Northwestern University, an academic program that would evolve into the university's groundbreaking Department of Performance Studies. He retired Professor Emeritus in 2006. For nearly forty years, he and his faculty peers seeded the city with emergent artists attuned to the ideas, presentational sensibility, and staging innovations of literature in performance. Galati took full advantage of the opportunity to investigate and critique new ways of telling old stories in Northwestern's laboratory setting. Within a decade of his hire, he would become a subject as well as a student and professor of his academic discipline.

Galati's theatre is spectacular in the Aristotelian sense, that is, having to do with all elements of the tragedy that contribute to sensory effects—voice, gesture, performance, costume, mask, music, anything that appeals to the physical senses. In Aristotle's analysis, spectacle functions as an emotional trigger or illustration and is the least important component of tragedy because it is not controlled by the poet, whose proper medium is words—logos. However, twentieth-century post-modern culture lost faith in the link between authenticity and logos. The poet's words, grown old and arthritic through endless repetition, seemed little more than empty rhetoric. Galati is a professor of literature whose overarching goal as an artist is to retrieve and reinvigorate the poet's voice. To this end, he deploys the full panoply of sensor effect unique to the theatre. This is not a knack for illustration but a genuine artistic voice embedded in the presentation of a tale already told. It is as a show-man that Galati is most notably an artist, a thinker, and an intellectual provocateur.

Galati's spectacular theatre depends on what Bert O. States describes as "a self-conscious theatricality that makes us forget we are in a theatre almost as soon as it reminds us that we are."[2] "Theatricality" is a slippery term in academic circles but is not so troublesome for theatre-makers, for whom it generally means an open acknowledgment of the medium in which they work. Playwright/actor Robert Bethune equates theatricality to the actor's mindfulness of the spectator's presence in the theatre. "That's the greatest theatricality of all" he exclaims, "to remember and act upon the fact that the performer and the audience, the preparer and the partaker share the same space and time and air together."[3] Galati would agree. In his estimation, "the best acting incorporates the energies of the spectator. In really good acting, the spectator fills the space, increases and raises the stakes for the actor." For most of the twentieth century, the theatrical self-awareness so valued by Bethune and Galati was scorned by mainstream theatre artists, teachers, patrons, and critics. In 1977, the influential New York critic Walter Kerr bemoaned the dangerous "invasion of theatricality" on and off Broadway, fare that abandoned climatic structure and psychological development in favor of spectacular presentation.[4] To Kerr, the trend toward theatricality and spectacle was a corruption of the artful, literary based drama that had dominated the American stage for generations. But unlike film and video, theatre—even realist theatre—takes place in the exchange between a performance and its audience. The unique dynamics and potential efficacy of this exchange are the primary focus of Galati's stagecraft.

His spectacular theatricality depends on an awareness of the theatrical frame. He believes that the frame "allows us to look at different possibilities, to ask different questions."

> You walk around the neighborhood and you look but you don't see the mailboxes. I mean, you do, but you dispense with them. The applications of that to conventions of theatrical space and performance are enormously interesting because the convention always has to be refreshed in order for it to be present, in order for you to know it's there even when it obviously is. The proscenium itself, the configuration of the theatre, all the ways in which we kind of jolt the familiar so it's no longer habitual, it's something. And it's ours. It belongs to the theater, but the proscenium has been conflated into realism because it got invisible. We stopped and were encouraged to stop seeing the frame around the pictures.

Galati's staging is not bereft of illusion and his dramaturgy depends on a compelling naturalism in performance. Even so, he takes care to refresh the spectator's awareness of the theatrical frame by calling on the unsolvable conundrum described by Joseph Roach as "the simultaneous experience of truth and illusion, presence and absence, face and mask."[5] Galati believes that this uniquely theatrical paradox allows us to see ourselves seeing what the mind has chosen to see. He explained, "perception, what we see, is a choice, a thing we *do*. What and how we know a thing in the world is the heart of who we are—the secret heart." States points out that with "real running water something indisputably real leaks out of the illusion."[6] When "something indisputably real leaks out" of Galati's stage illusion as it is intended to do, we are called on to see ourselves seeing and in crucial moments, to see beyond expectation and conditioning.

The story of his career runs remarkably parallel to and often anticipates artistic, social, and economic developments that amount to a cultural sea change in twentieth-century theatre production and spectatorship, including a turn toward self-conscious theatricality, empowered ensemble collaboration, and an ongoing reckoning with pervasive stereotypes largely unchallenged in realist drama. The story of Galati's career is, as Jason Loewith points out in a 2012 profile, "in large part the story of Chicago theatre's rise."[7] After 1986, Galati participated in annual season planning for Chicago's two premiere regional houses, the venerable Goodman Theatre and the increasingly famous upstart acting company, the Steppenwolf Ensemble. Between 1985 and 1995, he directed, wrote, or performed in ten productions for the Goodman and an equal number for the Steppenwolf, often staging his original adaptations of non-dramatic work. He directed multiple productions at Chicago Opera Theatre and oversaw the development and staging of a new opera for the Lyric Opera Center, the Lyric's incubator for emergent artists. Until 1988, he continued to accept significant stage roles when he could fit them in his demanding academic schedule. By the late 1980s Chicago theatre was hot and Galati's career was on fire.

Part I: The Rise of Off-Loop Theatre: Frank Galati and the Chicago Style

In a 1985 feature article entitled "Chicago Theatre: Second to None," *Christian Science Monitor* critic Hilary DeVries noted the recent achievements of Chicago-based theatre. He writes, "In seeking an explanation for such singular success, critics point to a unique production style – an invigorating blend of youthful energy and hip theatricality, which marries rock-and-roll rhythms with controversial topics and a no-holds-barred acting technique."[8] Galati was prominent among the pioneers of Chicago theatre who abandoned the implicit voyeurism of realist convention in favor of a riveting acting technique that acknowledged the presence of an audience in the shared space of the theatre. As an actor, a director, and the author of innovative stage adaptations, he was able to bind the city's indigenous in-your-face acting style to his own spectacular theatricality in cohesive productions with intellectual power and stunning emotional impact. The theatre in which Galati matured as an artist did not feature direct audience address, mandatory physical interaction, or artless spontaneity. It was, however, the kind of theatre that knows and shows itself to be theatre.

Before Galati became a revered professor of literature in performance at Northwestern, he completed BA, MA, and PhD degrees in the university's interpretation program. Interpretation, or as it was known to pre-WWII practitioners, oral interpretation is the study of non-dramatic literature through the selection and performance of verbatim passages of non-dramatic text. At Northwestern, he studied with and was mentored by two extraordinary teachers, Wallace Bacon and Robert Breen. "The most important element in my development," he explained with obvious conviction, "was the years that I spent experiencing the criticism of performances in these classes with these great teachers." He was excited and validated by the lack of pretense in the chamber theatre technique developed by Breen. Breen's technique for the adaptation of non-dramatic literature entailed a phenomenological shift in mode from the written to the spoken word intended to sustain and refresh the original author's voice and presence in performance. "What I learned from Breen," he explained in 1993, "led directly to *The Grapes of Wrath*." What he learned, he continued, was to "open the equation."

> The naturalistic equation is closed, that is, the observer of the representation is closed off from its operations. Presentation opens the equation so there is a direct relationship in both manner and substance between the representation and its observer. When the equation is open rather than closed, the mechanisms of illusion are in full view and the relationship between spectacle and spectator is defined by connection and interaction rather than separation.

"Performance," writes Bernard Beckerman, "alerts us to what the performer does … In a simple sense, it stresses the doing of the show while 'presentation' stresses the giving of it."[9] Galati's bailiwick as a director and author is the giving of the story but this giving is compromised if the doing of it—the performance—is poorly executed. On Chicago's off-Loop stages, his spectacular presentation was countered and completed by actors and designers who learned their trade in the city's intimate performance spaces, on stage and in the presence of an audience. In Chicago, the audience was unquestionably in a theatre and more often than not, the theatre was an exciting place to be precisely because it was a theatre.

Part II: Two Case Studies: Staging Stein and Steinbeck

Robert Breen described chamber theatre as a way of "novelizing" the stage. Galati embraced his mentor's technique and expanded it by calling on the visual, aural, and kinesthetic qualities of the stage—Aristotle's spectacle—to "theatricalize" the novel. If there is a "play" to be found in a work of non-dramatic literature, he will find it. But just as he "sees" the play in a novel, it is necessary to "see" theatrical space and an implicit acknowledgement of the audience written into his stage adaptations of non-dramatic literature. His playscripts no less than his staging take full advantage of the theatre's paradoxical copresence of real and fake, truth and illusion, presence and absence. His published scripts will be successfully produced and interpreted in new and compelling ways long after his achievements as a director are the stuff of memory. His staging is unique to him and not intended for resurrection. However, the mechanics and consequence of the conceptual exchange between performance and audience embedded in his text is manifest in his stagecraft which is available for close observation and critique. In addition, his published scripts were completed in production and are in many ways a product of it. For now, or at least for me, Galati's writing and stagecraft inform and complete each other in ways that are best understood in tandem. *She Always Said, Pablo* (Goodman Theatre 1987, Lincoln Center 1990) and *The Grapes of Wrath* (Steppenwolf Theatre 1987, La Jolla and London 1988, New York 1990) were conceived, written, and directed by Galati. The pleasure as well as the efficacy of both productions depended on spectacular effect and simultaneous frames of illusion and reality.

In his Cubist vaudeville *She Always Said, Pablo*, "She" is Gertrude Stein and Pablo is of course, Picasso. *Pablo* was the first of Galati's productions to be videotaped for the New York Public Library for the Performing Arts, Billy Rose Collection. It was an artistic as well as a professional breakthrough for the director because in this production the scaffolding of his spectacular theatricality was fully formed and in full view. The object of Cubist art is perception itself, not what we see but how we see. In this, Galati has shown himself to be a latter-day Cubist and his work is best, perhaps only understood in the terms, strategies, and agenda introduced by the Cubists themselves. Like Stein and Picasso, he depends on spatial and kinesthetic intelligence rather than linguistic reasoning and causal logic to make his point. Richard Axsom explains that in Cubism, "Normative, everyday knowing is thrown off guard. The tendency towards the stabilization of information is thwarted.... In this particular presentation of the everyday, the attempt is made to prevent congealing points of view and to maintain an open-ended attentiveness to the world which is forever amenable by new experience."[10] Like Stein and Picasso, Galati demands an open-ended attentiveness that "warns us against premature foreclosures."[11] *She Always Said, Pablo* asked the audience to look and look again. In dissociating attention from prior experience and conventional code, Stein, Picasso, and Galati each in their own way, positions "attentiveness" as an act of subversion.

"I hate pretending," Galati admitted somewhat ruefully. "I know that sounds odd coming from me of all people, but in *The Grapes of Wrath* we wanted to not lie. It wasn't necessary, ever, because the stage is always a stage and the story is always a story." Galati wrote the original draft for *The Grapes of Wrath* in January of 1987, less than two months before he went into rehearsal for *She Always Said, Pablo* at the Goodman Theatre. Steinbeck's rustic, muckraking novel is a far cry from Stein's elliptical prose and Picasso's revolutionary art but the phenomenological operations of Galati's script and mise-en-scène for *Grapes of Wrath* were rooted in a Cubist conception of reality as a unified field in which presence is manifold and ambiguous. "To yield not to the play as a play but to the illusion," writes Howard Pearce, is to "trivialize the theatre event."[12] Eugene O'Neil's *Long Day's Journey into Night* is, for example, not a play about a journey. It is a journey, an ordeal meant to be undertaken in the shared space of the theatre. *Grapes of Wrath* was conceived, in Galati's words, as "a dynamic process of communication in which the spectators are vitally implicated." He underscored perception as a willful and decisive act for which the individual spectator was obliged to take some share of responsibility. In order to achieve this end, he and his collaborators encouraged the audience to resist the compelling illusion they presented on stage and yield instead to the immediacy of the theatre event and the underlying truth of Steinbeck's resolve.

Part III: Backstage Process and Onstage Themes: Maternal Projects

In 1985, DeVries reported that "interviews with actors, playwrights, and artistic directors here reveal that the two most prized commodities within the Chicago theater scene are a sense of community and the opportunity to take artistic risks."[13] Galati is known among peers as a builder and shaper of empowered ensemble theatre. A strong directional presence is evident in all his productions but the final product is shaped in the process of its making and by its makers rather than predetermined by a single artist's sensibility. This entails risk for everyone involved. More than one production has spiraled out of his embrace because the ensemble failed to coalesce. However, the fact that his commitment to ensemble is vulnerable to disruption and failure begs the question of why and how the highly improbable collaboration he seeks works at all, which it does. When he is good, he is very, very good. Without overemphasizing the man's unique and admittedly charismatic presence, the central and organizing question addressed in Chapter 6 is: how can a director authorize creative collaboration and an open-ended journey of discovery while maintaining a personal voice in the process and quality control over the final product?

Galati's demeanor as a director is a noticeable departure from the popular conception of the stage director as a paternal decision-maker and father figure. Working through preproduction and rehearsals, he demonstrates competencies, values, and qualities culturally defined and generally denigrated as female and maternal: vulnerability, an appreciation of beauty, resourceful and ready adaptation to context and need, a capacity for empathy and, most important, mutuality. The challenge to establish and participate in viable mutuality by loving another while maintaining one's sense of self as separate from the other is a recurring leitmotif in his work on stage as well as behind the scenes. Maternal characters, issues, challenges, and interests are everywhere present in his productions. In his choice of material, casting, and staging, Galati's mise-en-scène honors the idiosyncratic voices of female artists and the language and visual literacy intrinsic to the stories his female protagonists want and need to tell. In this, he is atypical of his Chicago peers. Chapter 7 considers seven of the many productions initiated by Galati between 1986 and 1996 that featured female protagonists who told the truth of their own bodies and experience—dangerous women—and mothers who either fulfill their social role without sacrificing full personhood for themselves and their children or, overcome by desperation and betrayal, fail to do so, and fail gloriously.

The Paradoxical Professor

In a 1995 feature for *American Theatre*, John Dillon tagged Galati "The Paradoxical Professor."[14] The title suited him on multiple levels and it stuck. His staging is best known for a paradoxical juxtaposition of compelling naturalism and spectacular artifice. However, his demeanor, reputation, and personal qualities are no less paradoxical than his staging. He is a showman with an activist's agenda and an intellectual with an artist's eye. He is a profoundly learned man with a kinesthetic sense of the actor's craft and a creative artist with a critic's cutting sensibility. He is the most open and the most private of men. He delivers specific and executable directives in soaring metaphorical imagery and makes genuinely inspiring speeches laden with meticulous dramaturgical research. He is a tender caretaker and an unrelenting task master who expects as good as he gives. He is a bono fide intellectual and a shameless entertainer, a speech maker, a clown and a bit of a mystic, a genial teddy bear and a ferocious defender of art, justice, and the outsider. He is a complex person with surprisingly few complications. These paradoxical qualities permeate the interviews and conversations we shared between 1999 and 2006. They are evident in the rehearsals I observed, in published interviews, and in his public speeches, his written and spoken comments to colleagues, and in the commentary of collaborators and students. Paradox can reveal a hidden or unexpected truth that defies resolution—a fitting characterization for an artist who, while approaching his eighties, is still becoming.

In 2001, Galati returned to the Goodman Theatre after a six-year hiatus to direct the world premiere of *The Visit*, a new musical based on Fredrick Durrenmatt's play. It was the last collaboration of composer John Kander and lyricist Fred Ebb, who died in 2004. On the second day of dance rehearsal, choreographer Ann Reinking told a story about tracking a lion on an African safari. They waited for several days before their guide located tracks with a high degree of integrity. This, he said, was a matter of life or death because his ability to read the beast's speed, nature and, most important, its intent depended on the definition—the integrity—of its footprint. The dancer's footprint, she told the company, should have a similar integrity. In the following pages, I call on detail and witness to maintain the integrity of Galati's footprint. For all the twists and turns of his labyrinthine path, there are no dead ends, no side alleys. He is as he began, a showman and a storyteller. I approach his showmanship and storytelling from multiple angles, beginning with his role in Chicago's nascent theatre scene and the heady 1986–87 season in which his position as a pivotal figure in a pivotal theatre town was confirmed. In Part II, I trace the realization of two of his most well-known and vexing productions and in Part III, consider his style of working in preproduction collaborations and the remarkable vitality of the complex and dangerous women who inhabit his stage world.

Robert Frost's pithy couplet, "We dance around in a ring and suppose/but the secret sits in the middle and knows" is an appropriate introduction to the study of theatre history and text analysis. In the beginning of this project, I thought of Galati as a secret and my research as a dance. That was a mistake. He is not a secret. He's a dancer who dances and supposes along with the rest of us. Nearing eighty, his dancing and supposing is far from over. In spring of 2022, he will direct the world premiere of *Knoxville*, a new musical by Stephen Flaherty and Lynn Aherns, with whom he collaborated on *Ragtime* and *Seussical the Musical* as well as other projects. However, this will be the first time in his long and illustrious career that he directs his own stage adaptation of a non-dramatic book for a large-scale commercial musical—and *Knoxville* is very much a book musical. Based on James Agee's Pulitzer Prize-winning novel, *A Death in the Family* published in 1957, it is the coming-of-age story of the boy who will grow up to write it, James Agee and perhaps in some ways, Galati as well. The production will premiere at the Asolo Repertory Theatre in Sarasota, Florida on April 23, 2022. It may open and close with fanfare but little notice. It may move to Broadway and draw rave reviews or pans. It may travel the world or die on the vine. No matter what the future of *Knoxville* turns out to be, Frank Galati will take it all in as shimmering patterns and intriguing suppositions in an ongoing dance. This book is about that dance.

Figure 1 Writer and director Frank Galati speaks of the making of *Knoxville* at Asolo Repertory Theatre in February 2019. *Sarasota Herald-Tribune.* Staff photo / Dan Wagner.

Notes

1. Daniel Selznick, "Frank Galati: From Basement to Opera Stage," *Christian Science Monitor*, December 17, 1993, p. 14.
2. Bert O. States, *Great Reckonings in Little Rooms: On the Phenomenology of Theatre* (Berkeley: University of California Press, 1985), 98.
3. Robert Bethune, "Theatricality," *Art Times Journal*, September 2002. www.arttimesjournal.com/theater/theatricality.htm.
4. Walter Kerr, "The New York Theatre Is All Show," *New York Times*, June 11, 1977.
5. Joseph R. Roach, *It* (Ann Arbor: University of Michigan Press, 2007), 19.
6. States, *Great Reckonings*, 21.
7. Jason Loewith, *The Director's Voice*, vol. 2 (Theatre Communications Group, 2012), 154.
8. Hilary DeVries, "Chicago Theatre: Second to None," *Christian Science Monitor*, December 6, 1985.
9. Bernard Beckerman, *Theatrical Presentation: Performer, Audience and Act* (New York and London: Routledge, 1990), 1.
10. Richard H. Axsom, *"Parade," Cubism as Theater* (New York, NY: Garland Publishing, 1979), 177.
11. Ellen E. Berry, *Curved Thought and Textual Wandering: Gertrude Stein's Postmodernism* (Ann Arbor: University of Michigan Press, 1992), 35.
12. Howard D. Pearce, *Human Shadows Bright as Glass: Drama as Speculation and Transformation.* (Lewisburg, PA: Bucknell University Press, 1997), 71.
13. DeVries, 1985
14. John Dillon, "The Paradoxical Professor," *American Theatre*, October 1, 1995. www.thefreelibrary.com/The+paradoxical+professor.-a017524190

Part One

The Rise of Off-Loop Theatre: Frank Galati and the Chicago Style

Introduction to Part One

The last three decades of the twentieth century were a remarkable and expansive era for theatrical innovation, change, and discovery throughout the Americas. Newly founded university departments of performance studies deployed theatre as a formal model for studying cultural structures and social behavior. Brazilian Augusto Boal's Theatre of the Oppressed ignited social and political agitation in South America and beyond. In the United States, a mushrooming regional theatre movement continued to transform the profession while backstreet iconoclasts and entrepreneurial rebels challenged long-established commercial structures. In 2018, playwright Jon Robin Baitz recalled the excitement of his first Broadway show. Acting in New York, writes Baitz, "transformed in the 1980s into something post-Freudian and hypnotic ... Because in that era, being any kind of artist in New York meant you were living through the plague and you were one of its diarists."[1] In 1985, the National Endowment for the Arts funding was under attack. Times Square was awash with seedy vendors hawking sex, drugs, and knock-off electronics and AIDS was about to devastate the city's arts community. It was very much a time of plague. But Baitz was electrified by what he saw in the theatre. "My first Broadway play," he writes, "was the head-banging 'Hurlyburly,' by David Rabe." Interesting fact: the incendiary 1984 production and celebrity cast that so inspired and impressed the young playwright had transferred to NYC from Chicago's Goodman Theatre where it premiered earlier that year.[2] But Baitz was correct. *Hurlyburly* may have previewed in Chicago but it was essentially a Broadway show. Chicago-style theatre was a horse of a very different color.

Terry Kinney, a founding member of the Chicago's Steppenwolf Ensemble, explained that the company "really wanted to make the audience have a sense of being part of it and break the fourth wall as much as we can. That doesn't mean that we turn and include them. It means that we spill out. The activity on stage spills into the audience."[3] The Steppenwolf actors were and continue to be remarkable effective in challenging the isolation of realist drama by letting the energy on stage spill out into the auditorium. They were not alone. In new plays and old, in bars and improv clubs, basements, and storefronts, the Chicago actor's energy was directed out, into the house. In 1985, Hilary DeVries declared in the *Christian Science Monitor*, "After years of serving as a stop for third-rate touring companies and laboring under *The New Yorker*'s infamous nomenclature 'The Second City' and its theaters are now second to none."[4] Galati circulated the Chicago theatre community as a mentor, seer, mastermind, cheerleader, and exemplar of the paradoxical paring that would come to define Chicago theatre in the 1980s: a highly charged naturalism that celebrated the stage for what it is—a prepared space for telling stories.

In October 1982, the Steppenwolf ensemble decided to transfer their revival of Sam Shepard's *True West* to the Cherry Lane Theatre in New York City. The move was highly controversial within the company but after prolonged and heated discussions among ensemble members, it was agreed that only John Malkovich and Gary Sinise would travel with the production and that they would keep a low profile about the Chicago connection.[5] In 2005, *Newsday* critic Linda Winer recalled that in early 1983, "Nowhere in the program or the bios did it say these are people from Chicago, that this is from a company called Steppenwolf. And I realized that there had been so many shows imported from Chicago that had failed, that it was actually saying that being from Chicago was a liability."[6] Expectations among the company were not high. Malkovich claimed he packed his bag for a weekend. But the intense, head-butting performances of Malkovich and Sinise proved to be a turning point for Chicago. The production ran for 762 performances, finally closing in August 1984. And so it began. For better or worse, Chicago was identified as the home of raw, rough, rock 'n' roll theatre.

The press coverage after 1983 was extensive and exciting but the catchy sound bites ("rock 'n' roll," "gonzo theatre," "raw naturalism") and oft repeated abstractions ("gritty," "gutsy," "unpolished") of those early notices positioned much, perhaps most, of the innovative work that characterized Chicago's local theatre scene as atypical or marginal, including Galati's. Consider: The Organic Theatre's wacky sci-fi serial *Warp!* (1971) by Stuart Gordon and Lenny Kleinfeld; the electrifying theatricality of Remains Theatre's adaptation of Melville's *Moby Dick* (1983) directed by guest artist Steven Rumbelow; the stunning street theatre of Red Moon's 1990 adaptation of the same book featuring the capture, butcher, and consumption of a life-size whale constructed of barrel staves and wire; the poetic minimalism and shrewd detail of scenic design by Chicagoans Kevin Rigdon, John Paoletti, Mary Griswold, Michael Merritt, and Linda

Buchannan; and the Lookingglass Theatre production of episodic tales of long-ago-and-far-away magic, love, and forgiveness, *The Arabian Nights* (1988). Only a few of these examples of Chicago theatre can be characterized as raw or gritty, none were unpolished, and several abandoned the stage conventions of realism all together. Nonetheless, each of these productions represent the Chicago style at its best.

If the primary product of their labors had been sweaty bodies and gratuitous violence, Chicago theatre-makers would not have attracted international attention, much less extravagant and nearly universal praise. Robert Falls was the artistic director of Chicago's prestigious Goodman Theatre for nearly four decades, but in 1984 he was a charismatic young Chicago director who lived in a cold-water walkup. Nonetheless, his reputation had already reached well beyond the city limits. Falls described the Chicago style as "crude, rough, energetic ... There's this tradition in Chicago," he continued, "of performance which does not have polish."[7] Without a doubt, the storefront theatres that proliferated in Chicago lacked the high gloss of a heavily financed Broadway blockbuster but at its best—and Falls' work was among the best—Chicago theatre was intelligent, intensely focused, and highly crafted.

In 1986, Galati accepted the position of Associate Director at the Goodman Theatre and joined the Steppenwolf Ensemble as a permanent member. He established an artistic affiliation with the Chicago Lyric Opera, was a go-to Hollywood screenwriter of literary adaptations for film and television, and continued to carry a full teaching load at Northwestern University. In the fall of 1987, AT&T ran a full-page ad in the *Chicago Tribune* and sponsored a prominent billboard on a major highway with the banner heading: "AT&T Salutes Chicago Theatre Because, As the Song Says, 'They Do Things They Don't Do on Broadway.'" Throughout the 1980s, theatre was indeed done differently in Chicago and Galati played a pivotal role in the evolution of that difference.

Notes

1 John Robin Baitz, "The Stars Who Got Their Start on the '80s New York Stage," *New York Times*, April 16, 2018. www.nytimes.com/2018/04/16/t-magazine/broadway-1980s-actors-sarah-jessica-parker-willem-dafoe.html.
2 Mike Nichols directed a cast that included Sigourney Weaver, William Hurt, Harvey Keitel, Jerry Stiller, Christopher Walken, Cynthia Nixon, and Judith Ivey.
3 NEAarts, "Steppenwolf Theatre Company," video, YouTube, August 24, 2016. www.youtube.com/watch?v=qjowyJR52oU.

4 Hilary DeVries, "Chicago Theatre: Second to None," *Christian Science Monitor*, December 6, 1985.
5 Scott Elliot, "Interview with Gary Sinise," *Bomb Magazine*, January 1999. http://bombmagazine.org/article/2193/gary-sinise.
6 "Working in The Theatre: Steppenwolf Theatre Company." Directed by Margarita Jimeno, (NYC: CUNY TV, 2015) Video. www.youtube.com/watch?v=D60S0ZKDHQc.
7 Pat Collander, "Chicago Theatre Comes into Its Own," *New York Times*, May 27, 1984.

1

Theatre Chicago Style: Second to None

In the early 1950s, Chicago was not known as a theatre town much less a theatre center. Nonetheless, in 1953, a group of University of Chicago students formed the Playwrights Theatre Club and when the company dissolved in 1955, a few former members, including Shelly Berman, Paul Sills, Mike Nichols, and Elaine May, moved to the neighborhood Compass Bar in Hyde Park to perform short improvised comedy scenes in the back room. In 1957, the Goodman Theatre became the city's first not-for-profit regional theatre with an Equity contract and in 1959, former members of the Compass group founded the improv cabaret Second City on Chicago's near north side. And in 1959, Ralph Lane was a high school drama teacher and coach in the city's northern suburbs. "When the history of the growth of off-Loop theater is written," Albert Williams declared in a *Chicago Reader* profile, "Lane's name should loom large. As a teacher at Glenbrook North High School and later, at Illinois State University, he trained several waves of important talent."[1] Galati, a Glenbrook High student at the time, was in the first wave of important talent mentored by Lane. With Lane's encouragement, he wrote and directed his first play, an experience he described as "a formative event in my life." The fledging teenage author/director was surprised one morning to hear the school principal praise the play, *Hallelujah to the Stars*, on the school's PA system. "Ralph Lane," explained Galati with obvious delight, "got me my first good review."

A few years later, Lane completed his doctorate at Northwestern University and joined the theatre faculty at Illinois State University in Normal, Illinois. "There," writes Abarbanel in Lane's 2006 obituary, "in the early 1970s, he was teacher and director to John Malkovich, Terry Kinney, Jeff Perry, Laurie Metcalf, Tom Irwin, and Rondi Reed. When they joined other friends to form the Steppenwolf Theatre in the mid-70s, Lane continued to advise them."[2] A great many of Lane's former students found their way to Chicago and he eventually followed them to work as a freelance director, producer, and mentor to emerging talent. "Ralph was adamant," recalled producer Douglas Bragan, "about breaking down the fourth wall and using the audience as much as possible ..."[3] In the

1990s, Lane and Bragan founded Arts Lane, a Chicago production company that staged classic plays for thousands of teenagers and gave entry-level employment to young Chicago professionals. For over four decades, Ralph Lane preached the gospel of connection, commitment, and theatrical honesty in Chicago—qualities that would help define the Chicago style.

By the 1960s, it was clear that something theatrical was afoot in the Windy City. Good, bad, or indifferent, enough of the theatre produced in Chicago by Chicagoans between 1970 and 1990 shared sufficient aesthetic values and performance aspects—some more so, some less—to constitute what Ross Wetzesteon, longtime editor of *The Village Voice*, described as "the most talked-about innovation in acting technique since the heyday of the Actor's Studio."[4] By 1990, Chicago-based theatre would be recognized internationally as a transformational force in the performing arts and an emergent economic powerhouse. Throughout this era, Galati commuted weekly, even daily, between multiple artistic worlds in the city and its suburbs, each with a discrete institutional structure, mission, and patron base. He liked to say that he traveled far by staying home. In terms of mileage as well as the extraordinary breadth of his artistic and academic commitments, he was correct.

Many have wondered at the man's capacity to handle such a wide variety of simultaneous and challenging commitments with unflagging enthusiasm and remarkable goodwill. An extraordinary memory and searing intelligence, good health, supportive colleagues, and dumb luck certainly factor in. However, Galati's ability to negotiate his extensive commitments with relative ease and grace was sustained by a nexus of shared values and applied practices that characterized the theatre being made in his hometown between 1970 and 1990. He circulated the Chicago theatre community as a mentor, seer, mastermind, cheerleader, and exemplar of a theatrical style born of the conceptual minimalism and audacity of improvisational theatre, the imposed intimacy of the makeshift storefront venues where Chicago actors, directors, and designers learned their craft, and the financial and internal structure that empowered the city's artist-run ensemble companies to take artistic risks. The result was a new and different kind of experience in the theatre.

Theatre Chicago Style

In 1970, Chicago had not yet established a foothold in the business of putting on shows but it did have a long-established tradition of non-commercial theatre deeply rooted in an affirmation of the city's working and middleclass communities. In 1889, Jane Addams established the Hull House, a groundbreaking community center and kindergarten. She noticed that her young clients were engaged by theatre but what excited them, writes Richard Christensen, "was not complex or exalted. It was burlesque and vaudeville and melodrama . . . but it got to these young people as no amount of preaching would, and Addams, smart person and devout social worker that she was, knew that theatre, even of this variety, was a liberating force for them."[5] Addams envisioned an entertainment that empowered the players as well as their audience and developed a lively community-based theatre center that survived well into the twentieth century. During the 1920s and 30s, Viola Spolin, author of *Improvisation for the Theatre* (1963), was a social worker at Hull House where she created a series of performance games to help immigrant children cross language and cultural borders. Addams' vision materialized again in the 1960s as a few determined pioneers began to produce entertaining and fiercely independent, if not exactly lucrative, theatre in the city and its suburbs. By the 1970s, multiple social and economic factors, including an unprecedented influx of young talent, promoted a culture of theatrical daring and innovation.

Not all artists and critics agreed that new ground was being broken in Chicago. Many preferred to credit the city's theatre community with reinvigorating well-established conventions. Even so, by 1985, wherever Chicago actors and productions traveled, from New York and Washington DC to Los Angeles, London and Australia, the comments of critics, patrons, and artists suggested that a broad spectrum of Chicago-based productions shared a defining, if ineffable, pool of qualities and characteristics that constituted a theatrical style.

Throughout his long career, *Tribune* critic Richard Christiansen demonstrated a preference for the passionate naturalism he found in Chicago. But ever the astute and faithful chronicler, he readily acknowledged that naturalism "was hardly the only element in the makeup of the city's theater."[6] The theatrical context that Galati entered in the 1970s was conceived in the convergence of two distinct genealogical lines, the first linked to a compelling naturalism and the second to an iconoclastic theatricality. These two lines can be traced through the poetic and brawny naturalism of Robert Sickinger's Hull House productions (1963–1969), much honored and beloved by Christiansen, and the eclectic, audience-oriented performances staged at Rev. Jim Shiflett's Body Politic (1966–1979). Galati's most significant achievement was his ability to bind the traditions of Hull House naturalism and Body Politic theatricality with the immediacy of the city's improvisational theatre in a coherent and compelling production style.

The Theatrical Legacies of Bob Sickinger and Rev. Jim Shiflett

In 1969, columnist Jory Graham bemoaned the fact that Chicago theatre "simply isn't like theater in London or New York. The big shows are elsewhere and Chicago is left out."[7] Three years later Broadway had lost none of the razzle-dazzle that Graham found lacking in Chicago but many theatre artists no longer perceived Broadway as the epicenter of a vigorous artistic community. In 1971, director Alan Schneider voiced his dissatisfaction with the self-serving and competitive nature of New York's commercial theatre. "What we lack most," he wrote in *American Theatre* in 1971, "is that which might be called a sense of being involved in some purpose or process that extends beyond our own personal needs and ambitions, of being part of a larger theatre community, not just having lunch together at Sardi's to be noticed and envied."[8] Meanwhile, in Chicago's scrappy storefront theaters, working-class neighborhoods, and academic programs, a complex network of exchange had begun to yield a more intimate and immediate communication with the theatre audience than the prevailing norm. This emergent theater was venturesome, physically expressive, ensemble-based, and dared to reshape realist conventions and training.

In 1962, Hull House was an uptown social service center housed in the Jane Addams Center a few miles north of the Loop, Chicago's central financial and theater district. That year, the Center's Association Director Paul Jans brought in director Robert Sickinger to reinvigorate the theatrical tradition established by Addams in the nineteenth century. "Sickinger," writes Albert Williams, "intended Hull House to become an oasis in that desert by providing an alternative to the diet of Broadway road shows and conventional community groups that then constituted Chicago theater."[9] For nearly a decade, he produced work under the Hull House banner that was not represented in the palatial Equity tour houses in or near the Loop. He recruited local community members to staff his productions, which were often brutally naturalistic and always staged in intimate, makeshift spaces far afield from the city center.

In 1963, Richard Christenson was an eager young reporter on the lookout for something new and exciting. He found what he was looking for in Sickinger's production of Frank D. Gilroy's gritty melodrama *Who'll Save the Ploughboy* at the Hull House Hattie Caller Memorial Theater. It was a performance he would later describe as "a defining moment in Chicago theater life, and a revelatory experience."[10] Sickinger's production of the off-Broadway hit was daring, intimate, and aggressively naturalistic. Christiansen recalled, "Decades after I reviewed it in the *Daily News* as 'the most exciting, significant and promising

Chicago theatrical event in years,' I can still hear and see in memory the vivid power of the play's story. In its energy, passion, and commitment, it set the pattern."[11]

Playwright David Mamet was one of many local theatre enthusiasts who worked with Sickinger and credits him as the founder of off-Loop theatre.

> Bob Sickinger was one of the greatest directors I've ever known. He worked in the Hull House settlement house, at Broadway and Belmont in Chicago, and he invented the Chicago theater of today. He was a maniac. Grown men and women lived in fear of his wrath and blossomed at his praise. We were all amateurs, and so we worked nights, from six P.M. till three or four A.M. This was in 1964. I was sixteen years old. I was a member of the chorus, I tore tickets, I was on the scene crew, I fetched coffee. ... The company was the community: high-school students, housewives, businessmen and women, working people. We bathed in his pride and we became proud of ourselves.[12]

In 1969, concerned with the center's mission to serve the community's underprivileged population, the Hull House board of directors withdrew their support for what they saw as "avant-garde theater for an audience of basically well-to-do customers."[13] Sickinger returned to New York, leaving a legion of energized theatre makers and arts advocates to carry on the work he had begun.

Meanwhile, Reverend Jim Shiflett began community work in a near north side inner-city neighborhood under the auspices of the Christ Presbyterian Church where he was pastor. Outraged by the violent police action directed against antiwar protestors during the 1968 Chicago Democratic Convention, Shiflett founded the Community Arts Foundation in a converted storefront and second-story bowling alley on north Lincoln Avenue, a rundown transitional neighborhood with working-class bars and relatively free of drugs and blatant prostitution. He couldn't get a permit to call the location a theatre but his friend Paul Sills, a founder of the Compass, Second City, and Story theatres and the son of Viola Spolin, named the venue The Body Politic and it stuck.[14] The first production in the building, *Civil War*, was presented in 1970 by Patrick Henry's Free Street Theatre Company. Very quickly, a wacky regiment of artists, musicians, dancers, and activists flocked to the space. The Organic Theatre's production of the science fiction serial *Warp* (1971), co-authored by director Stuart Gordon and Lenny Kleinfeld (AKA *Chicago Reader* critic Bury St. Edmond) featured a lethal eggbeater ray gun among other outrageous effects and theatrical inventions. Theatre projects and independent companies spun off or sprang up in the vicinity, most notably Ruth Pyskacek's Kingston Mines

Theatre at 2356 Lincoln Ave where the musical *Grease* by Jim Jacobs and Warren Casey premiered in 1971.

Shiflett was a man with a mission and as he explained to Linda Winer in 1971, his mission was spiritual rather than aesthetic, political, or commercial. Passionately committed to the physical and mental wellbeing of the working-class members of his urban congregation, he told Winer, "They don't need their heads hammered. They need a way to enjoy their lives. These people feel so goddam guilty. It's pathetic—they've got to be told it's all right to enjoy." Shiflett admitted, "I know artists are bastards and bitches most of the time. But they are also very much concerned with life and the expression of life. And if we don't start protecting those expressions of life, we may not have a life. A community without the arts is not worth having."[15]

Shiflett was impressed by Spolin's non-authoritative theatre games, introduced to the Chicago theatre community through Sills' early improvisational work at the Compass Theatre on Chicago's south side. When the Compass folded, Sills was one of the founders of the improvisational cabaret theatre Second City. Shiflett was moved by the spontaneity of the Second City performers and the remarkable warmth and lively exchange between the players and their audience, particularly when they fielded audience suggestions for situation improvs at late night performances. "It was simple to see they weren't just dealing with games or theater, but with a basic communication between them and the audience."[16] The games and improvisations that Shiflett admired were conceived by Spolin to enhance creativity and spontaneity in the classroom. However, these "games" were readily adapted to the rehearsal room and supported a vibrant and direct connection between the actors and the audience in performance. Shiflett was convinced that this connection was capable of uplifting and empowering the community he served. The intimate spaces of the bare-bones performance venues at the Body Politic encouraged and supported audience-oriented performance that was directed outward, toward the audience in a lively and enlivening exchange that brought the energy and spontaneity of improvisation to dramatic storytelling.

At the time Rev Shiflett was stirring up Lincoln Avenue, Galati was a student of oral interpretation at Northwestern University. His teachers and mentors, Charlotte Lee (1909–1995), Wallace Bacon (1914–2001), and Robert Breen (1909–1991) maintained a close working relationship and friendship. "It was a very stable, healthy and secure environment," recalled Galati. "They had vitality, a sense of humor, compassion, they loved each other and we would do things. We had so much fun together so it was a very embracing and loving environment.

I never wanted to leave." Wallace Bacon was a close friend of Dr. Charles McGaw, dean of the Goodman School of Drama, the professional training program of the School of the Chicago Art Institute in the Loop and author of the popular Stanislavski based textbook *Acting is Believing*. Robert Breen was connected to David Shepherd and Paul Sills, who led the ragtag group of intellectuals developing a new kind of improvisational theatre on the south side campus of the University of Chicago. In *The Compass: The Improvisational Theatre that Revolutionized American Comedy* (1991), Janet Coleman notes that the famous Compass Theatre "Living Newspaper" segment

> was to be gleaned straight from the pages of the press each day. According to Shepherd, the technique (similar to one that later became the keystone of Paul Sills' Story Theater) was much like a device he and Sills had admired in Robert Breen's work at Northwestern University. Breen developed a technique called Chamber Theatre in which actors weave in and out of narrative and into character and dialogue.[17]

Breen, Bacon, McGaw, and Shepherd formed a triangulated web of exchange between the city's far south, north, and central academic institutions.

When Galati came on the scene in the early 1970s, the Chicago audience was already primed for openly theatrical, audience-oriented performance. What he brought to the table was the refined sensibility of a new form of theatre based on performance conventions and techniques developed by Breen in the interpretation program at Northwestern University and by Galati himself as a full-time faculty member from 1972 until his retirement from academia in 2006.

Chamber Theatre

The underpinning of Galati's stage adaptions and directing style lies in his study and exploration of chamber theatre, a technique developed by Breen for teaching non-dramatic literature through performance. His field, oral interpretation, is the study of literature through the selection and performance of dialogue, action and narrative from the original work. Breen was by all accounts a brilliant teacher and scholar but he was also a man of the theatre. As a professor of literature, he mobilized theatrical conventions to help his students transcend a diligent but superficial understanding of literature. H. L. Mencken argues that the critic is, or should be, an artist in their own right, one who brings their own unique insights to the literary enterprise. "It is precisely at this point," claims

Mencken, "that criticism becomes genuine criticism; before that it was mere reviewing."[18] Breen developed chamber theatre as a teaching tool intended to engage his student/interpreters as the literary author's artistic collaborator rather than a diagnostic scholar or academic champion. What Breen proposed was a new form of literary analysis, one "in which pieces of fiction are acted as drama; where the characters are brought onto the stage to say their lines and act out their actions, but where a new character, the Narrator, is given a speaking voice, too." He explains that "the essence of chamber theatre technique is in its concern for the narrative point of view."[19] Unlike a conventional stage or screen adaptation—a dramatization of literature—Breen set out to novelize the stage by combining the theatre's ability to represent action with the novel's capacity to reflect on that action from a point of view outside the story.

As a teacher, he posed a peculiar question that Galati continued to ask his own students: "What kind of person is this sentence?" This is not the same as asking "What kind of person would say this sentence?" Breen is calling attention to the unique character and distinct voice that arises from the structure, rhythms, inflections, and vernacular eccentricities of the narrative voice in literature. Galati explained the challenge of finding the person in a sentence by pointing out a passage in the fifth edition of *Oral Interpretation*, a textbook he co-edited with Charlotte Lee:

> Sentences are like people. Some are vague, distracted, and not all put together. Some are windy, effusive, and full of hot air. Some are blunt. Some are elegant and graceful, capable of balancing ideas ... making swirls and dips on the page ... letting the reader out at the end with a vivid "plop." Sentences give off vibrations like people do. They *reveal* and they *conceal* just as people do.[20]

The question, "What kind of person is this sentence?" initiates an exploration of the sensibility and point of view that permeates a literary text and this is key to Galati's stage adaptations of nondramatic literature. "One of the fundamentals that I was so excited to understand," continued Galati, "was that the persona in the poem is an entity that has ticks and twitches and tones of voice and that it's possible to really perceive and feel the stylistic contours of a sensibility that's speaking in the work." Galati has never abandoned Breen's central precept—to reflect on the action from a point of view outside the story—but his attention was increasingly drawn to the ways in which the theatre could allow the sensibility speaking in the original work expression beyond the limitations of linguistic content. He continued to pose the same questions Breen had asked his students, including "What kind of person is this sentence?" but he sought new and different answers in the kinesthetic, aural, and visual attributes of embodied performance.

Galati's focus on the performative aspects of chamber theatre are evident in his oral and written critique of student projects. In 2003, I watched a young woman perform a passage from his adaptation of *Blue Eyes Black Hair* by Marguerite Duras as a class project. Midway through the passage, she lifted a large vase into the air, tilted it, and threw her head back to meet the cascade of falling water full face, gulping convulsively at the downpour. Galati saw a deep sensuality and poetry in her action and described it in his critique.

> The flower has gone to the lover and Duras must slake her thirst. We are kicked in the gut by this. Tepid water, river water, the juice that will stream down on the woman's body, or pure mountain water made of rain—all this churns as we witness the gulping and observe the ordeal, the travail of the sacrifice, the priestess drinks from the bitter cup. This is my body, take and eat. Brilliant.[21]

In the same class, he noted how another student found the "voice" in a favorite nonfiction text by performing footnotes and a wry "ibid" with vaudevillian gestures and wit. Director and playwright Jessica Thebus, a former student, recalled that when she lifted the hem of her skirt in a certain way as she walked onto the platform, Galati noted that her gesture captured the anticipation and playful theatricality of her text. "The drape of your skirt," he told her, "was like the curtain rising on the stage. As if to say, 'Something is about to begin!'" Thebus recalled, "he always saw things we did—choices and details in performance we weren't aware of until he called attention to them." A former student told me, "He's like a magician who pulls a silver dollar from behind your ear. It's yours, but you didn't know it was there until he found it."

The audience response Galati seeks is physical, sensual, and in the end, emotionally charged and intellectually provocative. Breen links the theatre's ability to achieve this effect to the interaction of two "modes of existence." In chamber theatre, the mode of existence defined by the audience's apprehension of the actors and the stage is simultaneous to their apprehension of fictive character and place. Like Breen, Galati was interested in "the interaction of the two distances as they respond to each other."[22] In Galati's conception, the story is always a story, the stage is always a stage, and the actor must fully and paradoxically exist in both and neither at the same time. He could not have achieved this co-mingling of mutually exclusive possibilities without a powerful naturalism to counterbalance the spectacular theatricality of his staging. He found that counterpoint in the tough and uncompromising quality of the

Chicago actor. Together, they created an improbable fusion of virtuoso showmanship and compelling naturalism, a combination that characterized Chicago theatre in the 1980s.

Naturalism Chicago-style

Beginning as early as the 1970s, the term most often used by critics to describe the acting style of Chicago's native theatre was "naturalism." To this day, the terms "realistic" and "realism" rarely appear in critical commentary on Chicago based theatre. The distinction between naturalism and realism is telling. The philosophical underpinning of twentieth-century realism holds the idea of the stage as an enclosed fictive environment rather than the acting platform of antiquity, renaissance, restoration, and eighteenth-century performance. On the realist stage, performance is conceived as an ephemeral and self-contained aesthetic object, a highly crafted illusion to be observed and appreciated from a darkened auditorium. The nineteenth-century slice-of-life Naturalism of Gerhart Hauptmann rejected the cause-and-effect contrivance of realist plot structure and called for absolute fidelity to physical reality in representation. The naturalistic actor of the twentieth as well as the nineteenth century seems to "live" on stage rather than maintain the carefully constructed artifice of Realism. However, nineteenth-century Naturalism reinforced rather than challenged the realist innovation of an imagined fourth wall, a kind of one-way mirror that rendered the audience invisible and inaccessible to the performers. But Chicago actors learned to direct their energy outward, acknowledging the presence of living spectators. In doing so, they often left an impression of natural and spontaneous behavior so powerful it commanded the stage as an acting platform.

Naturalism in Chicago, whether in-your-face or lurking just below the surface, was not sustained by private introspection, elaborate backstories, or a determined erasure of the theatre environment and event. Many, if not most Chicago actors had some form of Stanislavski-based training. Nonetheless, in order to survive on the city's intimate off-Loop stages, the Chicago actor learned to assert the actor's material reality in the moment of performance. The overall effect of Chicago's most powerful onstage performances was not empathy but connection, that is, an awareness of self and other as different but connected. Empathy can mask difference and in doing so, release the spectator from accountability and agency. Galati explained the Chicago difference: "With Chicago actors, it's the action. You take the moment forward. The backstory is for fun or grounding. We are more interested in the consequence of the act than in the cause—by fully understanding the consequence of our acts, we might change behavior."

Chicago-style acting in its fullest maturity was famously and forcefully demonstrated in William Peterson's gut-wrenching performance as the convicted murderer and self-taught essayist, Jack Abbot, in director Robert Falls' Wisdom Bridge production of *In the Belly of the Beast: Letters from Prison* (1985). Falls took his script from letters written from prison by Jack Abbot to the author Norman Mailer and published by Mailer under the same title. Peterson delivered narrative solo passages that were neither traditional monologue (extended dialogue) nor soliloquy (externalized thought). The stage was his platform and the audience was clearly his intended auditor. *London Times* reviewer Irving Wardle described Petersen's performance as, "a revelation of human nature" played "at white heat and point-blank range." He declared it to be "one of the most important performances we're ever going to see in our lifetime."[23] As reviewer Sid Smith pointed out, "no matter what intellectual distance or glib analytical trick you employ, it's hard to doubt that Abbott is there, and that we, the audience, are on trial."[24] I saw the production several times and each time, it seemed to me, if only for a queasy moment, that we may all be sociopaths at heart and if so, no less accountable, abused, and doomed than the terrifying creature before us.

Washington Post staff writer David Richards described the performance as "a raw, abrasive production that hurls itself at an audience, jabs at its conscience and challenges its equanimity."[25] Richards tempered his praise by faulting the production for a failure to probe the inner life of the character. But in Chicago, the inner disquiet of the audience took precedence over that of the character. *New York Times* critic Frank Rich acknowledged the talent, energy, and skill of Peterson's performance but found the production lacking. "Unfortunately, the 90-minute script remains a mound of unintegrated material. It adds few facts and no insights to the existing Abbott dossier, and it usually sidesteps the New York literary world's curious role in the criminal's post-parole recidivism."[26] In the same article, he asserts that Chicago could fulfill its burgeoning potential only by producing "its own indigenous drama" with authors like Chicago-born Lorraine Hansberry and David Mamet who "flesh out and transcend the bare bones of naturalism with metaphor and psychological depth."[27] But *Belly of the Beast* did not set out to correct a social wrong, add to the dossier of a historic figure, or provoke empathy for the killer or his victims. It was conceived deliberately or instinctively to provide the audience with a personal and deeply felt experience in real time. Peterson provided a harrowing and unforgettable experience in the theatre, an experience that bypassed empathy in favor of shock, horror, and persistent unease.

In the *London Times*, Holly Hill described Chicago actors as "brooding, explosive—going right to the edge of the cliff of disbelief and hanging over by their nails but never slipping off."[28] The edge Hill speaks of is that point where actor and character, real and fake, truth and pretense exist simultaneously, rendering the imaginary barrier between spectacle and spectator porous and unreliable. This is an extremely precarious position to maintain but it is something Chicago's audience-trained actors were exceptionally good at. To maintain and support this precarious foothold on the cliff of disbelief, the city's theatre makers rid the stage of anything and everything that was not essential to the telling of their story, often achieving a dazzling clarity of purpose.

Simplicity and Presence

Breen believed that to "accomplish the end simply and without waste does not mean that a baroque style is to be stripped of its convolutions in the interest of simplification," but to achieve an "economy in style" with "as much elaboration as an elaborate end calls for, only as much polychromatic richness as is necessary to create a baroque effect."[29] By necessity and inclination, Chicago designers generally adhered to Breen's precept. Designer Kevin Rigdon was directly involved in the early success of the Steppenwolf productions. He described how, in the formative years of the company, scenic elements as well as actions and emotions were stripped to the bone, rendered "raw" by intense all-night discussions and demanding rehearsals. He recounted a telling compliment that acknowledges the achievements of that era.

> I worked with Peter Hall at the National Theatre [in London]. One day, Peter stopped me to say how much he enjoyed working with me, he felt that that I got it. He said, "Your work is like a sauce reduction. You take all these ingredients and reduce and reduce until you have a single spoonful of theatre, an intense experience when you put it in your mouth." That was what our work was like, what we learned in those early days with the company.

Far from being unpolished or undercooked, the process Hall described requires the constant and painstaking attention of a master chef.

Rigdon noted that the company's barebones aesthetic worked against the impression of calculated refinement. He recalled, "There was a roughness, a rawness to what we did, not messy or sloppy but never pitch perfect and very immediate." In the cramped and makeshift performance spaces of the Steppenwolf's early homes, Rigdon gave the actors what they most wanted and needed—a poor-theatre production style that enhanced and indexed the company's powerful actor/audience dynamic. In the Chicago production of *Orphans* (1984), the entrance door of the apartment bounced against the jamb when it slammed and shabby masking was exposed when it was pulled open on the small, cramped stage. Rather than distract from the performance, the lack of visual pretense underscored and enhanced the actor's unchallenged authority over the production. "Back then," he explained, "we weren't interested in windows and doors. The closer the actor gets to an item, the more real it needs to be. If you didn't touch it, you didn't need it."

In 1981, Robert Falls directed Bertolt Brecht's *Mother Courage and Her Children* for the Wisdom Bridge Theatre. Sonja Lanzener played Mother Courage, a war profiteer who enlists her three children to provision the various armies that ravaged Europe in the fourteenth and fifteenth centuries. In the end, she loses everything to the carnage of war, including the children she set out to protect and support. Falls cast Galati as an accordion-playing cook who sang for his supper and designer Michael Merritt fashioned an entirely different theatrical world for each scene. Using only a few, easily moved elements, the stage appeared gritty at one moment, whimsical or threatening in the next, until the final scene when the stage was bare save a raw wood platform on rickety wheels with a frayed rope pull, all that remained of the supply wagon that had sustained Courage and her children through the interminable wars.

Actor Glenne Headly played Courage's only surviving child, Kattrin—a deaf mute and the play's last vestige of human compassion. In the final scene, Kattrin risks her life in a desperate but futile attempt to warn a distant village of imminent danger. Headly stood splay-legged atop the wagon and at an earsplitting boom— the report of a gun the size of a small cannon—she collapsed. Lanzener cried out in anguish once, then heaved herself onto the wagon, stripped Headly's body, and rolled her onto the stage floor with a thud. She piled the girl's shoes, drum, and threadbare clothing on the empty wagon and without a backward glance, hauled it off stage, leaving Headly's naked body sprawled awkwardly on the stage floor under a dirty light. In those final moments, when the physical reality of stage and actor were most aggressively present to the audience, the production took on its greatest intellectual and emotional power. The scene was bleak, bone chilling, and surprisingly sensuous, a single spoonful of theatre intense on the tongue.

Galati generally works toward a simplicity that is sensual rather than austere. He is a self-described "arraigner" who likes to set things in interesting and unexpected juxtaposition to each other, to sequence and re-sequence events. He likes to play with ideas, images, and unexpected relationships. Sometimes, he plays too much. "My fault and limitation? To over organize and over compose and overregulate the way the work feels." Galati's love of spectacle can render him vulnerable to a little more visual elaboration than an elaborate end calls for, an inclination tempered by his Chicago collaborators. Rigdon designed sets and lighting for *The Grapes of Wrath* and was fully involved in the production as it took shape. He recalled an incident early on in rehearsal.

> One day we were working on the Hooverville scene in *Grapes of Wrath* and trying anything and everything to make this mess of a scene work. Frank said, 'I have this great idea to costume the mayor,' and he shows me this priceless drawing of a man wearing a chest of drawers like something from a bad Disney movie. I put it in my book and eventually Frank said, "Aren't we going to talk about this," and I said, "No. Consider me saving you from yourself." It wasn't the last time I kept him from moon-booting himself.

"Moon-booting" is a reference to a synthetic boot that was popular at the time. Mid-calf, Michelin Man puffy, and apparently made of aluminum foil, it was a questionable sartorial choice. Rigdon said, "I always looked out that Frank wouldn't moon-boot himself. Frank respected that." Galati respected Rigdon's editing because he understood that Chicago's stripped down aesthetic enhanced the actor's presence and connection to the audience.

The notion of presence saturates a theatrical style described as "visceral," "immediate," and "in your face." For the most part, the religious overtones and mystical undertones of the word "presence" were too esoteric to gain much purchase with working actors and designers in Chicago but Galati has never shied away from the term. Asked for an example to illustrate his understanding of "presence," he described a specific moment in a matinee performance of Margaret Edson's *Wit* on Broadway. Actor Kathleen Chalfant played the role of a stoic professor of literature undergoing excruciating experimental treatments for terminal cancer. To Galati, her performance was a small miracle.

> There's a wonderful scene in which she remembers an early encounter with a tough teacher who demands that she rewrite a paper. I was struck that this was a perfect example of a woman and an ensemble who's completely tuned in to the

audience, listening to them. She's shaping the speech in such a way that she's allowing the audience to breathe along with her in the speech. She would come to the end of a phrase and allow it time to settle into us. In that afternoon performance, she was completely in the moment, with us as an audience. I mean, I could feel her reaching for me and there was actually one point when someone coughed and she let it into the line. She was cooking along at a clip when there was, maybe a catch breath in which this miniscule disturbance began – and she let the disturbance in – and then just topped it so that there was no loss of momentum and no obscuring what she was saying by any kind of distraction. This is something I have felt and am really interested in and something I learned a lot about as an actor.

Galati's success as an actor in the early 1970s owed a great deal to his ability to maintain, in his own words, "a relationship between spectacle and spectator defined by connection and interaction, rather than separation." For him, Chalfant gave "a brilliant performance because she was there with us, in the theatre." As he described the incident, it struck me that the fierce presence on stage may have confirmed his own sense of presence in the theatre and perhaps, in the world.

Rigdon explained that presence and connection drove his designs for Steppenwolf's successive homes. "You start from the audience. What is the relationship between the actor and the audience? How can you create a space where an actor can have a dialogue with the audience? That," he explained about his design for the company's first purpose-built 515-seat theatre on Halsted Street, "is what drove the apron into the auditorium, the wrap of the balcony and the shallowness of the audience. Two thirds of the audience is in the front third of the space, close to the stage. And the middle row is eye to eye with the actor on the stage." He was not unconcerned with wing space, acoustics, sight lines, or auditorium capacity but his primary objective in designing a performance space for the Steppenwolf actors was to support the flow of kinetic energy between the stage and the audience. Theatre spaces with a similar agenda materialized all over the city and its suburbs, including the quirky asymmetrical platform at Wisdom Bridge, the original Victory Gardens studio theatre on the top floor of the Northside Auditorium Building on Clark Street, and the John Lennon Auditorium, a forty-two-seat storefront theatre designed by Louis DiCrescenzo for the Practical Theatre Co on the corner of Howard Street and Custer Avenue. In these off-Loop theatres, the primary objective was to sustain and enhance, as Rigdon says, the ability of the actor to be in dialogue with the audience. One of the city's earliest and most enduring audience-oriented performance spaces still exists in Piper's Alley as a shallow platform with three exits, a few bent wood chairs, and cabaret seating—home of Chicago's groundbreaking improv company, The Second City.

Improvisation and Ensemble Chicago-style

In an interview published in *The Director's Voice* (1993), Robert Falls observed: "There were two great and simultaneous influences on American theatre and American acting in the 1950s. One was the Actors Studio in New York, which is the one everybody knows about, and the other was the Second City in Chicago." Saint Nicholas, Victory Gardens, Steppenwolf, Wisdom Bridge, Body Politic, "All of them," observed Falls "had roots in the Second City."[30] Second City was founded in 1951 by Bernard Sahlins, Paul Sills, and Howard Alk as a cabaret theatre that featured a specific sketch-based form of improvisation. Unlike long form improvisation, which is devised on the spot in front of an audience, the Second City ensemble works together over a rehearsal period of weeks or months to develop carefully crafted scenes with a strong sense of character, situation, and message or theme. The "embryos" for these sketches arise from popular and raucous late night improvs with the audience but the final script is created by the actors and set for the run of each review.

Ross Wetzsteon observed that Chicago's long tradition of improvisation was formative in the development of the city's theatrical style. In 1984, he noted—correctly—that many of the younger theatre makers in Chicago regarded Second City as "a fossilized tourist trap." But Wetzsteon points out that Second City had a profound influence on the style of acting that characterized the city. The influence of that improvisational group, he writes,

> lies less in its nurturing of comic talent than in its development of an acting style. In fact, the two major legacies of Second City—improvisation and ensemble—form the very basis of the Chicago style currently altering the contours of American theatre ... Groups like Steppenwolf didn't grow up in a cultural vacuum—like it or not, Second City was in the very air they breathed.[31]

Second City was also in the air that the city's theatre and entertainment patrons breathed. By the time Galati came on the scene, the company had offered the Chicago audience good entertainment at an affordable entry fee and cover charge for twenty years. Because of Second City, Chicago theatre patrons were conditioned to expect and even demand something more lively, immediate, and engaging than a sophisticated reproduction of life staged in a silent auditorium.

Improv is not based on a script but it does have rules. The first and primary rule, "say yes, never say no," directs the actor to accept, never deny whatever word or action is introduced by a scene partner. "To accept" requires the actor to suppress intention in favor of a heightened awareness and receptivity in the moment of performance. The second rule, "say yes and ..." disallows passive or neutral acceptance on stage. The shared goal in improvisation is to keep the momentum of the scene alive by always adding something new, something of one's own that a scene partner can work with or against. For Chicago's ensemble actors and improv performers, acceptance meant that every intrusion, disruption, or obstacle was an opportunity.

In the early 1980s, guest artist and Steppenwolf member Lori Metcalf played a glamorous star of stage and screen in the Columbia Collage production of the 1938 comedy, *The Man Who Came to Dinner* by George S. Kaufman and Moss Hart. It was an unusual role for Metcalf and she was pleased but unaccustomed to the slinky backless evening gown and high heels she was fitted for. In an important second act plot point, her character realizes that she has been outmaneuvered and betrayed. In rehearsal, Metcalf found herself far upstage left with a barricade of fusty furniture between herself and the audience. It was a weak stage position but on cue, she turned her back to the auditorium, spread her arms out against the upstage wall and clawed her way along the flowered wallpaper until she reached an unblocked position center. The muscles of her exposed back rippled as a spasm flowed down her spine and expelled at the coccyx with a small butt-bump. Once she reached an unblocked position center stage, she lifted her shoulders in a deep inhale, smoothed the satin at her hips, raised her chin and turned out. When she faced the audience, she was upstage center, composed, dazzling, and clearly set on fanatical revenge. In a few beats, Metcalf went from privileged complacence to venomous determination—Carol Lombard to Cruella de Vil—and did so from an unfavorable stage position with her back to the audience. Director Sheldon Patinkin called her performance a masterclass in back acting.

Metcalf's choice was intuitive but her intuition was to "say yes" to what she was given and add a palpable shift in tone and tension before releasing the scene to her partners. Without missing a beat, she turned the obstacle of a weak stage position into an opportunity and exploited a unique costume element as an asset. Such choices are not unusual for a savvy actor but the nimbleness and invention with which Chicago actors could "say yes, and ..." created the strong impression of spontaneity, immediacy, and invention associated with the Chicago style.

Chicago improv guru Del Close is a legendary figure in the world of unscripted comedy. He was also an accomplished actor and very much concerned with the theatre. The "commandments" Close articulated for improv resonate with qualities that define the Chicago style: an unpretentious and energized intimacy, intense focus on each other, penetrating intelligence, rigorous and merciless editing of anything extraneous to the goal, a disregard for illusionism and the clutter of realist verisimilitude, and a mutual trust that authorizes exhilarating risk. Close preceded Galati by over a decade but his focus on relationships between actors, his emphasis on supporting and listening to each other, and his warning against condescending to the audience are mirrored in Galati's own work and foundational to theatre making in Chicago.

In 1984, Second City co-founder Bernard Sahlins declared, "Chicago is the risk capital of the world."[32] The city's reputation for risk-taking is directly linked to the ensemble structure that developed in Chicago's artist-run production companies. Steppenwolf ensemble member and acting artistic director Randy Arney explained, "We can take risks we'd never otherwise take because we're in our own theatre with people we love. And risk is a large reason for our success." Martha Lavey, the company's artistic director from 1995 to 2015, addressed the issue of risk-taking in the American Wing Theatre "Working in the Theatre" video series. "You have to take risks," she said with a small shrug. "What does that actually mean? That you go at things full throttle and not all of it works. I don't think of things we have done as mistakes. ... Ok. We learned from that, we'll do something else."[33] Lavey's shrug suggests that she considers risk to be implicit in making theatre or at least, in the way it was made in her theatre. By the mid-1980s, the Chicago audience and press core licensed risk and audacity by defining "failure" as a failure of courage, will, commitment, or energy rather than a failure to maintain aesthetic standards, dramatic continuity, authorial intention, or a director's vision.

Music philosopher Constantijn Koopman's description of ensemble music aligns with Chicago style ensemble acting: "When successfully engaging … as a group, we do not merely share a great experience; we also promote our sense of belonging together, our belief in our capacity for effective collective action, and our joint commitment to ideals that go beyond our private wellbeing."[34] For over two decades, Galati was drawn to, depended on, and inspired countless Chicago theatre artists who believed in the artistic muscle of collective action.

A Directorial Style in Embryo: University of South Florida, 1966–1969

In 1965, Galati entered the master's degree program in the Department of Speech at Northwestern University with an emphasis on interpretation. In 1966, on the strong recommendation of his teachers and mentors, he accepted the position of assistant professor of oral interpretation at the University of South Florida (USF). He was twenty-three years old when he arrived at the newly constructed state university in an undeveloped area of Florida. "It was the Wild West," he recalled decades later. "In those days, it was barren—not even a stop sign at the highway turn-off."

For nine thousand dollars a year, he taught five days a week, five classes a day in oral interpretation with twenty-five students per class. Each student prepared, memorized, and performed multiple ten-minute selections of non-dramatic literature per semester. In addition to his teaching load, he oversaw a weekly lunchtime reading hour and was required to write, produce, and direct a full-length adaptation of non-dramatic literature for the USF stage every academic quarter. He was also responsible for the physical setting and advertising for all productions. In a little over two years, he directed over thirty "Coffee House" performances and ten major adaptations for the Department of Speech.

> It was grotesque. And I <u>loved</u> it. I put up everything by every author I'd ever read. Many of my students were older than me and would have been sent to Vietnam without their student deferment. Some had already been to Vietnam and back and were in school on the GI Bill. I was this kid making it up as I went along and I just sort of ploughed on. You know, there's such a thing as too much rehearsal. Know your lines, master it and get it up. It's not a deadline—it's just a day. There's so much excitement in that. That's what we did and it was thrilling. Every day was a passionate adventure.

Many of his USF students had never been inside a professional theatre and few had heard of Vladimir Nabakov, Günter Grass, or Luigi Pirandello—authors whose work Galati assigned them to read and perform. They were unworldly and unschooled but years later he could still recall their exhilaration. "They felt privileged to be there. It meant everything to them. They were killing themselves to be a part of it all—and they loved it. They were devoted and I adored them. I always felt their humility and sincerity." The student body reciprocated his appreciation and at the end of his first year, voted Galati USF Teacher of the Year.

In a few frenzied years at USF, Galati's directorial style and interpretive technique emerged in embryo. The number and variety of projects he juggled was astounding, as it has continued to be throughout his career. His work with the USF students established the extraordinarily high standards of energy and passion he would inspire and expect. His commitment to contemporary issues and current events emerged in productions like *M Company*, his adaptation of a 1966 *Esquire* article about infantrymen in Vietnam. In *M Company*, he juxtaposed eclectic references, songs, sounds, and images in an evocative collage or sampling effect that would be a hallmark of his work in subsequent years, as would strategic interpolations of music, song, and narrative. Galati has created or commissioned an original musical spine or through-line for every adaptation he has written and directed, often performed on stage by musicians in costume. *M Company* ran an hour and forty minutes with one intermission—about right for Galati, who likes his shows short and intense. The cast included twenty-five students—extremely large for a dramatic reading but near to average for Galati whose view of the human condition tends to be panoramic. Visual elements were necessarily minimal. Students performed in street clothes, often on a bare stage. He used pencil and ballpoint pen on unlined paper to draw an evocative visual image for each production and had mimeograph copies distributed on campus. He saved dozens of these handmade poster/flyers and each one conveys significant information about the production in ways that words cannot.

Commitment and passion, social relevance, a musical through-line, brief in length and large of cast, boundless energy, and visual eloquence in staging and presentation—these elements and qualities characterize every theatrical adaption of non-dramatic literature Galati has written and directed. The storytelling style of *M Company* was eclectic, literate, and episodic, fragmented in form rather than linear in development—all hallmarks of his mature work. Finally, Galati drew on the powerful if unpolished presence of the young men and women who momentarily inhabited the imaginative realm of literature in performance. Throughout his career, immediacy, and presence, that is, the irresistible sense of a living human intelligence within the spectator's physical reach have preempted sophisticated illusionism and realist verisimilitude in his work. On his return to the Chicago area, these interests, preferences, and techniques would be embraced and enhanced in the style of theatre taking shape in his hometown.

Notes

1. Albert Williams, "Theater People: Ralph Lane Hooks Them When They're Young," *Chicago Reader,* April 26, 1990. www.chicagoreader.com/chicago/theater-people-ralph-lane-hooks-them-when-theyre-young/Content?oid=875565.
2. Jonathan Abarbanal, "Ralph Lane, 78, Mentor to Chicago Actors, Dies," *Backstage,* February 1, 2006. www.backstage.com/magazine/article/ralph-lane-mentor-chicago-actors-dies-34174/.
3. Douglas Bragan interviewed by Albert Williams, "Theatre People," 1990.
4. Ross Wetzsteon, "Can an Electric Theatre Style Revive New York?" *New York,* December 16, 1985, 50.
5. Richard Christiansen, *A Theater of Our Own: A History and a Memoir of 1,001 Nights in Chicago.* (Evanston, IL: Northwestern University Press, 2004), 47.
6. Richard Christiansen, "Revealing the Real Roots of The City's 'Rock 'N' Roll Acting,'" *Chicago Tribune,* May 18, 1987.
7. Jory Graham, *Chicago: An Extraordinary Guide* (Chicago; 1969), quoted in Richard Christiansen, *A Theater of Our Own* (2004), 133.
8. J. Robert Wills, *The Director in a Changing Theatre: Essays on Theory and Practice, With New Plays For Performance* (Palo Alto, CA: Mayfield Pub. Co., 1976), 137.
9. Albert Williams, "Theater People: In the Beginning There Was Robert Sickinger," *Chicago Reader,* April 27, 1989.
10. Christiansen, *A Theater of Our Own,* 127.
11. Christiansen, *A Theater of Our Own.*
12. David Mamet, "Why I Write for Theatre," posted to Robert Sickinger's memorial page, 2013. www.bobsickinger.com/.
13. Christiansen, *A Theatre of Our Own,* 130.
14. Richard Christiansen, "Does Anybody Care About the Body Politic?" *Chicago Tribune,* February 6, 1994, Arts Afield sec.
15. Reverend Jim Shiflett interview with Linda Winer, "Body Politic's Friendly Giant and A Miracle on Lincoln Ave," *Chicago Tribune,* August p 20, 1972, Arts sec., 7.
16. Winer, 1972.
17. Janet Coleman, *The Compass: The Improvisational Theatre that Revolutionized American Comedy* (Chicago: University of Chicago Press, 1991), 99.
18. Henry Louis Mencken, *A Mencken Chrestomathy* (New York: Vintage Books, 1982), 439.
19. Robert S. Breen, *Chamber Theatre* (Englewood Cliffs, NJ: Prentice-Hall, 1978), 86.
20. Charlotte Lee and Frank Galati, *Oral Interpretation,* 5th ed. (Boston: Houghton Mifflin Company, 1977), 148.
21. Frank Galati, "Notes to Class," Northwestern University, Performance Studies 324-1, Spring 2005, Galati private archives.

22 Breen, *Chamber Theatre*, 49–50.
23 Irving Wardle quoted by Richard Christiansen, "'Beast' Makes Its Mark on London," *Chicago Tribune*, May 24, 1985
24 Sid Smith, "'Belly of The Beast,' 'Coyote' Electrify D.C," *Chicago Tribune*, June 17, 1985.
25 David Richards, "Theatre Cry from the Heart ANT Imports a Powerful 'Beast,'" *Washington Post*, June 17, 1985.
26 Frank Rich, "Critic's Notebook; Chicago Has Blossomed into a Theater Center," *New York Times*, October 13, 1983.
27 Rich, "Notebook," 1983.
28 Holly Hill, "Theatre in the United States: 'Steppenwolfen' Take New York by Storm," *London Times* July 8, 1995.
29 Breen, *Chamber Theatre*, 35.
30 Arthur Barlow, *The Director's Voice; Twenty-One Interviews* (New York; Theatre Communications Group, Inc 1988), 93.
31 Wetzsteon, 56.
32 Pat Colander, "Chicago Theatre Comes into Its Own," *New York Times*, May 27, 1984, Sec 2, 4.
33 Margarita Jimeno, dir., "Working in The Theatre: Steppenwolf Theatre Company," February 5, 2015. www.youtube.com/watch?v=D60S0ZKDHQc.
34 Constantijn Koopman and Stephen Davis, "Musical Meaning in Broader Perspective," *Journal of Aesthetics and Art Criticism* 59 (2001): 261–73.

2

One Who was Working: 1969–1986

In 1969, Galati decided on a career in academia, resigned his teaching position at the University of South Florida and returned to Northwestern University to enter the doctorate program in interpretation, at that time a division of the Department of Speech. The prospect of a life in the theatre had not yet occurred to him. "That," he says, "just sort of happened by accident." To complete the requirements of the PhD, he prepared and performed a solo recital of material adapted from his dissertation subject, Vladimir Nabokov's *Pale Fire*. The novel's unreliable narrator, Charles Kinbote, is the self-appointed editor of a 999-line poem entitled "Pale Fire," allegedly written by his brilliant, murdered friend and neighbor, John Shade. Galati staged the piece as an academic Q&A led by Kinbote.

> I took questions from the audience and the answers were supposedly about the poem but I always had a "plant" in the audience and at some point, I'd call on her or him. He'd ask a critical question about some line or something about Shade—I wouldn't know what, it didn't matter. I'd say, "Yes, an excellent question!" and launch into a long passage from the novel, which, of course, had nothing at all to do with Shade or the poem or the question but was all about Kinbote.

Director John Dillon, a former classmate, described the performance in a 1995 profile as "an unforgettably funny hour of academic satire as Galati's Kinbote 'explained' the poem and took questions from the audience, all of which he answered with verbatim sections he'd memorized from Nabakov's book."[1] There was no tenure-track position available when he graduated but in 1973, he was offered and accepted a tenure track position as assistant professor of interpretation at Northwestern University. He retired professor emeritus in 2006. His academic career was illustrious and fulfilling. He had no expectations beyond it but the die was cast in 1971, two years before his appointment, when producer/director William Pullinsi offered him a pivotal role in his commercial Equity production of *The National Health* by Peter Nichols.

Pullinsi was the first Chicago producer and director with the financial means, the appropriate theatre, and the vision to produce the chancy new plays he had seen in London and New York. In 1971, he and his partners Tony DeAngelo and June Pullinsi, his mother, opened the Forum Theatre adjacent to the Candlelight Playhouse, the prosperous dinner theatre they had established in Summit, Illinois, a working-class suburb of solid bungalows situated just outside the city limits. The second Forum production, *The National Health*, is a dark comedy by the British playwright Peter Nichols. Pullinsi intended to offer the pivotal role of the hospital orderly to Galati's Northwestern classmate Mark Lamos, an actor who had impressed him in Equity roles at Chicago's Ivanhoe Theatre and Academy Festival Theatre in Lake Forest. However, Lamos was Broadway bound. On the recommendation of Mike Nussbaum, a well-known Chicago actor who had appeared in several Candlelight productions, Pullinsi auditioned and cast Galati as the orderly. Other opportunities followed and by the time he accepted a faculty position at his alma mater two years later, he had found steady employment as a professional actor, author, and director in the greater Chicago area.

1971–1975: *The National Health, Miss Lonelyhearts, Boss*

British playwright Peter Nichols's idiosyncratic theatricality was remarkably well suited to Galati's inclination for presentational, audience-oriented performance. Reviewing a 2001 revival of Nichols' *A Day in the Life of Joe Egg*, Ben Brantley wrote,

> It's not literature that Mr. Nichols is presenting; it's not cinema. What he creates for the stage are only and transcendentally plays. Mr. Nichols has written that he has consistently tried to shatter the "two-way mirror" between a play and its audience. He consciously draws attention to his works' artificiality only to dig more deeply under the skins of his subjects.[2]

In the double storyline of *The National Health or Nurse Norton's Affair*, half a dozen male pensioners languish in a British hospital ward as a mixed-race romance develops among the hospital staff. The foul-mouthed, clownish, and vaguely sinister orderly played by Galati addresses the audience directly as a master of ceremonies, mediating between the presentational style of British music hall, the gritty realism of the hospital ward, and the arch mannerisms of daytime TV soap opera. In the show's finale, Nichols calls for the orderly to dance out of the audience and onto the stage as a manic, banjo-wielding bishop in blackface. In high stepping minstrel-show fashion, Galati ascended a broad staircase to preside over the final bows and apparent death of the ward's inmates. *Chicago Daily News* critic and columnist Sydney J. Harris gave the show a "rave" review, contributing significantly to the stature of Pullinsi's fledging commercial venture. Harris saved "the best" for his last paragraph "and that," he writes, "is the diabolically effective performance of Frank Galati as the orderly-cum-commentator."[3]

Later that year, Richard Christiansen called attention to the notable fact that though the production "upset some customers, [and] thrilled many more," this was "contemporary theatre of high quality being staged in Chicago by Chicagoans."[4] Originally scheduled for a limited eight-week run, *National Health* was extended for six profitable months. Because Pullinsi operated under an Equity contract, the production qualified for the Joseph Jefferson Award. The Jeff, as it is called, was founded in 1969 to honor the city's professional theatre and has become the Chicago equivalent of New York's Antoinette Tony award. In 1972, the Forum had thirteen out of thirty-five nominations. *National Health* received five nominations, including best performance in a principal role for Galati. He did not win that year, but Pullinsi won best production and best direction.

After *National Health* closed, cast member John Mohrlein teamed up with actor John Ostrander to form the Actor's Co-Op, a loosely organized profit-sharing group of actors who planned to mount shows wherever they could find space. Galati was approached and agreed to a chamber theatre-style production of Nathaniel West's Depression Era black comedy *Miss Lonelyhearts*, a piece he had developed at Northwestern. Mohrlein and Ostrander were included in an ensemble of sixteen friends and acquaintances with thespian instincts. "One can only wonder," wrote *Chicago Tribune* lead critic Linda Winer, "where such a range of actors was found."[5]

They secured space in the basement of the Holy Covenant Church on Diversey Parkway abutting the elevated train tracks. Paul Appel, an Evanston-based artist, was recruited to design a set. Galati, Appel, and Mohrlein pounded together a "nest" of miscellaneous salvaged doors. "All kinds of doors—we thought they had some symbolic value and they were free," laughed Galati. "There were knobs and handles sticking out everywhere, in every direction." The title character of West's novella, Miss Lonelyhearts, played by Galati's Northwestern classmate Roger Muller, is an increasingly distraught personal advice columnist who answers the letters of desperate and pitiful readers under the pseudonym Miss Lonelyhearts. "The room was very low and energetic," explained Galati.

"Everybody was excited and turned on by using the letters as a physical presence in Miss Lonelyhearts's world and imagination." He explained that the multiple narrators, each with a distinctive and highly individual voice and physical quality, produced "an odd echo effect—everything was in double exposure. The redundancy was valuable. It was an interesting way to experience a text—the narration penetrated the moment along with the sporadic rumble of the passing 'L' train."

To everyone's surprise, *Chicago Tribune* theatre critic Linda Winer showed up at the church basement to review the small, non-Equity production. In her review, Winer singled out the director as "a peripatetic comer," but what Galati valued more than praise was her understanding and validation of his audience-oriented, presentational aesthetic. "She got it. And she was really eloquent about it," remembers Galati. "It was the first time someone was talking about the sort of thing I was doing, bringing a novel to the stage." In her review, Winer admitted that she did not immediately catch on. At first, the multiple narrators "seemed stilted and artificial, with verbatim readings by the various characters often distorting West's deadpan lines." But, she continued,

> before long ... this line-bouncing among actors begins matching the impersonal hideousness of the novel's tone. Miss Lonelyhearts views the horror of his correspondents' letters with the eye of a stunned observer. He can't get away from the suicidal sweet-sixteener born without a nose, the pregnant Catholic baby factory with the aching kidneys, the crippled husbands, the raped youngsters—nor can he ease their pain. In Brechtian fashion, we are held outside the sorrow so we can get a better look.[6]

Winer understood that Galati's goal was not to make the individual characters take on a psychological reality of their own but to embody, in performance, West's distinctive tone and mood, the emotional impact of his prose and the intellectual force of his voice.

Galati's mentor and teacher, Robert Breen describes this distancing effect in his text, *Chamber Theatre*:

> [The] audience, like the long-jumper who must move back from his mark a considerable distance if he is to lengthen his leap into the pit, must view the events on the stage from a certain distance that will eventually allow it to engage the events more deeply and with fuller understanding than if it indulged itself in slack-jawed wonder and sentimental identification.[7]

As Winer suggests, far from interfere with the production's impact on the audience, the hodgepodge of castoff doors, noise disruptions, unexpected juxtapositions, and ever-changing narrators increased the emotional as well as the intellectual impact of the production.

There was real human suffering in *Lonelyhearts* but Galati denied his audience the empathic catharsis associated with a carefully crafted illusion of suffering. As he explained many years later, "the distance established between representation and its observer allows the eye to focus on conditions and circumstances that are ignored, veiled, or transparent in everyday consciousness." A subtle hand is required to balance the distance between the observer and the observed. If illusion dominates perception, the spectator is absorbed into the emotional landscape of the story. But if the aesthetic distance is too great, the observer remains detached, even disengaged from the action on stage. Galati's productions don't always "land," but when they do, the spectator is hit as if by a stun gun, stopped, as he says, in their tracks in a moment of recognition. When he fails to achieve this effect, it is most often because the distance established between illusion and its perception is too great, the staging too self-conscious, the presentation overwhelmingly theatrical or just overwhelming. However, in the cramped basement of the Holy Covenant Church in 1973, the director and his friends got the balance between representation and presentation just right and West's tortured characters were rendered all the more horrific because of it.

While Galati was preparing his script for *Miss Lonelyhearts*, Pullinsi recruited him to write the book and lyrics for a musical adaptation of *Boss*, columnist Mike Royko's bestselling send-up of Chicago's infamous Mayor Richard J. Daley. The combined celebrity and celebrated antagonism between Royko and Daley attracted major local attention and national press coverage. "We were confronted," says Galati, "by the most formidable array of critics—including *Time* and *Newsweek*, local and national television." Despite tepid reviews, word of mouth and the extensive national press attention gave *Boss* a run of over nine months and Galati won that year's Jeff award for best original book and lyrics.

The production was a box-office success but neither Galati nor Pullinsi were entirely satisfied with the project. Galati wanted to stage the book in the presentational style of *Lonelyhearts* with author Mike Royko as an on-stage character and narrator. He told reporter Linda Winer that he had hoped to build the show around "a conflict between [Royko] and Daley on stage. It was felt, however, that any Brechtian approach or narrative would be unsuitable to a musical comedy format. Maybe it would have. Who knows?"[8] The book's most interesting and fleshed out character is Royko himself but in the final production, Daley, played by Dick O'Neill, was the central character in a cartoon production that played it safe. In retrospect, Pullinsi felt that Galati's unique sensibility as a performer and his understanding of Royko's biting humor never quite made it to the stage. He recalled, "It was never so funny on stage as when Frank read it to us. He has this charm, like there's a devil in him, but it's all fun. He's always in league with the audience, but bigger than life."

After *Boss* opened, Galati suggested that Pullinsi look at Leon Katz's adaptation of the commedia dell'arte scenario *The Three Cuckolds* as a possible Forum production. Pullinsi liked the idea but was busy with a Candlelight project so he gave Galati his first commercial directing assignment with the popular African American comedian Godfrey Cambridge cast in the lead. Cambridge was an outspoken activist for the civil rights movement and showed up for rehearsal carrying a gun. "He was sure," explained Galati, "that 'people' were after him. It was difficult because he couldn't remember the lines—he couldn't concentrate. I went to his hotel and we ran lines together for hours, but he couldn't keep them in his head." A few days before the scheduled opening, Cambridge and Pullinsi agreed to let him out of his contract and the show opened with Bob Roven playing the role with the script in hand. Despite the problems, *Cuckolds* opened to good reviews and earned Galati his first Jeff nomination for Best Director. Four years into a career that got started "by accident," he had earned Jeff nominations as best actor in a principal role, best director, and best supporting actor, won the award for book and lyrics of an original musical, been reviewed in *Time* and *Newsweek*, and had written and directed one of the most noteworthy non-Equity independent productions of the early 1970s. It was, to say the least, an auspicious beginning.

Chicago has a rich history of excellent arts journalism but the young arts reviewers, seasoned journalists, columnists, and reporters whose careers parallel the rise of off-Loop theatre brought a fresh enthusiasm and engaging journalistic style that inspired public interest. One of the most influential critics of the old guard was the much feared and much-loved columnist, Claudia Cassidy. Cassidy was a towering presence in the Chicago arts community but throughout the 1970s, she ignored or discounted the burgeoning off-Loop productions mounted outside the city's cultural hub. Sydney J. Harris, the legendary *Chicago Daily News* "Strictly Personal" columnist had been drama critic for the *Daily News* since 1946 and when the paper folded in 1978, transferred his column to the *Chicago Sun-Times*. Cassidy and Harris set an extremely high standard for arts coverage in the city. Their example of beautifully written, erudite, and consistently entertaining journalism set the stage for a new generation of theatre, music, and dance critics who played a crucial role in the development and richness of Chicago theatre.

By the mid-1970s, the voices of *Tribune* critic Richard Christiansen and the *Sun Times'* Glenna Syse were joined by an impressive list of urban and suburban journalists who reported on and promoted Chicago's nascent theatre scene, including *Tribune* writers William Leonard, Roger Dettmer, and the paper's Nite Life critic, Larry Kart. The popular *Sun-Times* columnist and television talk-show host Irv Kupcinet regularly featured Chicago theatre in his interviews and comments. Bury St. Edmond's by-line first appeared in *The Chicago Reader* in 1975 and Anthony Adler began reviewing for the same paper shortly after. Intelligent and well-crafted reviews by Lawrence Bommer and Jonathan Abarbanel were published in the *Windy City Times* and Roy Leonard consistently promoted local theatre as host of WGN's immensely popular midday radio show. In the suburban press, Scott Fosdick and Dorothy Andries reported on theatre, dance, and performance in the greater Chicago area.

The list of significant reviewers who contributed to the development of Chicago theatre between 1970 and 1986 is extensive but during those years, it was primarily Syse and Christiansen who encouraged, chided, amused, and demanded attention for homegrown Chicago theatre. They made theatre a hot topic in bars, restaurants, and board rooms, on the street and in city hall. In the early 1970s, Syse used her position at the *Sun-Times* to lobby for and win alterations in the rigid Chicago fire code, making it feasible for non-profits to convert abandoned storefronts for theatre use. At her memorial in 2000, Dennis Zacek, artistic director of Victory Gardens Theatre, said, "There would not have been an off-Loop theatre if it weren't for her. It's as simple as that."[9] Second City founder Bernard Sahlins gave a similar tribute. "Glenna and Dick Christiansen were in a large part responsible for the burgeoning theater movement in Chicago."[10] By 1976, Chicago arts reporters guaranteed that theatre would not be ignored in the city's bicentennial celebrations and by the end of the decade, live theatre was as integral to the Windy City's public image as Wrigley Field, broad shoulders, and machine politics.

The Bicentennial: CETA, *Ladies Voices*, *The Mother of Us All*

In 1976, the US economy was in a substantial downturn but state and federal funds were nonetheless available for arts and culture projects to mark the country's bicentennial celebration. Chicago was no exception. The city's architecture, public sculpture, opera, journalism, and jazz were promoted and events planned by Chicago's world-class opera, symphony, and art institute. Theatre was not yet recognized as a potential economic engine but in 1976, the city's powerful working-class mayor Richard M. Daley suddenly died of a heart attack in his sixth term of office. His successor, Michael A. Bilandic, may have been "Mayor Bland" (so-named by *Sun-Times* columnist Mike Royko) in comparison to the colorful Daley, but shortly after assuming office he married Heather Morgan, director of the Chicago Council on Fine Arts and an influential arts advocate. Morgan's support alerted major Chicago philanthropists to the quality and economic potential of the performing arts. In the two and a half years Bilandic served as mayor and in the subsequent administration of Jane Byrne, the performing arts were supported in Chicago as never before.

Heather Bilandic's office used federal economic rehabilitation funds, the Title VI program of the Comprehensive Employment and Training Act (CETA), to support a WPA-style Artist-in-Residence program that put musicians, poets, directors, actors, designers, and performance artists as well as painters, sculptors, muralists, and photographers on the city payroll with full medical benefits and social security. I was a CETA Artist in Residence for two years. I made costumes for Ida B. Wells at the Historical Society and created life-size puppet creatures in an unventilated attic on Navy Pier. When the program ended, the city made substantial sustaining grants available to emerging and established off-Loop theatre companies, including Victory Gardens and Kuumba Workshop among many others. The notion began to take hold that making theater might turn out to be a viable profession in Chicago. Sharon Phillips, business manager for the Body Politic in the 1970s, told Richard Christiansen, "Before CETA … you made what money you could and split it up at the end of the week. But the CETA checks changed that. They were real salaries, $650 a month in two paychecks. They gave us a taste of a real life."[11]

In the 1975–76 Bicentennial season, twenty-seven-year-old playwright/actor/director David Mamet reconnected with former students William H. Macy and Steven Schachter. Patricia Cox, a recent graduate of the University of Chicago, joined them to revive Mamet's St. Nicholas Theatre, a company he had established at Goddard College in Plainfield, Vermont. Later that year, Robert Falls, still an undergraduate and newly arrived in the city from downstate, attracted considerable attention when he directed a highly praised late-night production of Michael Weller's *Moonchildren* in the basement of Mamet's theatre. Gregory Mosher, the newly appointed Associate Director at the Goodman Theatre, opened the Goodman's 1975–76 Stage II series with the premiere of *American*

Buffalo, a new play by David Mamet featuring Macy and Chicago actor J. J. Johnson. The production was staged at the Ruth Page Auditorium and ran weekends only.

In a far north suburb of Chicago, a group of young actors who called themselves the Steppenwolf Ensemble commandeered a vacant high school auditorium to produce a series of weekend shows. In 1976, critics Larry Kart (*Tribune*) and Dorthy Andries (*Pioneer Press*) traveled to the unlikely location in Highland Park to report on their earliest efforts. Andries announced, "Powerful new theater opens in Highland Park."[12] Kart agreed: "Steppenwolf's twin bill shows flashes of artistry."[13] A year later, Kart discovered the Summer Comedy Theatre production of Leonard Bernstein's *Candide*, directed by Michael Maggio, produced by Fred Solari, and designed by Maher Ahmad and Christina Scholtz. The musical played a four-weekend run at the Athenaeum, a decommissioned Catholic high school auditorium on the north side. *Candide* was produced on a wing and a prayer but with Maggio's buoyant staging and the inventive no-budget solutions concocted by the design team of Scholtz and Ahmad, the show was a sellout and Kart declared it "second to none."[14] The off-Loop theatre scene was still uncharted territory and Kart wasn't sure how to characterize the company. "For lack of a better term, this 'Candide' has to be classified as 'community theater,' but in conception and execution it rivals any musical presented on any stage."[15]

In 1976, Roger Dettmer reported that Actor's Equity estimated "on average, actors [in Chicago] can expect to work 42 weeks out of every year vs. New York City's 14 weeks."[16] There was no mention of what income those working weeks brought in. Even with the support of CETA funds, theatres struggled to meet union minimums. But the point wasn't what Chicago actors got paid. The point was that in a depressed economy and an environment where the number and variety of opportunities for professional theatre work were historically limited, Chicago actors, designers, stage managers, and directors worked. What's more, the work was good and getting better.

In 1976 a remarkable number of talented Chicago-based directors were making a name for themselves in the Windy City, but of the "local boys" who made their reputations as professional stage directors in Chicago, Frank Galati, Michael Maggio, and Robert Falls were among the most prominent and influential artists of their generation. These three men matured together and collaborated or worked in direct proximity to each other throughout the 1970s and 1980s. In 1986, Falls was named Artistic Director of Chicago's Goodman Theatre with Galati as Associate Director. Shortly after, Maggio joined the

Goodman team as Resident Director. With Falls in the lead, this triumvirate of Chicago directors enlivened the Goodman stage and the Chicago theatre scene for over a decade.

The three men had much in common. Each was a college-educated Midwestern baby-boomer. Each came from a working-class background. Each managed to make a virtue of necessity with an ingenious use of limited resources. Nonetheless, each man established a distinct signature that balanced and complemented his peers. Falls was a striking presence in his own productions. A big man with big ideas, he invigorated the stages of off-Loop theatre with richly conceived concepts and a postmodern sensibility. As artistic and resident director of the Wisdom Bridge Theatre—a second story dive on Howard Street with a urinal-turned-planter in the theatre lobby—he established a reputation for daring and often breathtaking productions. Michael Maggio had a lighter touch. Versatile, and stylish, his productions were marked by wit and a masterful sense of timing. He managed sophistication without a trace of arrogance or elitism and a heartfelt poignancy without succumbing to sentimentality. In 1983, Maggio was appointed artistic director of the Northlight Theatre in Evanston, Illinois. At that time, Northlight was an Equity house situated in a suburban grade school auditorium with a more sedate subscription audience than Falls' scruffy Wisdom Bridge.

Falls and Maggio both graduated from university theater programs where they studied acting and directing technique. Galati, a professor of literature, has never taken or taught an acting or directing class in his life. He learned his craft on his feet, as an actor in front of an audience or a classroom, listening and watching as he was watched. Falls and Maggio each found an artistic base in small, professional, not-for-profit theatres with a loyal subscription audience. Galati's artistic base was the interpretation program at Northwestern University, a hothouse environment where he explored theatrical framing, audience address, and narrative voice with a passionate and eclectic company of student performers. The intentional theatricality and audience-oriented aesthetic of *Miss Lonelyhearts* were atypical of his Chicago peers. In the early seventies, he was a popular and in-demand actor but his work as a director was seen as "different." His staging was distinctive and his storytelling coherent but he had not yet developed the spectacular showmanship of his mature work. However, in 1976, he began a long and fruitful relationship with the Chicago Opera Theatre. The fledging but ambitious company allowed him to explore theatrical presentation in the context of the standing-on-the-edge-about-to-jump emotionalism of grand opera and to do so in the English language. The unlikely conduit for his crossover to the opera world was a woman: the perplexing expatriate author of non-linear prose and plays, Gertrude Stein.

In 1974 the Museum of Contemporary Art (MCA) commissioned Professor Galati to adapt and stage a short selection of what he considered to be Stein's most playful pieces for an intimate performance at the museum. He prepared the text for a piece entitled *Ladies' Voices* and invited two accomplished colleagues from the Northwestern Speech Department, Lila Heston and Sandra Singer, to perform. He assumed that the project would be a straightforward reading of the text by two bold and witty women with extensive experience as oral interpreters. However, with text in hand he noticed that "the ladies were <u>not</u> happy." They didn't understand and therefore couldn't learn Stein's convoluted lines. They wanted Galati to coach them through the piece and help them make "sense" of it, but he was seriously pressed for time. He was shuttling between three different theatre commitments at the time and teaching a full load of classes at Northwestern. "So I told them," he recalled, "that every single sentence makes perfect sense—there is no smoke screen or abstraction. In 'Miss Furr and Miss Skeen,' the word 'gay' is exhausted out of existence. I said to them, 'It's not <u>about</u> exhaustion—it's <u>exhausted</u>. It's all absolutely real'—well [*expressive eye roll*]—if looks could kill!"

In Stein's prose ballad *Miss Furr and Miss Skeen*, two women meet and gaily thrive in their relationship for a time, then drift apart without comment or reflection. Stein's writing is experiential rather than discursive and he directed Singer and Heston to perform the words rather than an action. He gave notes on projection, posture, tempo, and clarity of speech rather than motivation or characterization and encouraged them to enjoy and savor the words rather than look for meaning or interpretation. He understood—and helped them to understand—that the power of Stein's language is sensual and this sensuality is released in the sound, rhythms, and flow of the human voice.

The MCA performance turned out to be an unmitigated triumph. "<u>Very</u> classy," he recalled, "done in long gowns and gloves, with a piano player and fresh roses on the piano. It had this wonderful erotic and intellectual energy. And in the end," Galati added with a grin, "it became one of their calling cards. They did it for <u>years</u>." The piece had a life beyond the MCA performance because Heston and Singer used their considerable vocal talents to capture the inherent sexiness and poignancy of Stein's words. The rhythmic verb-less phrases, the gowns, the roses, the beautiful voices, the very formality of the setting established pathos and longing as a sensory experience without feigned emotion.

Galati understands that the power of Stein's language "is not reportage, but its ability is to communicate feeling and emotion in the manner of an electric conductor."[17] Assuming an academic manner and tone, he explained that what might at first appear to be "stylistic eccentricity" in Stein's writing is "a very carefully crafted, carefully thought-out use of materials. She always dismantles the expected syntactical arrangement in order to surprise the ear and arrest listeners." He continued, "You hear the line and it sort of stops you in your tracks."[18] Stein's language challenges habitual rationalization and assumption to capture, in Galati's words, "a moment of mindfulness in which you are stopped in your tracks, present and fully alert to yourself and to the world."

Chicago Opera Studio (renamed Chicago Opera Theatre in 1979) Artistic Director Alan Stone selected the Virgil Thomson/Gertrude Stein opera, *The Mother of Us All* for his 1976 season. It was an appropriate Bicentennial choice because it linked two remarkable and distinctly American women: the author Stein and the activist Susan B. Anthony, the mother of Stein's title. Stone invited Marcus Overton to direct. Overton had a conflict but he had seen *Ladies Voices* and recommended Galati. At that time, Galati had zero experience and little knowledge of the genre but he was excited by the opportunity to work with an audience delighted by artifice and accustomed to virtuoso theatricality.

In retrospect, is seems inevitable that Galati would be drawn to the opera world. Sheldon Patinkin was a passionate and lifelong patron of the opera. He was also Chair of Theatre at Columbia College and my boss for seventeen years. Challenged by an undergraduate student to defend his inexplicable love for a theatrical form that featured farfetched stories, improbable ingénues, and "bad acting," his answer was characteristically pithy: "It isn't about what happens to them. It's about what happens to me." Patinkin understood that the power of opera is essentially visceral, physical, and profoundly personal. Galati took full advantage of the latitude COT allowed him to explore, pressure, and exploit this power.

His production of *The Mother of Us All* delivered what critic Thomas Willis judged to be "an ingenious, authoritative, and often captivating presentation" with "several moments of imaginative brilliance, matching the sometimes-paradoxical relationship of words and music with precisely focused business."[19] The production marked the beginning of a long and productive association between Galati, the design team John Paoletti, Mary Griswold, and Geoffery Bushor, and the opera company. In 1977, he directed Richard Hoiby's adaptation of Tennessee Williams' *Summer and Smoke*. "A refreshing American opera of real persons and love."[20] In 1978 he staged Otto Nicolai's *The Merry Wives of*

Windsor and in 1979, Benjamin Britten's *Albert Herring*. "Britten operatic comedy hits its mark."[21] In 1981, he directed the Chicago premiere of Robert Kurka's opera based on Jaroslav Hasek's satiric anti-war novel *Good Soldier Schweik*. The *Tribune* headline announced: "'Schweik': Brilliance amid excess humor."[22]

The success of his work at COT was due in no small part to Stone's expert vocal coaching and to the polish and energy of music directors Robert Frisbie and Steven Larson. However, Galati is generally credited with the company's early reputation for what were, by operatic standards, dramatically cohesive productions with a strong sense of character and story. COT allowed him to play with the opera's intrinsic theatricality and at the same time, encourage his young singers to, in his words, "tell the story." In 1985, Robert C. Marsh wrote in the *Sun-Times*, "It is the particular strength of the Opera Theatre that each character registered in sharp focus without going overboard in the direction of caricature."[23] In the same article, Marsh chided COT for having neglected what it did best. Of the six productions Marsh cites as exemplary of the company's strengths, four were directed by Galati.

1977 to 1981: *The Dick Gibson Show, Travesties, Good Soldier Schweik, Strider*

In 1977, he directed his adaptation of Stanley Elkin's *The Dick Gibson Show* for Novel Ventures, a production company formed by friends and classmates from Northwestern. Elkin's novel is regarded as a comic masterpiece and beyond politically incorrect. In his review of the novel, Dwight Garner wrote, "[it] squeezes the blackheads behind the ears of your imagination; it's a Diane Arbus walk on the unreconciled side. It's among the most powerful and funny American novels . . ."[24] Elkin was initially hesitant to grant the rights for a stage adaptation but acquiesced when he saw Galati's early draft. I designed thrift store costumes for the sleazy talk-radio host Dick Gibson and the panel of eccentric guests he interviews on a midnight broadcast.

Elkin came to Chicago to see the play and, as Galati explained, "He loved it! And he was extremely generous to us. Later, some people in Hollywood optioned his next novel, *The Living End*, and asked Stanley to write the screenplay. He didn't want to, but he'd just seen our show, and he recommended me."[25] Galati was on a sailing vacation with his family when he got the call from California and was whisked off St. Thomas on a private plane to discuss the project with

Elkin and the producers. Helen Tillman reported, "He said, 'I didn't exactly know what they wanted,' but he flew back to St. Thomas and for the next two weeks, sailed and wrote a ninety-page first draft in longhand. The producers were surprised when he showed it to them and said, 'Keep going. Do anything you want.'"[26] Which he did.

The comedian Richard Prior was interested in the property and Galati rewrote the screenplay to suit him but the film was never made. Nonetheless, this first commissioned screenplay led to many more adaptations of nondramatic literature for the screen. He got an agent and quickly became one of those celebrated writers who get paid for Hollywood treatments and scripts that never actually make it to the screen. However, in 1989, his treatment of Anne Tyler's popular novel *The Accidental Tourist* was filmed by Lawrence Kasden who did additional work on the script. Galati shared an Oscar nomination for best screenplay with a reluctant Kasden. Once again, the first time he was eligible for a major award—the Oscar—his name appeared on the list of nominees.

Immediately after *Dick Gibson* opened, Galati went into rehearsals for Tom Stoppard's intellectual farce, *Travesties* (1981), directed by Michael Maggio at the Wisdom Bridge Theatre with setting designed by Michael Merritt. I designed costumes for the production and Galati played the central role of Henry Carr, a retired minor British consulate officer engaged in writing a memoir of events that took place in Switzerland during WWI. The plot requires abrupt, onstage shifts between old Carr's disjointed ramblings at his desk and young Carr in 1917 Switzerland, a world inhabited by the Dadaist Tristan Tzara, author James Joyce, and Vladimir Lenin. In old Carr's memory each of these historic figures is in some way connected to a pair of trousers and his role as Algernon Moncrieff in an amateur production of Oscar Wilde's *The Importance of Being Earnest*.

It would be difficult to overstate Galati's success in this role. The extended opening monologue is set in 1974 with the elderly Carr at his desk rambling and raving something about trousers and Switzerland. His speech establishes the main action of the play as a product of Carr's lurid but unreliable memory. Bruce Mays described the opening scene in a seven-page profile published in *The Chicago Reader*: "He's out there, alone for 15 minutes . . . It is his play; it lives or dies on his performance."[27] The theatre had 150 seats but according to Managing Director Jeff Ortmann, *Travesties* regularly sold out 175 tickets with people crammed into aisles, standing on chairs, or wedged into exits. Spare tickets advertised in the local alternative newspaper sold immediately. Mays said of the thirty-six-year-old actor, "The Wisdom Bridge Theatre is wishing they could bottle whatever it is he does to an audience and sell it at the door."[28]

The Wisdom Bridge stage was a low asymmetrical platform nearly forty feet wide at one diagonal. The configuration was basically a shallow thrust stage with odd angles and irregular corners. Carr's desk was on a small, off-center triangle that jutted into an aisle. Speaking more like a director than an actor, Galati described the position of the desk as a framing location. He explained,

> In a conventional proscenium, you would tend to put it at the side of the stage, making the whole play a kind of balloon coming out of this burst of energy over to the side. But because of the peculiar triangle that thrust the stage floor into the aisle, the desk was placed downstage and squeezed from center to right. It was a hot spot, but it didn't block and it allowed me as the person playing the framing location, to be part of the frame, but at the same time in the picture.

Galati played directly to, with, and at the audience in "a style," Mays points out, "he had begun during *Pale Fire* and would use again and again, as Aston in *The Caretaker*... until by the time he became Henry Carr in *Travesties* he was all but consuming his audience."[29]

The second act opened with Galati again seated at the desk. Old Carr is holding forth about Switzerland when he is overcome by a visceral flashback of being shelled and gassed in the trenches of World War I, the gargantuan travesty at the disturbing heart of Stoppard's farce. Galati emphasized the character's encroaching dementia and lingering shell shock by casting those near him as indifferent bystanders in his anguished delusion. From his "framing" position, he used the cadence, pauses, and spiraling patterns of Stoppard's language to trigger a visceral and immediate effect in the theatre, much like Singer and Heston had done with Stein's prose in their MCA production. BJ Jones played the glib Dadaist poet Tristan Tzara and compared the effect Galati achieved in this speech to a fleeting sense of shell shock. "He sneaks up on you," said Jones, "and you're just... stunned. It's stunning."

As an actor, Galati was adept at placing himself simultaneously within the frame and within the picture. In *Travesties*, he demonstrated a mastery of this technique as an actor but in his 1981 production of Robert Kurka's opera *Good Soldier Schweik* for COT, he was still exploring the technique as a director. The opera is based on Czech author Jaroslav Hašek's unfinished and darkly comic novel about the First World War. The production was designed by Galati's long-time collaborators Mary Griswold and John Paoletti (sets and costumes) and Geoffrey Bushor (lights). It was a financial and critical success for COT but music critic John von Rhein felt that Galati's ebullient staging tended to overwhelm the opera's darker shadings.

> So much of this "Schweik" ... veers so far toward snazzy-comic production values and nonstop stage busy-ness that after a while we lose the bitter undercurrent of the satire. What emerges is a fast-paced dazzler of a show, quite the most imaginative integration of music and stagecraft COT has given us. But this "Schweik" lacks the sardonic bite that the subject demands ...[30]

Intoxicated by their own showmanship and stagecraft, Galati and his collaborators dazzled rather than stunned the audience. The distance between spectator and story was too great for Von Rhein, who felt that the brilliant showmanship overwhelmed rather than heightened the story's impact.

However, Von Rhein was impressed by the impact of the opera's final scene. Galati scattered multiple victims of the war, tattered civilians as well as uniformed soldiers, across the stage and held them in stasis as Schweik slowly threaded his way through the haggard frozen bodies and then literally walked out of the theatrical frame. Von Rhein described the scene in the *Chicago Tribune*:

> A phalanx of soldiers, hollow-eyed and dressed in bedraggled World War I uniforms, advances toward the footlights, spitting out an angry chorus. "Pray for the ragged soldiers," they shout. In a tight circle in front of them, a group of orphans—the pathetic victims of war—lay dead or dying. Pvt. Joseph Schweik, the opera's central figure, makes his way across the stage, slowly stepping over the bodies, which he regards over his shoulder with no horror, only silent curiosity. His whole manner is calm, accepting. Perhaps he has learned the hideous truth; perhaps he will remain the sweet fool to the end. In any case, off he marches, in precisely the opposite direction of his orders—to what fate we are never quite sure.[31]

"This is powerful theatre," wrote von Rhein of the final scene, "and here director Frank Galati gets the tone just right."

Outside of his work for COT, the production that best anticipates and introduces Galati's mature work as a director/adapter was his 1981 production of *Strider*, an ensemble musical based on Leo Tolstoy's story about the triumph and decline of a piebald horse and the parallel decline of his owner, an arrogant Russian aristocrat. In the winter of 1980, Maggio and producer Fred Solari formed a new not-for-profit summer production company in Woodstock, Illinois, a village fifty miles northwest of Chicago with a small but exquisitely renovated turn-of-the-century opera house complete with belfry and a resident ghost named Elmira. Galati opened the company's first season with a musical adaption of Tolstoy's story developed in Leningrad's Gorky Theatre. The piece had been translated and brought to New York in a 1979 Off-Broadway production at the Chelsea Theatre.

The project, a literary adaptation with music and extra-dramatic narrators, was seemingly ideal for Galati. However, he was dissatisfied with the original book, lyrics, and orchestrations and commissioned Xenia Youhn, a friend and professor of Russian literature at Northwestern, to provide an original translation of Tolstoy's story. He asked music director Les Stahl to put together an original score of incidental Russian folk and classical music. He wrote new dialogue and lyrics and when choreographer Dennis Grimaldi left the show during rehearsals, he and Peter Amster staged the musical numbers together. The reviews were good, some of them very good. Rick Kogan of the *Sun-Times* wrote, "It is an exciting, delightful, brilliantly staged, and acted production of a proud, funny and dazzling piece of theatre."[32] Scott Fosdick, who felt that the production "takes a great story, makes brilliant theater of it and, in the process, destroys the story," nonetheless felt that the productions strengths were noteworthy. "The superbly realized theatricality of 'Strider' makes the musical well worth the trip up Route 4, about 45 minutes past the racetrack to Woodstock."[33]

Christiansen was not a fan. "It takes more than I can muster," he wrote, "to suspend the disbelief that these are only men and women trying to act like horses."[34] But Galati had set out to dissuade the audience from the conditioned "suspension of disbelief" and discouraged the appearance of "acting" like or imitating horses. I was the show's costume designer and we agreed to dress the horses in dance rehearsal clothes—tights, legwarmers, lose torn sweatshirts and scuffed character shoes—with detailed theatrical costumes for the human characters. Set designer Joseph Nieminski's raked wooden stage and rough sliding doors could have passed for a well-worn dance studio as well as a weathered horse barn. Robert Shook's lighting evoked the atmosphere of a well-used rehearsal hall with frankly theatrical effects added in dialogue scenes to indicate a fictive location, season, and time of day. The actors focused on connecting to the dancer's animal joy in movement and physical display.

The ensemble devised a form of visual codeswitching to cue shifts between narrator, dramatic character, and non-speaking horse character. Collectively, the *Strider* narrators assumed the anonymous but relaxed intimacy of a master storyteller speaking directly to the audience. When they switched into a fictive character, tensed muscles and calculated gestures left the impression of being "on," that is, knowingly observed while feigning ignorance of the observer. As human characters, they "cheated out" toward the audience and gazed into a distant horizon. They posed and postured like aristocratic figures in a court

Figure 2 Barbara Robertson center, Maria Racossa far right. Woodscock Music Festival production of *Strider*, 1981. Courtesy of the photographer. Photo by Lisa Howe-Ebright.

portrait, oozing subtext, mysterious desires, and barely suppressed fears. Horse characters, on the other hand, had no subtext. The switch to a horse role was marked by a palpable shift from feigned disinterest to a disinterested awareness of observers on stage and off. The "horses" went about their business in the attitude of Degas's self-absorbed dancers marking time in the wings. Barbara Robertson played a glamorous circus bareback rider and an equally beautiful show horse. As the celebrated bareback rider, she performed dance movements in spangled Russian folk dress and maintained the demeanor of a diva center stage. As the thoroughbred horse, her warmup *rond de jambe* simultaneously recalled the coiled energy of a tethered thoroughbred and the self-absorption of a dancer at the barre.

All but one of the ensemble members took on multiple roles, appearing as an extra-dramatic narrator as well as a horse and a human character within the story. The anomalous figure who did not join in the dancing, singing, or storytelling was Vaska, a taciturn Russian stable hand who lived with the horses and communicated with characters, horses, and occasionally, the audience in grunts, shrugs, and low rumbles. Actor Mike Genovese's Vaska watched the horses and he watched us, the audience, watching the horses watch. Genovese—a craggily handsome actor, possibly typecast as the cranky Vaska—hunkered down in a corner, slouched in the shadowed wings, or leaned incongruously against the ornate carving of the theatre's permanent proscenium. At an early preview matinee, he sat in his usual position downstage right with his gaze fixed on a young woman seated in the first few rows. When she noticed him looking, he pulled his head into the folds of his ragged cowl and continued to watch the front rows from its shadow. As the applause for the dance subsided, he scowled up toward the balcony rail where a bus load of "matinee ladies" were noisily resettling themselves. It was not at all clear if Genovese was "acting" or just being Genovese—a little bored and irascible—but Galati, who sat next to me in the house, was delighted with the effect and whispered, "We are watched!"

Vaska/Genovese was empowered to look into the house by the authority Galati granted his actors in rehearsals and I felt that he did so without the knowing wink or ironic nod that acknowledges a clear distinction between theatrical frames. To be fair, Richard Christiansen did not "read" Genovese's actions as I did. In his review he wrote, "Unfortunately, Galati and some of his actors (including Mike Genovese in his overdrawn caricature of an eccentric peasant) cannot resist winking about the quaintness of it all."[35] For many theatregoers, a look into or acknowledgment of the audience is tantamount to a "wink," but on the occasion of that preview, Genovese did not convey such knowing to me. The actor could be seen looking, a meaningful and "readable" gesture to be sure, but the situation remained open to the unsettling possibility that the man who looked did so not to be seen looking but to look. If one attributed Genovese/Vaska's action to the intention of seeing rather than a representation of seeing, the character was simultaneously inside and outside the theatrical frame of Tolstoy's story.

By the end of the *Strider* run in summer 1981, Galati's work as a stage director was well known and generally admired but he was perceived by many producers and patrons as an accomplished actor who also directed distinctive and unconventional productions. Christiansen's reviews of his acting were highly appreciative, even glowing, but the critic was never entirely comfortable with the unabashed theatricality of Galati's directing projects. But like it or not, theatricality was Galati's stock in trade and whenever the opportunity arose, he continued to direct extremely popular and successful non-musical and musical productions in a frankly presentational style. Whether or not Galati's theatricality was an unmitigated success in *Strider*, it was a prototype of work yet to come.

1982–1984: *Division Street, Christmas Carol, Heart of a Dog*

In 1982, Maggio was approached by commercial producers to direct a production of Steven Tesich's *Division Street*. He wasn't available and felt that the script—an over-the-top farce about a crew of misfits who inhabit a Felliniesque apartment building on Chicago's Division Street—was more in Galati's line than his own and recommended his friend for the project. The plot of *Division Street* is little more than a pretext for a theatrical rant against political correctness and trendy liberal causes and Galati framed the entire production as the maniacal soapbox tirade of a brilliant pissed-off playwright.

The production I saw on opening night was memorable not for its argument, plot, or character development, but for the boisterous energy and sheer audacity of what took place in the theatre. *Division Street* was immensely entertaining, but once again, Galati's staging proved to be too much of a good thing for Christiansen who did not appreciate the show's extra-dramatic antics and

Figure 3 BJ Jones (seated) and Jo Lauck. *Division Street*, New Broadway Theatre, 1981. Courtesy of BJ Jones. Photo by Mary Griswold.

exuberant theatricality. His *Tribune* review began, "'Division Street,'... wants mightily to please, so mightily that is strains a little too hard much of the time."[36] He praised specific moments of inventive stagecraft and performance but felt that overall, the production was "overdone." Again, he was not alone. Nonetheless, the show was a surprise box office success, extended twice past its announced run and was videoed for the local NBC television station. The production was not without pathos or intellectual underpinning but it was memorable primarily as a celebration of human imagination, exuberant vitality, and an unrepentant theatricality that fully acknowledged the presence of an audience in the cramped auditorium of the New Broadway Theater.[37]

In 1981, he appeared as an accordion playing cook in Robert Falls' much acclaimed production of Bertolt Brecht's *Mother Courage and Her Children* (Wisdom Bridge Theatre). In 1982, he played the backstage dresser to James O'Reilly's aging Shakespearean actor in *The Dresser* by Ronald Harwood (Body Politic Theatre) and in 1983 he was Clove to Nicholas Rudall's Hamm in a heartbreaking, laugh-out-loud production of Samuel Beckett's *Endgame* (Court Theatre) directed by Maggio. In 1984, Greg Mosher cast—or miscast—him as Ebenezer Scrooge in the Goodman Theatre's revisionist production of *A Christmas Carol*, about which Galati says, "the less said the better." The extravagant production threw the Goodman into financial disarray and left Galati physically depleted and depressed. Nonetheless, a few weeks after *Christmas Carol* closed, he began work on a new project with Maggio at Evanston's Northlight Theatre.

The two planned an original adaptation of Mikhail Bulgakov's satire of the New Soviet Man, *Heart of a Dog* (1925), directed by Maggio. Galati would write the script and appear in the production. Once again, he commissioned his friend Xenia Youhn to prepare a literal translation of Bulgakov's novella. The production was designed by Linda Bucannon (sets), Robert Shook (lights), and me (costumes.) In the story, an egomaniacal Russian surgeon/mad-scientist, Dr. Preobrazhensky, played by Galati, inadvertently creates the perfect soviet bureaucrat by transplanting the pituitary gland and sexual organs of a deceased criminal into a stray dog. "It's a little grotesque," Galati explained. "A gothic tale of impossible medical transformation for the purposes of looking at Soviet society."[38] The ensemble improvised a zany *Young Frankenstein*-inspired surgery scene and Maggio staged a manic multidirectional chase scene. Sid Smith wrote, "The slapstick is merciless, the mugging is shameless, but the theatrics are inspired tour de force; in the end, this screwball treatment, a kind of Nikolai Gogol meets the Marx Brothers, does Bulgakov little harm and may win him additional fans."[39]

Maggio managed Bulgakov's farce with finesse and his direction was as always, clean, and well-paced. However, his staging was more screwball comedy than cutting satire. Galati's script was published by Dramatists Play Service and independent productions in Chicago, New York, and west coast universities received excellent reviews, particularly if a balance was found between caricature and dark despair and the ensemble was able to break through the conventional fourth wall of realist representation. In 1988, Galati received a letter from a Professor of Slavic Languages and Literatures at Princeton University. She writes,

> This is an unsolicited fan letter from a Russian literature professor just recently returned from New York, where a colleague and I saw your adaptation of Bulgakov's *Heart of A Dog*. What a magnificent job: not just the text, which completely captured the tautness and '20's raciness of the original, but the production as well, with its Meyerholdian mix of stylization and pathos ... I have never seen so accurate and enriching a transposition of Soviet material on the stage.[40]

Vsevolod Meyerhold was a Soviet theatre director who challenged the style of realist representation championed by his contemporary, Konstantin Stanislavski. His presentational techniques and experimental manipulation of realist convention are clearly indicated in Galati's original pre-production text. However, these elements were atypical of Maggio's work and the celebratory theatricality imbedded in Galati's text did not surface in the Northlight production.

In the early 1980s, Galati was a much sought after and highly acclaimed local actor with an interesting resume of eclectic directing credits. By the end of the 1986 season, he would be a nationally acclaimed stage director with—if anyone asked—notable acting credits in the Chicago area. This quickening of his directing career and reputation ran parallel to the extraordinary expansion and international reach of Chicago theatre in the late 1980s and early 90s. The remarkable events of the 1985–86 theatrical season would confirm his local, national, and international stature as an innovative and influential theatre artist.

Notes

1 John Dillon, "The Paradoxical Professor," *American Theatre*, October 1, 1995, 35.
2 Ben Brantley, "Revival of A Playwright Who's Funny and Upsetting." *New York Times*, February 14, 2002, Arts sec., 2.

3   Sydney J. Harris, "'The National Health's' a Triumph," *Chicago Herald*, April 21, 1972.
4   Richard Christiansen, "'National Health' Extended at The Forum," *Chicago Tribune*, June 30, 1972.
5   Linda Winer, "A Powerful Unlovely, 'Miss Lonleyhearts,'" *Chicago Tribune*, January 12, 1973, Arts sec., 8.
6   Weiner, *Lonelyhearts*.
7   Robert S. Breen, *Chamber Theatre* (Englewood Cliffs, NJ: Prentice-Hall, 1978), 49–50.
8   Frank Galati, Interview with Linda Winer, "Galati's New Musical Booked for Opening—in 2073!", Chicago *Tribune*, June 24, 1973.
9   Dennis Začek, Quoted in Marla Donato, "Glenna Syse, 73, *Sun-Times* Critic," *Chicago Tribune*, March 5, 2001.
10 Bernard Sahlins, Quoted in Donato.
11 Sharon Phillips, Interview with Richard Christiansen, *A Theater of Our Own* (2004), p. 190.
12 Dorthy Andries, "Powerful New Theatre Opens in Highland Park," *Pioneer Press* (Highland Park), July 29, 1976, Arts sec., 17.
13 Larry Kart, "Steppenwolf's Twin Bill Shows Flashes of Artistry," *Chicago Tribune*, December 17, 1976, Arts and Entertainment.
14 Larry Kart, "A Musical Treat with The Best of Everything," *Chicago Tribune*, August 26, 1977, Arts and Entertainment.
15 Kart, 1977.
16 Roger Dettmer, "At 50," *Chicago Tribune*, July 11, 1976, Arts and Entertainment sec., 6.
17 Frank Galati, Interview with Connie Lauerman, "Thinking of Her; Galati Revives Gertrude Stein at Goodman," *Chicago Tribune*, February 12, 1995, Arts and Entertainment sec., 16.
18 Galati, Interview with Lauerman, 1995.
19 Thomas Willis, "'Mother of Us All': Timely Pageant," *Chicago Tribune*, May 3, 1976, Arts sec. 3, 11.
20 Robert C. Marsh, "A Refreshing American Opera of Real Persons and Love," *Chicago Sun-Times*, April 17, 1977.
21 John von Rhein, "Britten Operatic Comedy Hits the Mark," April 13, 1979.
22 John von Rhein, "'Schweik': Brilliance Amid Excess Humor," *Chicago Tribune*, May 25, 1981.
23 Robert C. Marsh, "Opera Theater Forgets Its Heritage," *Chicago Sun-Times*, March 31, 1985.
24 Dwight Garner, "A Late-Night Radio Drama, With Hints of the Internet to Come," *New York Times*, September 21, 2017.

25 Frank Galati, Interview with Helen M. Tilman, "'Dynamite' Galati." Feature. *Northwestern Alumni News* October 1980:9.
26 Tillman.
27 Tillman.
28 Mays, 9.
29 Mays, 36.
30 Von Rhein, 1981.
31 Von Rhein, 1981.
32 Rick Kogan, "Tolstoy's 'Strider' an Exciting, Delightful Winner," *Chicago Sun-Times*, June 19, 1981, Arts sec., 56.
33 Scott Fosdick, "Adaptation Saddles the Noble 'Strider'" *Daily Herald* (Arlington Heights), June 19, 1981.
34 Richard Christiansen, "Vibrant 'Strider' Opens Woodstock Season," *Chicago Tribune*, June 19, 1981.
35 Christiansen, "Vibrant 'Strider.'"
36 Richard Christiansen, "'Division Street' at Broadway Lost in Too Much Farcical Traffic," *Chicago Tribune*, September 2, 1982.
37 The New Broadway Theatre was an intimate, short-lived, for-profit rental house on Broadway Avenue in Chicago, 1982–1984. It had a small proscenium stage and precariously raked seating.
38 Frank Galati, Interview with David Prescott, "A Carol's Song: Days of 'Christmas' at the Goodman," *Chicago Tribune*, December 15, 1985.
39 Sid Smith, "'Heart' a Three Ring Circus with Plenty of Style," *Chicago Tribune*, March 30, 1985.
40 Caryl Emerson letter to Frank Galati, "Heart of a Dog," February 6, 1988, Box 25, Folder 7, Frank Galati (1943–) Papers, 1948–2014, Northwestern University McCormick Library of Special Collections and University Archives.

3

The Hottest Theatre Artist in Chicago

In 1985, Peter Sellers, director of the Kennedy Center American National Theatre, declared Chicago to be "the hottest theatre town in America right now."[1] Few could argue the point. By the end of the 1985–86 season, Chicago's position at the forefront of theatrical growth and innovation in the United States was indisputable. Local productions transferred to London, Australia, New York, and the Kennedy Center in Washington DC. Chicago theatre-makers were courted by Broadway, film, and television producers. In 1984, Galati commented that "those of us who are privileged to work in theater are feeling a giddy excitement over how much exciting theater is springing up around town. There's such a tremendous, contagious energy."[2] By the end of 1986, he would be appointed Associate Director at the Goodman Theater, join the Steppenwolf Ensemble as a member and go-to director, and be established as a Hollywood screenwriter. He was full professor at Northwestern University and engaged by the Lyric Opera of Chicago to direct the first and last subscription season productions of the company's decade-long Toward the 21st Century Initiative. It was a time of giddy excitement for anyone invested in Chicago theatre, particularly Frank Galati.

The Goodman Theatre, 1986

In 1973, Goodman Theatre Artistic Director William Woodman brought in former Julliard student Gregory Mosher as Associate Director. Woodman resigned the position in 1977 and Mosher, who was twenty-eight years old at the time, was appointed Artistic Director. During the next seven years, Mosher infused the Goodman with youthful passion, energy, and driving ambition. In his first two years on the job, the theatre lost 16,000 of the original season subscribers and gained 18,000 new ones.[3] In his seven-year tenure, he brought greater diversity to the theatre, produced thirty-seven world premieres, and staged innovative revivals of classic plays, including Henrik Ibsen's *Enemy of the People* with African American actors William Marshall and Paul Winfield in the leading roles. Under his leadership, playwrights, actors, directors, and designers with hometown credentials were featured with increasing regularity in the Goodman subscription season. He produced and directed nine of Chicago native David Mamet's plays, including the 1984 American premiere of *Glengarry Glen Ross*. The production transferred to Broadway with the Chicago-based cast and creative team, including designers Michael Merritt (setting) and Kevin Rigdon (lighting). Mamet won the New York Drama Critics' Circle award that year for best American play and the Pulitzer Prize for drama. Chicago actor Joe Mantegna won the Tony Award for Best Featured Actor in a Play and Mosher received a Tony nomination for best director of a play. In July 1984, Samuel Freedman declared in the *New York Times*, "At this moment, the Goodman Theatre of Chicago may be one of the most exciting theaters in America."[4] That November, Mosher produced, adapted, and directed a daring but financially disastrous revisionist production of Charles Dickens's classic *Christmas Carol* with Galati cast—or miscast—as the parsimonious Ebenezer Scrooge.[5]

Early in 1984, Mosher decided to move the Goodman's annual holiday offering and perennial cash cow, *A Christmas Carol*, from the Goodman's 683 seat house to Chicago's historic Auditorium Theatre with nearly 4,000 seats. The production would have new sets, costumes, extravagant special effects, and a new script co-authored by Mosher and Larry Sloan, artistic director of the audacious Remains Theatre. But when rehearsals started in October, the script wasn't ready and Mosher was often absent. Although innovative and bold, Mosher's *Christmas Carol* suffered from a serious lack of planning and an excess of hubris. Construction of the elaborate set was plagued with a series of technical setbacks and rehearsals progressed in fits and starts. Nancy Coons reported on a rehearsal she attended a few weeks before the scheduled opening:

> ... the cast was as yet not tackling the expected theatrical details of mannerism and pacing, but rather, was engaged in a sort of group therapy, mixing improvisation, confession, and confrontation to project motivations appropriate to Dickensian emotions. With Mosher pacing back and forth, coaching and goading the cast as they sat around a conference table, two young actors played out improvisations about drugs, sex, and other contemporary themes in order to play more authentically a scene of desperate bargaining in the script.[6]

Mosher explained that he didn't want an ordinary *Christmas Carol* and in that at least, he succeeded. Sloan reflected, "it was a million-dollar show the size of a

Broadway production—we all need more time, more planning, and more money."[7] With better planning and an appropriate budget, the production may have found greater financial and critical success. But even so, as Sloan observed, it would have been a Broadway-style production rather than Chicago-style theatre. Chicago was identified with a robust and visceral acting style, integrated ensemble work, and a storefront sensibility that distained production values that upstaged the performance.

In 1984, the Goodman board of directors announced the formation of the New Theater Company, an ambitious project conceived and promoted by Mosher as a permanent, Chicago-style ensemble of playwrights including David Mamet and John Guare, ten actors, and several resident designers. The New Theatre would operate with an independent administrative structure in a separate dedicated space. A location for the 350-seat house was identified on Briar Street several miles north of the Goodman's Loop location. Renovations begun but the space wasn't ready in time for the first scheduled production in spring 1985, so Mamet's adaption of Anton Chekhov's *Cherry Orchard* was staged in the Goodman's miniscule studio theater off the main lobby. Samuel G. Freedman reported in the *NYT*, "While 'The Cherry Orchard' received mixed-to-poor notices—the general sense was that it was earnest but arid—the union of artists like Mr. Mamet, Mr. Mosher and the actors Lindsay Crouse, Peter Riegert, and Mike Nussbaum has created palpable excitement."[8] But on April 16, 1986, shortly before the second production was scheduled to open in the new building, Mosher announced that he had accepted former mayor John V. Lindsay's invitation to head the struggling Vivian Beaumont theatre at Lincoln Center in New York. When Lindsay finalized the appointment in the press on April 29, Mosher had already relocated to New York City. Mosher's sudden departure was a shock but not necessarily a surprise. For all the enthusiasm, talent, and excitement he brought to Chicago, his sensibility was more Julliard than Illinois State, more Big Apple than Second City.

The New Theatre Company's second production opened to negative reviews and poor box office returns. With only part-time and mostly absent artistic leadership, mounting debt, and mediocre critical response, the New Company was abandoned. With Mosher's abrupt departure, the Board of Directors were forced to announce the 1985–86 subscription season without artistic leadership in place. In the first months of the search for a new artistic director, backstage gossip was rampant in Chicago. Rumors circulated among the theatre community about dissent and possible acrimony among factions on the theatre's board but when the dust settled, it was clear that the Goodman intended to look to local talent for a replacement. All of the front-runners, Robert Falls and Frank Galati with Michael Maggio mentioned as a possible third candidate, were native Midwesterners who had come of age in Chicago storefront theatre.

Before his departure, Mosher had talked to Galati about directing a mainstage production in the upcoming season. Nikolai Gogol's nineteenth-century farce, *The Government Inspector*, was mentioned but nothing was confirmed until the board announced that Galati was slotted to direct Gogol's play as the 1985–86 season opener. It was a daring, even a dangerous choice for a theatre in financial straits and far from a safe choice for a director in line for the top artistic position. "It's a stubborn play," Galati told Christiansen shortly before the opening, "determined to go its own cranky and sometimes coarse way."[9] In a *Sun-Times* pre-opening feature, Glenna Syse wrote, "The choice [of Gogol's play] is a major and expensive commitment, with 20 actors in 30 roles and costumes by the truckload.... [It] will be the theater's only new in-house production until 1986. Everyone will be watching."[10]

Galati's research for the project was comprehensive. In a one-hundred-page, densely written spiral notebook, he compiled notes on reviews of contemporary production, questions, thoughts, and sketches.[11] The notebook includes detailed biographical material and lengthy quotations from over sixteen academic books and countless critical articles. He notes reviews and feature articles on contemporary productions staged by theatre luminaries Richard Eyre and Liviu Cuilei. Both productions were faulted as excessively farcical and lacking balance. Two quotations from the reviews were highlighted: "The worst of this treatment is that it often drives actors in pursuit of broad farcical clowning" and "vulgar theatrical camp without a sustaining rationale." He was clearly aware that he needed to let Gogol's bitter humor serve a purpose greater than its own end and needed to find a balance that had eluded Eyre and Cuilei. He explained to Syse, "You have to walk a tightrope because the whole thing teeters above the abyss. It's about the bogus and the genuine, it's about the difference between being authentic or being a sham ... It's about genius and invention."[12]

Galati was aware that the Goodman's antiquated stage and auditorium posed equally significant challenges to a director. The theatre had not been substantially remodeled since its construction in 1922 and the stage was essentially a nineteenth-century structure with limited capacity to fly scenery and an ornate proscenium frame of imposing height and width. The archaic auditorium had a steep rake with curved rows of seating that stretched across the entire width of the seating area. Extra space was needed between rows to allow access from the side aisles, providing patrons with comfortable leg room but increasing the distance between the stage and seating substantially. With only 683 seats, the house felt—and was intended to feel—much larger than it was. Antique wire frames installed under theatre seats provided convenient storage for a gentleman's fedora or top hat and the inspirational aphorism, "You, yourself, must set fire to the fagots you have brought"—much quoted by Hedley S. Dimock, a guiding light of the early twentieth-century camping movement—was emblazoned across the top of the proscenium arch, only recently hidden under a false façade on Mosher's order.

The building's interior had been designed for a society not unlike Gogol's own, one in which theatre architecture affirmed the entitlement and privilege of its enlightened audience. A grand staircase descended from the street-level entrance to the sunken lobby—reportedly designed in the style of Kenneth Sawyer Goodman's mausoleum—and the deco grandeur of the auditorium had a strong sense of occasion. Galati played with and against the innate elitism of the building's architecture, breaking through the facade of the proscenium with exuberant theatricality and dowsing the possibility of refined aesthetic appreciation with low humor, rapid fire slapstick jokes, and indecorous laughter. Played against the Goodman's restrained classicism, the outrageous "bits" improvised by the cast had the subversive edge of a street urchin slapping a pie in the face of a robber baron.

The show opened to excellent reviews with general agreement that Galati had found a balance that had eluded other directors. He made so strong an impression on critic Glenna Syse that his name was mentioned in the *Sun-Times* headline as if he had bested the author in a sporting match: "Galati proves Gogol's match; Director enhances wit of 'Inspector.'" Doors slammed shut with cartoon sound effects and a carpet unfurled as if by magic. The town mayor's alcoholic mother-in-law, played by composer Polly Liontis, accompanied the action on an electronic synthesizer. Nonetheless, Gogol's scathing indictment of government corruption was as chilling as it was entertaining and connections between Chicago's infamous political corruption and Gogol's Russia were obvious. However, Galati successfully linked the darker moments of the production to deeper human fears and insecurities about knowing fake from real, the counterfeit from the genuine. In an interview with Larry Bommer, he said, "What attracted me to Gogol as a theatre artist is how he skirts the irrational and introduces questions about identity, illusion, reality, the nature of personality, and fear and terror that are really contemporary. That, more than the political satire, is what I find incredibly relevant."[13]

Galati cast actor/playwright Keith Reddin in the central the role of Ivan Alexandrovich Khlestakov, a minor civil servant mistaken for the dreaded and powerful government inspector of the play's title. Reddin, a former student of Galati's, was a mercurial young actor whose apparently rubber limbs and mobile features were well suited to Gogol's farce. But more important, Galati knew him to be a "smart actor," well equipped to grasp "this ungraspable character ... who is what he is fully only when he's fully in disguise, when he feels the comfortable mantle of an audience's acceptance and approbation ... He's a sort of genius of deception—which is after all the epitome of theatrical art.... everyone in the play wants to be somebody else—and Khlestakov most of all."[14]

The action was super-charged, improvisational in spirit, and uncluttered in execution. B.J. Jones, one of Galati's ensemble "irregulars," played one of four greedy supplicants who beg favors from the fake inspector general. Jones recalled the way Galati and the ensemble worked together to solve a staging problem and streamline the action.

> Four of us show up, one after the other, to ask a favor of Khlestakov. Four in a row. Grovel, grovel, ask for a favor. It was the same scene over and over again. I was just acting, getting the job done the way actors do but I guess the action was bogged down and Galati saw it. So the next day he shows up with new pages of dialogue for each of us. He had reduced each speech to the specific intentions of each supplicant. It was brilliant. We walked in together and each of us asked for what we wanted, bang, bang, bang. A 25-minute scene reduced to 5 minutes. But we didn't know how to stage it. So, I said, "let's go to the front of the stage, kneel, and talk directly to the audience with our backs to Keith, the Inspector General." And we did, with Keith kind of lounging behind us. We took it out to the audience. This was so typically Frank.

Empowered by Galati and accustomed to ensemble collaboration, Jones and the company were well-equipped to direct their energy outward, into the audience. *The Government Inspector* was a Chicago-style ensemble collaboration inflated to farce on a grand scale.

In January 1986, the Goodman Board of Directors announced the appointment of Robert Falls as the theatres next Artistic Director and Galati as Associate Director. Christiansen reported in the *Tribune*, "Goodman's search committee, having gone through several interviews with Falls and Galati, has had a hard time choosing between the two men; so, in the last few days, the innovative plan has been to hire Falls for the principal post, with Galati coming on board as his associate."[15] Soon after these appointments, Falls and Executive Director Roche Schulfer invited Michael Maggio to join the Goodman artistic team as Resident Director and announced that he would direct the final production of their first season, Steven Sondheim's *Sunday in the Park with George*. For more than a decade, this hometown triumvirate joined forces to shape an extraordinary era for the Goodman Theatre. Their artistic collaboration stands as a striking tribute to Chicago's ensemble ethic.

The Steppenwolf Ensemble, 1986

By 1985, members of the Steppenwolf ensemble were increasingly unavailable for new productions due to New York transfers, film and television commitments, and pending stage offers. At the same time, the company's remarkable success and national reputation prompted greater public scrutiny and high audience expectations. It was clear that the core company would need to expand or disband and the founding members, Gary Sinise, Jeff Perry, and Terry Kinney, were determined to see the company survive as a permanent acting ensemble.

You Can't Take It with You, by George S. Kaufman and Moss Hart (1936) was selected for the 1985–86 holiday production and Galati, who was not yet a member of the ensemble, was invited to direct. The *Tribune* headline declared: "'You Can't Take It with You' a Sublime Celebration of Screwball."[16] Galati was delighted to be working with the Steppenwolf actors and gave the company full credit for the production's success. "I had almost nothing to do. I went there and watched them and laughed.... once they trusted me not to interfere with the process, they had established among themselves, the artistic conversation just sort of flowed." But, he added, "In terms of comedy I could be useful." A few weeks into rehearsals, he accepted Sinise's invitation to become a permanent Ensemble member and as a member, he would participate in season selection and propose projects that interested him as a director.

The ensemble was renowned for its "raw energy" and Sinise is "the actor most closely associated with the company's intensely physical 'rock 'n' roll' acting style."[17] Galati is a man of impressive erudition, genuine modesty, and something of a public intellectual. Sinise's invitation struck a few outsiders as counterintuitive but Galati and the core Steppenwolf company were truly kindred spirits. The Ensemble was known for a powerful, in-your-face performance style that acknowledged the presence of an audience in the shared space of the theatre. This acknowledgement was demonstrated and to large extent accounted for the success of the company's critically acclaimed, pre-Galati production of Langford Wilson's *Balm in Gilead* (1980), a production Jeff Perry described as "absolutely the most defining, challenging, vibrant, and fun example of what we had set out do."[18]

Twenty-nine actors appeared in the production, including founding and original members of the ensemble as well as several soon-to-be members. John Beaufort reviewed the production in the *Christian Science Monitor* as "a verbal folk opera with set pieces for arias recited by several of its 29 characters."[19] He also, inexplicably, described the production as "a quaint reminder of the era when actors fraternized with audiences." In fact, the company's choice to challenge the conventional fourth wall of realist drama was anything but quaint. Ensemble members aggressively dismantled any inclination to imagine a separation between actor and audience and the ways in which they did so were integral to the theatre event. Faux tiles painted on the floor and walls of the seating area doubled as the walls and floor of the sleezy bar where the play takes place. Action was overlapping and simultaneous. Cast members gently hassled or acknowledged non-actors in their vicinity. Dopey, the freaked-out drug addict played by Sinise, served as a liminal narrator and all-around Greek chorus, cuing light changes and music from the stage. Director John Malkovich recalled, "Somehow we hit upon the idea of Gary's character being the kind of master of ceremonies, narrator, observer, participate, or all of the above, so that he gave sound and light cues and moved the action forward and backward or had moments where he controlled repeat action. He became a kind of director on the floor."[20] Sinise directed his intense gaze like a follow spot, focusing the spectator's attention on a specific character or action in the crowded milieu. He was a constant presence hovering in the margins of the story and the stage.

By 1985, the original company members had spent over a decade in close and sometimes volatile proximity to each other. Shortly before Galati became a member, Kinney explained that "in the first couple of years we were always fighting; we were all strong personalities, and we were young. But we don't fight much anymore. We're very accepting of each other now."[21] Nonetheless, company decisions were still intensely argued and the niceties of backstage decorum were often ignored. Company members placed a high value on the positive energy of what outsiders might see as unproductive combativeness. "I can do work here I couldn't do anywhere else," Sinise explained in 1986, "because we've a history together. You can ... head bash and it can be misread as a creative assault. But Terry Kinney and I can have enormous conflicts, and we know what we're really doing; we know we're forcing each other to dig deep and not settle for something easy."[22] This sort of active engagement was not limited to company meetings and rehearsals. If a company member felt that a moment or an exchange had grown stale by repetition, it was not uncommon for an actor to throw a "monkey-wrench" into a scene in progress, actions so off-putting that in a more conventional Equity company, sanctions could be leveled. "It's the way we interact during performances," explained company member John Mahoney. "Sometimes we cover up weakness, sometimes we goose each other if we're off, sometimes we break the pattern."[23]

"The great thing about them," explained Galati, "is they never stop working—or let each other stop. They are out there every night, together and completely present to each other." Nonetheless, his innate diplomacy and ability to contain his own ego—qualities that would prove invaluable in projects with divas and overbearing commercial impresarios—were a welcome anodyne in the tightly knit family of talented and outspoken actors. As their director, he took care to honor each of them as individuals within the ensemble. "You know," he mused, "*You Can't Take It With You* was the first show they ever had a choreographed curtain call. They all just came out and bowed together. They were thrilled that they each got applause." His respect for the Ensemble's work ethic meshed smoothly with the Steppenwolf's non-hierarchical structure and balanced their feistiness without diminishing the company's legendary vitality. In 2002, veteran Ensemble member Rondi Reed agreed that company members were remarkably forthright. "This is no place for sensitive souls or tender feelings. That's not us. If you've got something to say, you say it." True enough, but in 2020, over thirty-five years after Galati joined the Ensemble, she reflected on his presence among them. "I believe that Frank was sent to us specifically to help us embrace our 'sensitive souls and tender feelings.' He did it with love and spoke with truth, engaging with grace, respect, discipline, and artistic responsibility. I am so so so so grateful," she continued, "to have worked with him."

Plays like *Balm in Gilead*, Sam Shepherd's *True West* and Lyle Kessler's *Orphans* provided "meat" for the young company's raw energies and physical intensity but the ensemble's early productions were memorable primarily and often only for remarkable performances. As Rich noted in the *New York Times*, the Steppenwolf was a "theatre for the senses and emotions, not for the mind."[24] The Steppenwolf actors could deliver a whopping punch but as they entered their second decade together, they needed a better set-up for that punch and a target worth punching. By 1985, Galati was a proven showman with an artist's eye for staging, composition, and spectacular effect. As for the target, he came to the table with a vast knowledge of dramatic literature and a sophisticated understanding of cutting-edge international performance theories and styles.

He knew and had taught the work of Mikhail Bakhtin, Richard Schechner, Peter Handke, Sam Beckett, Gertrude Stein, Vladimir Nabakov, Eudora Welty, Joseph Beuys, John Cage, Antoine Artaud, and Bertolt Brecht. He quoted poets, philosophers, and the pioneers of performance theory from memory—Yeats, Heidegger, Sartre, Arendt, and Husserl as well as Pina Baush, John Cage, and Peter Brook. He was well prepared to integrate the cutting-edge currency of the company's dynamic acting style with contemporary stagecraft and dramaturgies.

In the spring of 1987, he directed company members in Wallace Shawn's *Aunt Dan and Lemon*, a play described by Frank Rich as about "nothing less than the central moral question of our age."[25] Glenna Syse noted in the *Chicago Sun Times* that the production posed the troubling question: "How can we continue to exist in a society that permits us to put the responsibility [for evil] elsewhere? The finger of blame is clearly pointed at every one of us."[26] Shawn's disturbing play was an inspired choice for the iconoclastic Steppenwolf actors. His dialogue furnished the kind of actor's "meat" the company reveled in and the cast featured not one, but three powerful female roles played by Martha Lavey, Molly Regan, and Rondi Reed. Performed in two hours without intermission, it was not an easy evening's entertainment. It is "an adult play," wrote *Sun Times* critic Hedy Weiss, "not just because it deals with themes of politics, morality, sex, violence, money and intellect, but because it requires a certain hindsight about the way we become the people we are."[27]

Christiansen, who had observed and supported the company's development since its inception, declared that "Rondi Reed, as Lemon's sad mother, and Tom Irwin, as the brutish father give the performances of their Steppenwolf ensemble careers."[28] The acting and directing were as seamless as any earlier Steppenwolf production but this time, the director and designers shared significant credit with the acting ensemble for the powerful effect achieved on stage. Richard Christiansen wrote, "With the perceptions of a poet, [Galati] has reinforced and amplified Shawn's text at every turn, using light, space, and music to underline the play's argument through revelatory imagery."[29]

Lemon, "a frail young woman, who 'honestly' admires the thoroughness of the Nazi killing machine ..." was played by Galati's former student, Martha Lavey.[30] Lavey was not an ensemble member at the time but would join in 1993 and served as the theatre's artistic director from 1995 until 2015.

Lavey died in 2017 and in a tribute published in *American Theatre*, Galati described an incident that captures her performance in *Aunt Dan and Lemon*.

Figure 4 Martha Lavy, Steppenwolf Theatre production of *Aunt Dan and Lemon*, 1987. Courtesy of the photographer. Photo by Lisa Howe-Ebright.

Near the end of the play, Lemon, luminous and beautiful in the pinafore of a young postulant, uncoiled an argument that embraced and all but condoned the atrocities of the Nazis and the extermination of millions. She imagines the victims as bugs to be squashed. The contrast between the purity and elegance of a young novice and the ideas she was pondering was so shocking that many audience members were deeply upset. At one matinee, a woman stood up in the middle of the speech and shouted, "Are you going to sit here and listen to this?" Martha continued. "I'm leaving!" the woman shouted. She gathered her coat, climbed over numerous audience members and marched up onstage—the only exit in that old Halsted Street space was at one end of the room and the only way to get there from the woman's seat was across the stage. The woman stormed behind Martha, smashed open the double doors, and ran out into the small lobby where she continued to rail against the show. Martha, the embodiment of irony, was as poised as the Virgin Mary. Her courage and absolute devotion to the lucid delivery of the text was palpable. It was a "great reckoning in a little room."[31]

Lavey's ability to live on the stage rather than create a convincing imitation of life was empowered by her director and achieved through an uncompromising commitment to the moment she shared with the audience and the story she was there to tell them.

Lyric Opera and Broadway "Popera," 1986–1996

In the heady days of late twentieth-century postmodernism, master narratives went the way of the albatross and once venerated conventions were subjected to aggressive deconstruction. Nothing was sacred, especially grand opera. By the 1980s, opera was no longer an elaborately costumed pageant played out against a painted backdrop. Opera was high drama and mind-bending innovation. Galati's predilection for theatricality and spectacular storytelling meshed seamlessly with the postmodern sensibility of late twentieth-century opera.

The outcome Galati generally oversees examines the human condition in the stop-time of narrative reflection and repetition. Kasper Holten, director of opera, Royal Opera House (Covent Garden), explains the overall outcome of the opera in similar terms.

> Through the combination of music and theatre, we can identify with characters, but then – when they feel love, despair, loneliness, fear, hope, jealousy – stop time and explore these moments further through music and movement, finding a language for the emotions it can be difficult to talk about, although they define our lives. Opera can make us see, feel and hear the world differently, and remind us about being in touch with the things beneath the surface, the things that really matter.[32]

Little wonder that Galati was attracted to and embraced by an all-encompassing art form with emotional peaks and abysses that unfold in the novelesque stop-time of lyric song.

In *Believing in Opera* (1996), Tom Sutcliffe offers an insider's account and critique of the remarkable achievements in direction, design, and narrative structure in contemporary opera, including the work of such luminaries as Ruth Berghaus, Peter Sellers, and Graham Vick. He points out that, like the theatre director, the opera director is a relative newcomer to the creative team. In earlier eras "when the content of the acting and how the actors behaved on stage were settled through conventions understood by both performers and audience, the musical director or conductor often took charge of the staging." Just as theatre was reinvented in the first quarter of the twentieth century, opera followed a similar pattern in its final quarter. "These days," writes Sutcliffe "even if the designs are in principle decorative and aesthetic rather than conceptual, there has to be a [director] with a genuine sense of artistic commitment to pull all the elements of a theatrical realization of opera into proper coherence and focus."[33] Galati's conception of the stage director as an editor who oversees, as he says, "the coalescence of many voices" aligns with Sutcliffe's description of the director's role in opera. "The producer (or stage director)," writes Sutcliffe, "is usually the strategist of the production ... It may not always be the producer who has the best ideas. It is just his or her responsibility to decide the outcome, to edit, to select, to receive what the design and lighting team and dramaturgs and conductor and singer-actors can offer."[34] Galati was able to bring the sprawling monster that is grand opera into a cohesive and meaningful whole and at the same time, honor the best ideas of his remarkable collaborators.

Sutcliffe looks primarily to England and continental Europe for innovation. In his estimation, "American companies mostly do not offer artistic autonomy to the more innovative and adventurous directorial talents."[35] The Lyric Opera's general director Ardis Krainik was a notable exception to Sutcliff's generalization. Krainik was determined to usher the company into the twenty-first century as a world-class institution. Toward that end, in 1982, she announced the Lyric Opera Center for American Artists. The Center would support two years of professional workshops for a young composer and a third year to prepare a full production. She described the ambitious program as an opportunity for talented young artists to have the experience of total immersion in the atmosphere of opera and theater on a year-round basis. After a six-month nationwide search, thirty-year-old William Neil was selected for the three-year immersive internship and Galati was Krainik's personal choice to direct and mentor the talented young composer into the heady international world of grand opera.

In June 1984, Galati staged the prologue and first scene of Neil's opera-in-progress based on Nelsen Algren's novel about a prizefighter falsely convicted of manslaughter, *The Devil's Stocking*. However, the Algren estate was unwilling to make the rights available at a price the Lyric was willing to pay and the project was abandoned. Neil turned to the 1920s trial of Lillian Sloan and her lover for the murder of her husband. "Although the only incriminating evidence was a handful of letters in which the woman, Lillian Sloan, had poured out her dreams about living an unmarried life, she and her paramour, Owen Evans, were convicted of the crime and died on the gallows."[36] Sloan's conviction and execution were based on a judicial interpretation of literature. This was Galati's bailiwick and it was decided that he would serve as librettist and lyricist as well as direct Neil's new opera, *The Guilt of Lillian Sloan*.

"For me," explained Neil, "the real learning started when I began to collaborate with Galati."[37] Under his mentoring, Neil learned that "a successful opera is based on a quick exchange of visual, sonic, and dramatic elements, a kaleidoscopic arrangement that makes the attention constantly shift from one element to another.... I learned that a successful opera composer uses [their] control over the listeners' emotions to get to their minds." Galati's theatrical sensibility had a profound effect on Neil.

> By the time I entered the third year of the residence, my ideas about intervallic structuring and "symmetrical" harmonies had taken a back seat to the needs of musical theatre. No matter how valid they may have been from a purely intellectual point of view, their stock value seemed to go down and the more I concentrated on making the score dramatically effective. That's the main thing.

Galati mentored Neil in the creation of carefully orchestrated shifts and jumps between progressive and repetitive time, between the dramatic and the lyric, and between mimesis and narration. As director and librettist, he crafted what he described to von Rhein as "a highly theatrical, though somewhat abstract interior landscape" that oscillated rhythmically as well as visually between courtroom realism and "a gauzy kind of neo-romantic lyricism" in Sloan's imagination.[38]

The opera was staged in June 1986 at Northwestern's Cahn Auditorium with a full orchestra and professional singers, sets, and costumes. The invited audience included the Lyric Opera board of directors, major donors, city officials, and important music critics. The production featured all the hallmarks of Galati's directorial style: non-linear storytelling, compressed action, passages of static reflection, stunning visuals, and unconventional juxtapositions. Under his guidance, the opera's making had been an ensemble effort from beginning to end. The *Chicago Tribune's* celebrated critic, John Von Rhein, acknowledged Galati's collaborative process: "In a more fundamental sense, the new opera is a true ensemble effort that has been shaped and refined by many people inside and outside the company."[39]

The following year, he returned to the Opera Center to direct Dominick Argento's seldom produced chamber opera, *Postcard from Morocco* with a libretto by John Donahue. Set in 1914, a group of strangers identified by the objects they carry—a hand mirror, a hat box, a coronet case—wait at an unnamed railway station. The Man with a Paint Box has a name but no paints, only a box and The Puppet Master may or may not have a puppet in his case. "The opera," wrote Tim Page in a *New York Times* review, "belongs to a proud American tradition: It is an opera, like 'Four Saints in Three Acts' by Virgil Thomson and Gertrude Stein, or 'Einstein on the Beach' by Philip Glass and Robert Wilson, that has no clearly discernible plot but makes its effect through a powerful series of images and inferences."[40] Critic Robert C. Marsh noted Galati's considerable contribution to the acting and mise-en-scène:

This was a piece of total music theater in which the skills of Frank Galati, who directed, were of equal or greater importance than those of conductor Lee Schaenen. The excellent musical preparation was matched by the quality of the acting, the persuasive force of the characters drawn, and the skill and ease with which 90 minutes of unbroken drama moved effortlessly.[41]

In 1986 Krainik was planning an ambitious, decade-long Lyric Opera project and determined that Frank Galati would play a significant part of it.

Toward the Twenty-first Century; *The Voyage of Edgar Allan Poe, Peleus and Melisandre, View from the Bridge*

In 1989, Krainik announced that the Lyric would stage two new or newly conceived twentieth-century operas on the Lyric stage every season for the next ten years, alternating between American and European composers. Galati told Dorothy Andres, "Ardis was such a visionary. She planned to produce ten 20th century operas in the final decade of the 20th century and she asked me to direct the first one—'The Voyage of Edgar Allan Poe' and the last."[42] The Lyric's toward the 21st Century initiative was launched with a newly conceived production of Christopher Gluck's *Alceste* (1767) featuring the Chicago debuts of soprano Jessye Norman and director/designer Robert Wilson. A few months later, Galati made his Lyric debut as director of the first America entry in the series, a lavish production of *The Voyage of Edward Allyn Poe*, composed by Argento and first produced by the Minnesota Opera in 1976.

With a libretto by Charles Nolte, *The Voyage of Edward Allyn Poe* "takes its point of departure from a bizarre incident in the great fantasist's life. In September 1849, Poe took a steamer from Richmond to Baltimore that seems, for whatever reason, to have languished at sea for days. Less than a week after arriving in Baltimore, he died, dissolute and destitute, at the age of 40."[43] The score is not Argento's finest and the libretto was judged by critics to be weak. However, critic John von Rhein declared, "such is the ingenuity of Chicago stage director Frank Galati and his design team of John Conklin (sets), Virgil Johnson (costumes), Duane Schuler (lighting), and John Boesche (projections) that one hardly notices any structural problem."[44] Conklin's setting evoked Poe's hallucinations in a surrealist dream world in which a bloodied child bride appeared in a plexiglass showcase and a flock of beds floated ominously across the horizon. Boesche projected off-kilter supertitles on the header with background information as well as short lyrical passages. Handwritten quotations from Poe's manuscripts appeared graffiti-style on the walls, often fading from view as quickly as they appeared. In contrast to this dreamscape, Virgil Johnson's detailed period costumes were consistent with operatic verisimilitude. Poe was real. His environment and most of the characters who populated it were figments of nightmare. Von Rhein wrote in the *Tribune*, "The images, which transmitted an almost kinetic quality, became larger, and larger and, then—with the focal point on the dark, deep-set eyes—blurred into haunting portraits of seeming madness."[45] The critic observed wryly, "With his fondness for murky psychological melodrama, the real-life Poe, one suspects, would have adored it."[46]

I saw the production from the Lyric's highest balcony seated among a small group of impoverished but friendly and surprisingly loquacious twenty-something opera nerds. As the audience settled, the group hashed over the Lyric's last production, *Alceste*, literally note by note. Their reviews were favorable but contentious. I was impressed. They were impressed that I knew and had worked with the director and two of the designers of the production we were about to see. At the final curtain, it was generally agreed among them that *Voyage* was "cool," that the projections were totally creepy, and with a few caveats, the score—"not Argento's best"—was well conducted by Christopher Keene. The staging and flow of movement between scenes achieved by Galati and his design team were admired with general agreement that transitions are the Achilles heel of grand opera. It was determined that the production never slipped out of the director's artistic control. I wondered aloud if the floating beds might not be too clever by half but my new acquaintances did not agree. "My dear," one of the young aficionados declared, not unkindly, "It's opera!"

Galati's Lyric debut was well reviewed in the press and the following season he returned to stage Debussy's *Pelleas and Melisande* with Teresa Stratas singing the lead and Robert Israel, a leading light in postmodern opera design, as production designer. *Pelleas* had been in the opera repertory since the early twentieth century but was seldom produced. Stratas did not appear until the third performance but was universally acclaimed when she did. The decidedly unconventional staging was not so well received. The *Tribune* headline announced, "Subtlety Gets Lost in Stagey 'Pelleas' Orchestra Rescues Debussy."[47] Von Rhein wrote: "Galati's theatrical brilliance can burn up the stage under the right circumstances, but here his attempt to treat Claude Debussy's masterpiece (offered as this season's European entry in the 'Toward the 21st Century' initiative) as a kind of postmodern ritual-theater was done in by its own conceits."[48] "The weak links in this production," wrote George Grass in a snarky *Chicago Reader* review, "are in the direction, set design, and costuming." Grass describes the director's contribution as "mostly adequate" but Galati staged a rape scene in the third act that Grass described as "unspeakably brutal and did literal and metaphorical violence to the spirit of the work."[49] Rape is, by definition, unspeakably brutal and Golaud's violent rage against Melisande is both sexual and essential to the opera's denouement. However, as critic Thor Eckert Jr. pointed out, the opera "is a work that has never been a crowd pleaser, yet whose admirers are generally fanatic partisans."[50] Galati and Israel's rendering of the opera offered very little to appease fanatic partisans and old-school sensibilities.

In the 1993–94 season he staged two classic operas for the Lyric: Verdi's *Traviata*, which opened the subscription season and the Puccini classic *Tosca*, a production that was shared with San Francisco and originated there a year earlier. June Anderson, who sang the role of Violetta in *Traviata*, is renowned as a fine dramatic actress as well as a powerful coloratura soprano. She did not disappoint. Von Rhein reported that "she internalized every emotion of the role with her usual intensity and conviction, from desperate gaiety to startled joy at her first stirrings of love for Alfredo, right on through to her deathbed scene, which tugged mightily at the heartstrings of even the most jaded opera-goers."[51] The critic was also enthusiastic about the psychological verisimilitude Galati had drawn from the performers:

> This is one of the best opening nights in recent memory owed primarily to several factors, notably the extraordinarily moving Violetta of June Anderson, Frank Galati's sensitive direction and the handsome, dramatically apt designs by Desmond Heeley. But this was a "Traviata" in which every aspect—singing, acting, conducting, stagecraft—signaled a true team effort and served to breathe musical and dramatic freshness into a familiar opera.[52]

This was the first time I had seen and heard *Traviata* performed on stage. All I can say is that I wept unashamedly in the upper balcony. I was not alone.

Reviews for *Tosca* (1993) were mostly positive and Galati's contribution was significant enough to be featured in the *Christian Science Monitor* review headline, "Galati's Production of 'Tosca' Worth the Trip to Chicago." David Selznick wrote, "Galati, [designer Tony] Walton, and conductor Bruno Bartoletti pursue every opportunity to make the melodrama plausible on a moment-to-moment basis, delineating one character's motivations with nuance and feeling and another's change of heart with gradual awareness."[53] Shortly after the opening of *Tosca*, Canadian impresario Garth Drabinsky announced his plan to mount a major musical production of E. L. Doctorow's award-winning novel *Ragtime*, an epic story of turn-of-the-century America. His Toronto-based production company Livent had secured the rights for the novel, Terence McNally was contracted to write the book, and Drabinsky began a highly unusual process of "auditioning" artistic collaborators. McNally had worked as a tutor for the Steinbeck family in the 1960s and remained a close friend to Elaine Steinbeck. He admired Galati's *Grapes of Wrath* and recommended that Drabinsky add his name to the list of candidates invited to submit their work. Galati was instructed to write a detailed critique of McNally's early draft. After submitting a lengthy document, he was invited to meet with Drabinsky in Canada for a personal interview and further discussion of the script and staging. It went well and Galati was invited to join the *Ragtime* artistic team. Ten composer/lyricists had been invited to write and submit a selection of original audition material for consideration and Lynn Ahrens (lyrics) and Stephen Flaherty (music), the team that created *Once on this Island*, were hired. The musical went into two years of preproduction and a year of previews prior to the 1998 Broadway opening.

In February 1995, he directed *Gertrude Stein: Each One as She May*, his 90-minute adaption of a story from Stein's 1909 book *Three Lives*. It was staged in the Goodman's intimate studio theatre. The cast of four African Americans included Jacqueline Williams as Melanctha and Johnny Lee Davenport as the suitor who abandons her with Rick Worthy and Cheryl Lynn Bruce as narrators. He staged the piece around a central staircase designed by Mary Griswold with a ragtime underscore created and played by violinist Miriam Sturm with pianist Reginald Robinson. The following November, he staged a joyful and iconoclastic production of the medieval morality play *Everyman* at the Steppenwolf Theatre. Twenty-eight members of the Windy City Gay Men's Chorus performed Gregorian chant, Christian hymns, and popular Christmas songs from upstage bleachers and Everyman was chosen by lottery at each performance from a group of four non-white males and one white female. But from 1996 until the Broadway opening of *Ragtime* in 1998, he was seldom seen in the Chicago area. In 1997, one year prior to the Broadway opening of *Ragtime* and two years before Galati was scheduled to return to the Lyric for the final production in the 21st Century series, Ardis Krainik died unexpectedly and William Mason replaced her as general manager of the Lyric Opera (1997–2011).

Under Krainik's leadership, the Lyric had commissioned a new opera from William Balcome to premiere in 1999 under Galati's direction. This final entry in the company's Toward the 21st Century Initiative would be *View from the Bridge*, based on the 1955 stage play by Arthur Miller with Arnold Weinstein and Miller collaborating on the libretto. The production was a joint venture with the Metropolitan Opera and the *New York Times* published a series of lengthy feature articles prior to the opening, including an extended interview and feature on the director. Invited to reflect on the appeal of opera, Galati commented on the form's combination of immediacy and virtuosity: "It's the kind of virtuosity you see in those who test themselves to the absolute limit. What if they fall? What if the pianissimo cracks? You live in fear in the audience, just as the singer does. It's the most difficult test the human voice can endure and it's happening in front of us. Now."[54] He commented in conversation that the most difficult notes "are linked to a pitch of emotion that cannot be expressed in any ordinary way." The virtuoso voice embodies rather than represents the soul's terrible longing to express the inexpressible.

Matthew Epstein, the Lyric's esteemed and outspoken artistic director, placed high value on Galati's ability to create a cohesive ensemble. "That's what he comes out of, ensemble theatre, and it's what opera should be about, but isn't always. Frank would not work well with a superstar. And in this case, even a big name like Catherine Malfitano, she's someone who prefers to work in an ensemble situation."[55] In 2004, "a terse press release from Lyric Opera of Chicago announced the severance of Epstein's twenty-four-year connection with the company."[56] Epstein and William Mason, the company's general director, had come to an impasse concerning programing. "In Chicago," said Epstein, "we sold out *A View from the Bridge. Mourning Becomes Electra* was a big hit, and we were preparing to mount revivals of *McTeague* and *The Seagull.* There was suddenly a decision to remove American opera from the 2005–06 season, and then another decision to remove American opera from the 2006–07 season as well." Under Kranik's leadership, the Lyric had mounted an American opera every year for the past fifteen years. Reflecting on his departure from the Lyric, Epstein said, "The fact is, that the cessation of Lyric's leadership – in its championship of American music, in stage direction, in smart productions of neglected music – was not something I could countenance." Mason responded, "The creative decisions and wishes of a music director and/or artistic director can only be realized if there is the money to pay for them."[57]

In 2000, the politics of the opera world, notoriously byzantine in the best of times, were increasingly fraught as costs soared and conflicts escalated between management and artistic leadership. *View* was a critical and financial success but it was also Galati's last foray into grand opera. Perhaps the challenges and pressures of opera production finally outweighed the advantages and rewards. Perhaps his decision was influenced by the loss of leaders like Epstein and Krainik, an artistic director and producer who valued daring creativity and genuinely mentored innovative and adventurous talent. However, his work in the opera and in the theatre attracted the attention of ambitious commercial producers and composers inclined toward the style, scale, and themes—passion, betrayal, vengeance, and death—of grand opera. After *View From the Bridge*, he directed three premieres of original, mostly sung-through musicals intended for Broadway: *Seussical the Musical* (New York premiere 2000), *The Visit* (Chicago premiere 2001), and *Pirate Queen* (Chicago premier 2006, New York premier 2007). Each of these productions rightly falls under the heading of "popera," a pejorative term coined by opera buffs for a new form of musical theatre that originated in the commercial houses of Broadway and threatened to displace more traditional fare in the opera house.

In 1990 *Chicago Tribune* critic Richard Christiansen had good reason to describe Galati as "Chicago's hottest cultural export."[58] He has continued to grow and develop new interests, strategies, and partnerships but by 1996 he had established the signature style and unique artistic voice that characterize his body of work into the twenty-first century. In his stage adaptations of non-dramatic literature for the Steppenwolf and Goodman theatres, he layered artifice into naturalism with increasing finesse and gave the elevated language of classic literature spectacular physical expression. The two productions that most clearly demonstrate the interests, strategies, and stagecraft of his mature work are his adaptation and staging of Gertrude Stein's Cubist innovations, *She Always Said, Pablo* for the Goodman Theater and his adaptation of John Steinbeck's *The Grapes of Wrath* for Steppenwolf Theatre. Both projects are consistent with Chicago-style theatre and both demonstrate the unique sensibility and aesthetic insight of a spectacular theatrical storyteller.

Notes

1 Peter Sellers, quoted in Hillary DeVries, "Chicago Theatre: Second to None." *Christian Science Monitor*, December 6, 1985.
2 Frank Galati. Interview with Larry Bommer, "An Interview with Frank Galati," *Windy City Times* (Chicago), October 24, 1984, 19.
3 Ross Wetzsteon, "Can an Electric Theater Style Revive New York?" *New York*, December 16, 1985, 52–61.

4 Samuel G. Freedman, "Will Success Spoil Nonprofit Theater?" *New York Times*, July 22, 1984.
5 Nancy Coons, "An Unlikely Mr. Scrooge: This Ebenezer Is a Lovable Actor in a Truly Nasty Role." Feature. *The Daily Herald*, December 6, 1984, sec. 9, pp. 3–4.
6 Coons.
7 Coons.
8 Samuel S. Freedman, "Chicago Theater World: A Moment of Suspense." *New York Times*, April 10, 1985.
9 Frank Galati, Interview with Richard Christiansen, "Frank Galati's Balancing Act Stands 'Inspection,'" *Chicago Tribune*, October 13, 1985.
10 Glenna Syse, "A Make or Break Show for Goodman; Much Rests On The Fate of 'Government Inspector,'" *Chicago Sun Times*, September 20, 1985.
11 Frank Galati, *Inspector General* spiral notebook, Box 22, Folder 10, Frank Galati (1943–) Papers, 1948–2914, Northwestern University McCormick Library of Special Collections and University Archives. Archives.
12 Galati, Interview with Syse, "A Make or Break Show," 1985.
13 Frank Galati, Interview with Larry Bommer, "An Interview with Frank Galati," *Windy City Times* (Chicago), October 24, 1984.
14 Galati, Interview with Bommer, 1984.
15 Richard Christiansen, "Goodman Improvises on Top Post," *Chicago Tribune*, October 27, 1985.
16 Richard Christiansen, "'You Can't Take It with You' a Sublime Celebration of Screwball," *Chicago Tribune*, December 2, 1985.
17 John O'Mahoney, "The Guts and The Glory," *The Guardian* (London), July 14, 2000. www.theguardian.com/books/2000/jul/15/books.guardianreview3
18 Jeff Perry, in John Mayer, *Steppenwolf Theatre Company of Chicago: In Their Own Words* (London: Bloomsbury Methuen Drama, 2016), 75.
19 John Beaufort, "Definitive revival of Lanford Wilson's First Full-Length Play; 'Balm in Gilead'; Play by Lanford Wilson. Directed by John Malkovich," *Christian Science Monitor*, June 18, 1984.
20 John Malkovich in Mayer, 73.
21 Samuel G. Friedman, "Steppenwolf theater's 10-year climb to success," *New York Times*, July 15, 1985.
22 Pat Colander, "Chicago Theatre Comes into Its Own," *New York Times*, May 27, 1984.
23 Ross Wetzsteon, "Can an Electric Theater Style Revive New York?" *New York*, December 16, 1985, 51.
24 Frank Rich, "Theatre: Steppenwolf Presents 'Orphans,'" *New York Times*, May 8, 1985.
25 Frank Rich, "Stage: Wallace Shawn's 'Aunt Dan and Lemon,'" *New York Times*. October 29, 1985.

26 Glenna Syse, "'George' and 'Aunt Dan and Lemon' Better Than New York," *Chicago Sun Times*, June 28, 1987, 8.

27 Hedy Weiss, "'Aunt Dan and Lemon'" *Chicago Sun Times*, June 1987, 40.

28 Richard Christiansen, "'Aunt Dan and Lemon' A Magnificent Play," *Chicago Tribune*, June 15, 1987.

29 Christiansen, "Aunt Dan."

30 Christiansen, "Aunt Dan."

31 Frank Galati, Members of Steppenwolf Ensemble, "How Did We Love Martha? Let Us Count the Ways," *American Theatre*, June 23, 2017. www.americantheatre.org/2017/06/23/how-did-we-love-martha-let-us-count-the-ways/.

32 Kasper Holten, Interview with Richard Mantel, "'Opera Can Make Us See, Feel and Hear the World Differently': The UK's Opera Chiefs Tell Us Why Their Art Form Matters," *The Guardian* (London), May 9, 2014. www.theguardian.com/music/2014/may/09/inside-opera-live-why-opera-matters-uk-opera-chiefs.

33 Tom Sutcliffe, *Believing in Opera* (Princeton, NJ: Princeton Univ Press, 2016), 82.

34 Sutcliffe, 83.

35 Sutcliffe, 167.

36 John von Rhein, "'Godparents' Of Lyric Opera Center's 'Lillian Sloan' Awaiting Blessed Event," *Chicago Tribune*, May 25, 1986.

37 William Neil, interview with Nancy Malitz, "New Opera Sparks New Hope." *Detroit News*, June 9, 1986. http://williamneil.net/wp-content/uploads/2018/04/Detroit-News-Review.pdf

38 Von Rhein, "Godparents."

39 Von Rhein, "Godparents."

40 Tim Page, "Opera 'Postcard from Morocco,'" *New York Times*, February 25, 1984,

41 Robert C. Marsh, "Aims High in Second Program of Argento", *Chicago Sun Times*, April 5, 1987.

42 Frank Galati, Interview with Dorthy Andries, "Galati Shares His View of 'Bridge,'" *Evanston Review*, September 23, 1999.

43 James R. Oestreich, "A Hallucinatory Voyage for an Artist at Sea," *New York Times*, Oct. 29, 1990.

44 John von Rhein, "Lyric's 'Poe' Is a Grim But Gripping Voyage," *Chicago Tribune*, October 29, 1990.

45 Clifford Terry, "Slide, Boesche, Slide! 'Voyage of Edgar Allan Poe' Designer Has Certain Images to Project," *Chicago Tribune*, November 25, 1900.

46 John von Rhein, "Fantastic 'Voyage' Lyric Opera Takes a Mystical Journey with Edgar Allan Poe," *Chicago Tribune*, October 21, 1990.

47 John von Rhein, "Subtly Gets Lost in Stagey 'Pelleas,'" *Chicago Tribune*, October 29, 1990.

48 Von Rein, "Pelleas."

49 George Grass, "Debussy's Masterwork," *Chicago Reader*, November 26, 1992, www.chicagoreader.com/chicago/debussys-masterwork/Content?oid=880933
50 Thor Eckert, Jr., "'McTeague' Opera Gambit Pays Off," *Christian Science Monitor*, November 25, 1992.
51 John von Rhein, "Curtain Rises on the Lyric: 'La Traviata' Is Memorable," *Chicago Tribune*, September 20, 1993.
52 Von Rhein, "La Traviata."
53 David Selznick, "Galati's Production of 'Tosca' Worth the Trip to Chicago," *Christian Science Monitor,* December 17, 1993, www.csmonitor.com/1993/1217/17142.html
54 Frank Galati interview with Bruce Webber, "The Opera's Director, Yes, but Not a Dictator," *New York Times*, August 11, 1999.
55 Matthew Epstein interview with Bruce Webber, "The Opera's Director," 1999.
56 Matthew Epstein interview with Tim Page, "The Book of Matthew," *Opera News*, December 2004.
57 William Mason interview with Tim Page, *Opera News*, 2004.
58 Richard Christiansen, "Frank Galati's 'Pablo' Opens in Washington as One More Highlight in a Remarkable Year," *Chicago Tribune*, July 1, 1990.

Part Two

Staging Stein and Steinbeck: Two Case Studies

Introduction to Part Two

Galati's Cubist collage, *She Always Said, Pablo* (Goodman Theatre 1987, Lincoln Center 1990) and his adaptation and staging of John Steinbeck's *The Grapes of Wrath* (Chicago 1988, La Jolla and London 1989, New York 1990) represent a distinct theatrical style that is simultaneously spectacular and thought provoking. Both productions were written and directed by Galati and both have been described as beautiful, stunning, and unsettling. While his spectacular "voice" is certainly expressed in the material manifestations of concept, casting, transitions, and blocking, Galati's unique artistic presence is most clearly felt in the ways he frames and manipulates theatrical space. "The problem," writes Antonin Artaud in *The Theatre and Its Double*, "is to make space speak."[1] Perhaps, but the problem is that many theatre patrons are unsettled by ideas not readily expressed in words and downright distrustful when such ideas arise from something spectacular or pretty. Nonetheless, while refusing to legislate precisely what should be thought, Galati's staging animates the theatre space in ways that cause one to stop and to think. How then, does one begin to chart a discourse initiated by space?

Art historian W. J. T. Mitchell proposes that a certain kind of metapicture—a picture that reflects on the nature of pictures—has "a tendency to look back at the beholder, or seemingly to respond to the presence of the beholder, to 'want something' from the beholder."[2] In such a picture, images are nested or framed within images but the viewer's conception of space is troubled by a pronounced and deliberate "transgression of this clearly demarcated 'nesting' structure."[3] Some element, image, or exchange passes through the metapicture's multiple levels of reality without acknowledging or even disturbing the spatial distinctions between them. Mitchell observes that when the boundaries between concentric spaces and levels of framing are deliberately transgressed, the metapicture can pose a challenge to the self-knowing of the onlooker. He calls on Diego Rodríguez de Silva y Velázquez's *Las Meninas* (1724) as an example of metapicture "in its most complex, articulate, and exalted status."[4] The composition appears to be classical but on closer inspection, the picture offers a confusion of absence and presence. Are the young ladies the subject of the picture, as the title suggests, or are they looking on as the artist assesses a subject standing in the space occupied by the onlooker? In the background, a strange ambient light calls attention to a framed image of Velázquez's patrons, the king and queen of Spain. Is the royal couple an effigy within an effigy or is this a mirror's reflection of figures that are absent from the picture but present to the figures represented? However it is interpreted, Velázquez's painting is unsettling and thought provoking because of how, not what, it represents.

The pleasure as well as the efficacy of Galati's mise-en-scène depend on the ways in which space is manipulated through simultaneous but contradictory frames of illusion and reality. Even as he shifts between presentational and representational frames, he inserts a wild card, some stable but roving agent able to traverse multiple frames of illusion and reality without destroying or even disturbing the distinctions between them. He described *She Always Said, Pablo* as "a vaudeville, a side-show, a visit to a gallery at night after they lock it up and the guards are gone."[5] But for all its celebratory theatricality, actor Marji Bank's unflappable portrayal of Alice B. Toklas circulated through the show's multiple conceptual frames without pause or comment. Alice was both a fantastic creature of the stage and one of us, familiar, trustworthy, solid, and comforting. It was primarily for her sake that wary spectators allowed themselves to be lured down the rabbit hole of Galati's Cubist vaudeville, willfully ignoring the fact that of all the creatures on stage she was the least reliable because she alone claimed to be "real."

Pablo was very much a playground but in *The Grapes of Wrath*, Galati had a compelling and gritty story to tell. Even as the company lured the audience into a momentary suspension of disbelief, realist representation was unsettled by intrusions either too real for artifice or too artful for reality. This effect was most powerful when, as Burt O. States says, things on stage "are what they appear to be."[6] Galati explained:

> The audience experiences the travail of the actor embedded in the narrative. Soaking wet, exhausted, covered with dirt, having hung around a real fire, dug a pit—these things are really endured by the actor. When you come to the final scene, the time for a conclusion, a statement, an utterance is long past. The gesture itself takes on the level of the sacrament an enactment you've witnessed. You've been there with them.

"To yield not to the play as a play but to the illusion," writes Howard Pearce, is to "trivialize the theatre event."[7] Eugene O'Neil's *Long Day's Journey into Night* is, for example, not a play about a journey. It is a journey meant to be undertaken in the shared space of the theatre. Pearce points out that to yield completely to the illusion of O'Neil's play trivializes that journey. Galati's *Grapes of Wrath* was conceived, in his words, as "a dynamic process of communication in which the spectators are vitally implicated." To achieve this end, the company encouraged the spectator to resist illusion and yield instead to the immediacy of the theatre event and the truth of Steinbeck's resolve.

Galati's staging produces a palpable tension between effects that accentuate the artificiality of the medium and effects that seem to anchor the story in the bedrock of realism. This is one of many Cubist strategies deployed by Galati whose career achievements, objectives, and strategies as an author and director are best understood in the terms, strategies, and agenda introduced by the Cubists themselves.

Notes

1 Antonin Artaud, *The Theatre and Its Double: Essays*, trans. Mary C. Richards (New York: Gross Press, 1958), 98.
2 W. J. T. Mitchell interview with Asbjørn Grønstad and Øyvind Vågnes Grønstad and Øyvind Vågnes, "What Do Pictures Want?" *Image and Narrative*, November 2006. www.visual-studies.com/interviews/mitchell.html.
3 W. J. Thomas Mitchell, *Picture Theory: Essays on Verbal and Visual Representation* (Chicago, IL: University of Chicago Press), 1995, 42.
4 Mitchell, 60.
5 Frank Galati, Interview with Hedy Weiss, "'She Always Said' Speaks to Genius: Pablo and Stein Will Lead Parade at the Goodman," *Chicago Sun-Times*, March 8, 1987, Arts sec.
6 Bert O. States, *Great Reckonings in Little Rooms: On the Phenomenology Of Theatre* (Berkeley: University of California Press, 1985), 21.
7 Howard D. Pearce, *Human Shadows Bright as Glass: Drama as Speculation and Transformation*. (Lewisburg, PA: Bucknell University Press, 1997), 71.

4

A Cubist Dramaturgy: *She Always Said, Pablo*

In 1987, Galati described *She Always Said, Pablo* as "a kind of intellectual circus. An opportunity for the Rose and Blue Periods of Picasso to cavort to the music of [Igor] Stravinsky and [Virgil] Thomson; for Picasso's clowns to juggle the words of Gertrude Stein."[1] The 90-minute Goodman Theatre production premiered on February 27, 1987 and was remounted in 1990 at the Kennedy Center in Washington DC. Galati did not write a single word spoken on stage but is rightly credited as the author as well as director. In lieu of a conventional script, he created an assemblage of typed or photocopied passages from Stein's essays, prose, and lyrics, photographs of paintings, people, sculpture, and drawings pasted together with cellophane tape. The material is collected in a 132-page three-ring binder organized in four sections: I Portraits; II Vaudeville; III A Prologue 4 Saints; and IV Simply Complicated and Interesting. The binder includes fragments of sheet music composed by Virgil Thomson and Igor Stravinsky and a cacophony of marginalia written in Galati's hand.[2] Asked if *Pablo* was a play, he said, "it's a play the way the word 'play' plays. 'Play' is the name of a form of literature, but it is also what children do. It's also what light does when it shimmers. It's also what you do when you pick up a violin. So in the full ample sense of the word 'play,' yeah, it's a play."[3] Ever mindful that "play" is a verb as well as a noun, Galati set out to occasion an experience in real time rather than a representation of some experience long ago or far away.

There was a great deal of anticipation about the production in the press but audience response to the first preview performances did not bode well. After only two previews, an alarming number of subscription patrons had filed complaints with theatre management. Steve Scott, a member of the Goodman's creative staff, recalled that about ten minutes into one preview performance, nearly an entire row of patrons walked out. Scott suspected that the Goodman's stalwart subscription patrons were put off by the production's unconventional format and lack of narrative logic. The cast and creative team were undaunted by the walkouts but word had gotten out and the word was not good. Sam Lesner, a reporter for the popular suburban *Skyline Newspaper,* had heard the rumors. He began his review by admitting, "Frankly, I came to scoff."[4] But only minutes into the show, he was charmed and exhilarated. Lesner's recommendation was unconditional and he assured his suburban readers that "Galati is no less than a genius."

> This is an extraordinary work, a hauntingly beautiful vocal work, a ballet, a shimmering fantasy, a beautiful operetta, a confoundingly complex series of tableaux, a totally abstract work that, to borrow a moment of Stein's literary style, abstracts all the abstractions of Stein's repetitions, sentence fragmentations and extreme simplifications without unduly abstracting abstraction.[5]

Lesner's praise and pleasure were undimmed by the fact that by his own admission, he didn't entirely understand what was going on. He was not alone. *She Always Said, Pablo* filled the head with ideas without knowing exactly what they were. Happily, understanding proved to be a moot point. Excellent reviews and word of mouth won the day and the entire run was sold out within two weeks. When the theatre announced the availability of tickets for a one-week extension, a line of customers extended for a city block outside the Goodman box office. Scott described the extension audience as "people who didn't regularly attend the theatre. Art Institute folks who had heard about the performance. It was a new audience for the Goodman."

When the production was remounted at the Kennedy Center in 1990 with the original cast and design, Louise Sweeney described it in *The Christian Science Monitor* as "a beautiful and heady excursion into the arts, unlike any other evening of theater."[6] Richard Christiansen summarized national press coverage in the *Chicago Tribune*: "Reviewers described the work as 'one of the most innovative plays I've seen this or any other season' (Bob Davis, WGMS) [and] 'a show for anyone who craves a challenge' (Robert Merritt, *Richmond Times-Dispatch*)."[7] Pablo was a financial and critical success for the Goodman and was videotaped for the Billy Rose Archive at the Lincoln Center Library of the Performing Arts.

Pablo Picasso famously told a reporter, "It took me four years to paint like Raphael, but a lifetime to paint like a child." *She Always Said, Pablo* was as illegible, irrational, and charming as a child's painting and playfully subversive from beginning to end. In her essay "The Berger Mystery," Mira Schor describes John Berger's 1967 essay "A Moment of Cubism" as thrilling because it "opens up a double vista to the past and to the future of an instance of radicality, whose promise is not completely fulfilled but yet may be ahead of us."[8] Within the changed cultural conditions of the late twentieth century, the Cubist's moment resurfaced on the stage of the Goodman Theatre. It is right and proper that Galati's collaboration with Gertrude Stein and Pablo Picasso marked a career breakthrough. Right because he showed himself to be a latter-day Cubist.

A Latter-day Cubism

Galati's affinity with Cubism begins with a shared love of surface and a rejection of high art elitism. Stein and Picasso loved the physical sturdiness of the ordinary, the everyday, the commonplace and the popular. "Picasso," writes Richard Axsom, "desired to rehabilitate the commonplace and to surprise everyday objects out of their banality."[9] The Cubists placed ordinary things—string, newsprint, flowerpots—in surprising juxtaposition to create an entirely new image without challenging the integrity of the original objects. Galati is also an artist of juxtaposition. He and his design team, John Paoletti, Mary Griswold (sets and costumes), and Geoffrey Bushor (lighting) created a Cubist collage from words, wheels, gossip, balls, socks, flags, sounds, and familiar shapes with unexpected color and texture. He placed these ordinary material things in transitory and often irrational relationships, totally familiar and at the same time, disconcertingly strange.

Stein conceived her plays as landscapes that offer a vista of shifting allegiances, an evolving environment where many things are happening at once and no one thing dominates perception for long. This, says Galati, "is a haunting idea in so many ways. I've used it in class a lot because it's a really playful way of saying to students that making theatre can be an alternative means to activism in politics and in social struggles." He continued: "a playground is also a battlefield in which children stage and imagine battles, a kind of rehearsal for the transformation of a landscape into a battlefield where the forces of society are in conflict." Galati's production was an actual landscape in which the unstable forces of sense and nonsense, truth and perception were in conflict. Alice, Lewis Carroll's remarkably self-possessed heroine said of *The Jabberwocky* poem, "Somehow it seemed to fill my head with ideas—only I don't know exactly what they are!" Galati's ever-changing landscape had a similar thought-provoking and for some patrons, objectionable effect.

Critics have identified a powerful political subversion in Cubist constructions and the politics of Stein have been rehabilitated by late century feminist critics. Linda Watts writes,

…in the years since her death, critics have expanded their definitions of the political. This redefinition is key to recovering a political reading of Stein, for while it is true that her writing is far from the social protest fiction of a Sinclair Lewis or a Steinbeck, Stein nonetheless responds in her writing to the social issues, relations and inequalities which prompt such writing.[10]

In the years prior to the First World War, Cubists critiqued ideologies that isolated art, its makers, and its audience from political and social realities. In an angry response to accusations of insincerity when he joined the Communist Party in 1944, Picasso demanded, "What do you think an artist is? An imbecile who has only his eyes if he's a painter, or ears if he's a musician, or a lyre at every level of his heart if he's a poet...? No. Painting is not done to decorate apartments. It is an instrument of war for attack and defense against the enemy."[11] Galati is no more a mystic than Picasso was. Nor is he in any sense an aesthete. He approaches theatre art as simultaneously poetic and pedestrian and, in this duality, it is or can be a powerful instrument of attack and defense against intellectual and economic elitism and political apathy.

It was not ideas the Cubists rejected but aesthetic and linguistic rationalizations that discipline the unruliness of images, rendering them silent and suitably decorous. Picasso's political agenda is the subject of Patricia Leighten's *Re-Ordering the Universe: Picasso and Anarchism*. "Style here is not a neutral vehicle for the disinterested esthetic play of line, color, and form, but a formal attack on artistic tradition that Picasso's contemporaries understood to be an attack on the forms and tradition of society itself."[12] His intentions, writes Leighton, "were to transform the mind of his age, not to obliterate it."[13] Picasso, Stein, and Galati each in their own ways, set out to galvanize meaning through lived experience rather than a transference of rational argument or linguistic meaning.

Galati shares with the Cubists a general love of surface and ordinary, commonplace things. He links the physical act of creating and apprehending images to intellectual cognition and believes that making art, literature, and theatre can be efficacious in political and social struggles. Besides these general concepts, three specific Cubist strategies are key to understanding the operations of design, structure, and staging in his body of work as a dramatist and director: first, a playful subversion of status quo forms and assumptions; second, a call to extra-ordinary attention; and third, the strategic co-presence or multistability of reality and illusion, absence and presence, representation and presentation.

Playful subversion. In an era of fervent manifestos proclaiming total and uncompromising artistic revolution, Stein and Picasso preferred to manipulate and explore the limitations of existing codes rather than begin or claim to begin from ground zero. Though clearly innovators, both artists remained within institutional structures. This allowed them to play with and subvert conventional linguistic and visual codes and thereby destabilize established categories and expose covert assumptions within artistic form. Their unorthodox manipulation of shape and form was the carrier of content that could not be expressed in words.

Their world and its communication apparatus seemed to have grown old, arthritic, and dysfunctional. But Stein loved language and literature and rather than dismiss language per se, she moved "through a gradual displacement of realist principles, writing within conventional forms—and the ideological agendas they imply—and simultaneously pushing against the limits of these forms."[14] Linda Watts argues that Stein is "not fashioning a cipher so much as refashioning ciphers already in cultural and linguistic place."[15] Stein plays with the orderliness of grammar in order to shake conventional form lose from its moorings. "Now listen!" she demanded,

> Can't you see that when the language was new—as it was with Chaucer and Homer—the poet could use the name of a thing and the thing was really there? ... And can't you see that after hundreds of years had gone by and thousands of poems had been written he could call on those words and find that they were just worn-out literary words?[16]

Stein understood that it was still possible to love but given centuries of use and misuse, it was no longer possible to say, "I love you." The phrase is only a phrase, words detached from any real-world consequence or meaning.

Extra-ordinary attention. Picasso's Cubist treatment of surfaces, materials, genre, and subject was a calculated attack on traditions and conventions that reduce artists to apolitical aestheticians at best and interior decorators at worst. Cubism is intended as a provocation, a call to attention that stands in opposition to normative, everyday apprehension of the world. Under normal conditions of consciousness, attentiveness is defined and directed by prior experience and conventional code. The stylistic characteristics of Cubism were a practical response to this problem. In Cubism, "normative, everyday knowing is thrown off guard" with the idea of maintaining an open-ended attentiveness to the world.[17] The Cubists defined attentiveness as a subversive act of "new-seeing."[18]

The co-presence of reality and illusion. The stylistic attributes of Cubist representation—fractured surface, repetition and multiple viewpoints, vertical stacking, the juxtaposition of pictorial styles and modes of expression—call attention to the physical reality of the artist's medium. In the years prior to the First World War, Cubism was hailed by its advocates as the New Realism.[19] The poet and critic Guillaume Apollinaire described their art as "an attempt to make of each picture a new, tangible reality rather than an illusory image either of some imaginary ideal or of some purely visual sensation of reality."[20] According to the painter Georges Braque, a passionate and lifelong advocate, the Cubists aim was not "to reconstitute an anecdotal fact, but to constitute a pictorial fact."[21] To Braque, a "fact" was any object or thing with solid material presence in the world. The elements of Galati's Cubist collage—flags, balls, socks, wheels—maintained their material integrity and at the same time, coalesced as a new reality independent of the original objects.

In Stein's writing, character, and event are repeatedly and self-consciously refracted through a single fixed moment, a technique she called the "continuous present and using everything and beginning again."[22] Galati explained, "It is important to return again and again to the same syntactical event only slightly altered and to feel what happens in the overtones when those keys are slightly changed, if that's the right word ... like chord progressions." He paused to think a moment, then said "There are narrative events but the return and advance, the return and advance is part of the emotional condition of the event."

In the decades since *She Always Said, Pablo* closed, I have interviewed a dozen or more theatre patrons who recalled the production with enthusiasm. When I asked, "What do you remember?" the answers almost invariably focused on what happened to the individual rather than what happened on stage. People remembered being "engaged," "caught off guard," "emotional and I don't know why," "frustrated but also—joyful? Yes, I was joyful," and my favorite answer, "It was great. I remember wanting to go home and play with my kids." In *Pablo*, Stein's words seemed to chase after the present with dogged determination, closing in as the speaker replayed a phrase with minute variations that shifted the onlooker's perspective ever so slightly and then shifted again and again until ... something happened. Hard to say exactly what happened but whatever it was, it happened there, in the theatre. The play on stage was a Cubist fact, a lived experience rather than a mirror or comment on experience.

Staging Stein

Stein insists that to understand her work, it may be necessary to learn a new meaning for the word "understanding." "Look here," she said in a 1947 radio interview,

> Being intelligible is not what it seems, after all, these things are a matter of habit ... <u>You</u> mean by understanding that you can talk about it in the way that you have the habit of talking ... putting it in other words ... but I mean by understanding—enjoyment.[23]

With the word "enjoyment" Stein calls attention to an erotic link between cognition and pleasure, a link that anchors comprehension in time and place, rendering it contextual and experiential rather than conceptual. Galati's appreciation of Stein's work is experiential. "Her language makes a certain kind of goofy sense to me," he explains. "I can't pin a meaning on it, but I <u>know</u> how I feel when I <u>hear</u> it." Galati's words acknowledge a link between knowing, feeling, and experience and this link is central to what he set out to achieve in his Cubist vaudeville. He knew that the youthful exhilaration and life-long bond between Stein and Picasso could be understood by entering the profound artistic and intellectual understanding—the enjoyment—they shared. He set out to cajole, seduce, or compel the Goodman audience into listening and understanding their work as he did, that is, to enjoy and take pleasure in it.

He recruited local actor/director/playwright/teacher Steve Iveich to help the cast develop a shared physical vocabulary. Larry Russo, who played the young Picasso, recalled how Iveich emphasized the inherent duality of the actor's presence on stage.

> Iveich wanted you to accept and acknowledge the fact that you were on stage—not pretending but appearing. Sure, we were playing parts, but we were also always ourselves. And once you're there—on stage—you have to BE there. You had to focus—really focus, not on who you're pretending to be, but on what you actually are doing. He used to say that the best thing you can have on the stage is a dog, because a dog is completely involved in what he is doing—like scratching himself or smelling something. If you can have the dog-thought onstage, the audience is never shut out. They get involved the same way you get involved in watching the dog watching or scratching or sniffing. I guess we were learning to always be doing exactly what we were doing. Frank would come and watch us work out every day. He was mesmerized by all this.

Iveich led non-verbal improvisations with repetitive movement and contact exercises that encouraged the ensemble to define the physical space they inhabited together. Viewed from the sidelines, the room looked more like a playground than a rehearsal hall and the sense of play established in rehearsals carried over to the stage. David Richards of the *Washington Post* declared, "This is not a play, but a playground."[24]

"To play" is a statement of intention, as in the declaration "I'm going out to play." Such activity demands a certain mental agility and duality in that an extraordinary level of awareness is required at the same time normal sense-making activity is abandoned. In *Pablo*, Galati needed his audience to play rather than sit and watch a play. Toward this end he established a series of conceptual frames, each with a hint or promise that the spectator's expectations of "a play" would be fulfilled, only to have each successive frame topple like a child's tower of blocks and reconstructed in new and unexpected arrangements. He initiated this doubling-back process with a striking pre-show image.

As the audience found their seats, Cubism was simultaneously represented and presented on stage. Exposed lighting instruments and swags of electric cable hung above the stage between scallops of draped, translucent fabric. Upstage, a monumental, sixteen-foot-high reproduction of Picasso's famous portrait of Stein balanced precariously akimbo on one corner. The portrait marks Picasso's irreversible break with the classicism of his Rose and Blue periods. To the right of the portrait's pivot point and below the slant of its lower edge, the silhouette of a powerful, bull-headed man sat alert but relaxed. The seated figure, seen in outline against a strong backlight, was from the famous 1967 *Life* magazine photograph of Picasso taken in his studio. The scene was a collage in which exposed lighting and a bare stage floor asserted themselves as the ordinary objects of a theatre. Scale and dimension were manipulated and skewed. Form was simplified in order to concentrate on the relationship between forms. Artistic styles—abstraction, realism, theatricality—were mixed. Identity was multiplied as a larger-than-life "Picasso" hovered over the "real" Picasso. The scene was a Cubist construction.

The exaggerated Stein portrait—a revered icon of twentieth-century art—suspended in a catapulting somersault established a sense of play. The mischievousness of this image was the result of designer John Paoletti's manipulation of a scaled model of the stage. Paoletti was a long-time friend and collaborator of Galati's and the two men shared an understanding, that is, an enjoyment of each other's ideas and insights that was anything but habitual. Galati described the first time they worked with the model,

> I had placed the portrait against the cyclorama, like a painting in an artist's studio, but it wasn't right. John made a face and just reached in and turned it so

that it was on a point and instead of being flat, it was leaning. It was genius. And I knew, but he didn't, that it was in keeping with a story from Penrose's biography [of Picasso]. On a visit to Picasso's home, he saw a painting hanging crooked, but Picasso wouldn't let him straighten it "because," he said, "akimbo is more interesting."

In pre-production sessions, the director and his designers felt increasingly empowered to abandon the constraints of traditional representation. "I felt, well, ... Why can't I ... make a collage, or a painting out of a play or a play out of paintings. So I started getting into the spirit of their own avant-gardism—just ... play and see what happens."[25]

The upstage silhouette of the seated artist called on the spectator's imagination to "see" a living actor in the crisp contours of its outline. The impression was reinforced by the fact that several Chicago productions had recently opened the house with an actor already positioned on stage, including Michael Maggio's Court Theatre production of *End Game* with Galati as Clov to Nicholas Rudall's Hamm. I knew he liked the idea of the watchers being watched and watched to see if the actor shifted in his seat. Stravinsky's *Pastorale*, performed by a small pit orchestra conducted by Ed Zelnis, signaled that the play was about to begin. The pastel circus performers of Picasso's Pre-Cubist Saltimbanque paintings paraded in one by one, silhouetted against an ombre backlight (cover photo). They carried or pulled effigies of the artist's work or props associated with him, including a tasseled beach umbrella and a miniature of the unmistakable "Chicago Picasso" sculpture on Daley Plaza. Galati explained his choices to Hedy Weiss,

> The Pastorale was a sort of nostalgia piece. It was composed late in the 19th Century and it looks back at the 19th-Century idyll—much the way Picasso's work in his rose and blue periods looked back. It's never sentimental or academic, but haunting, simple, somewhat sad. And the forlorn figures in the Saltimbanque paintings move across the stage to his music like refugees fleeing before the modern world comes seeping in—before the major earthquake in Picasso's vision known as Cubism.[26]

Each figure adopting a distinctive pose and eccentric pattern of movement. A youthful Stein, played by Susan Nussbaum, rolled across the stage and positioned her electric wheelchair far left.

The wheelchair was not an affectation. In the late 1970s, Nussbaum's career had been short-circuited by an automobile accident that left her partially paralyzed. Galati's casting was a surprise to many, including Nussbaum herself. However, in January, he submitted a tentative cast list to the Goodman's producing team for final approval and was adamant that Nussbaum should be offered the role of Stein. He wrote,

> I am PASSIONATE about Susan Nussbaum for G.S. She and Marji [Bank/Alice Toklas] will both use body mikes. They need to have a different vocal impact and must seem, both, to be each in her own very private space. But Susan will bring a depth of feeling and humor that we'd be hard pressed to find in anyone else.[27]

Emotion and humor are key to Galati's understanding of Stein and it is not surprising that he sought these qualities in casting the part.

Nussbaum had concerns about how her wheelchair could be integrated into the production but in Galati's hands, the chair proved to be an asset. She explained, "Frank exploited it. He began to bring other wheels into the design of the play—a cart, wagons, a painting on bicycle wheels. And things began to move in circular patterns just like Stein's language." As Nussbaum worked with the script, she began to see how her physical presence could support Galati's effort to make the audience see differently. "In the same way that the audience had to reorient and open their minds to enjoy the play, they had to reorient and open their minds to accept me as Gertrude Stein. And they did! Most of them." Leaning slightly into the forward movement like a figurehead on the prow of a ship, she seemed to be propelled by will or destiny rather than electricity, drawing the ensemble into her wake as she passed. It was magical but it was also ordinary, pragmatic, and as Nussbaum noted, a provocative break with the normative world of theatrical representation.

Larry Russo joined the opening parade in the costume of a matador, one of Picasso's many alter egos. He held a Chinese umbrella on high just as Picasso had with Francoise Gilot in the famous 1948 Robert Capa photograph. Steve Ivcich danced into view as a lithe Minotaur, a blind creature of myth with the body of a man and the head of a bull and another of the artist's recurring alter egos. It was a very pretty scene and in its calculated disorder, seemed to be fraught with meaning without any indication of what that meaning might be. Then, in a flurry of activity the ensemble and the multiple "Picassos"—the painting, the silhouette, the matador, and the Minotaur—exited the stage. A pair of Saltimbanque figures hoisted up by the portrait and paraded it off leaving the seated artist poised against the upstage horizon. I expected him to rise and begin the play but an ensemble member hurried back in, took hold of the seated "Picasso," swung it around and propelled it offstage on caster wheels. In that half turn, the famously arrogant Spaniard whose art had transformed the world was transformed into a plywood torso perched on a wheeled frame—a stage prop. The shift from sense to non-sense and from purpose to play was instantaneous. I had expected him to stand because I saw what I expected to see.

The insignificant or, rather, non-signifying moment in which the initial stage picture dissolved was the first of many gestures in which solid objects changed in perception but not in form. In such moments, Galati called attention to the fact that looking is not a passive project of reception but an interpretative process of cognition. This insight is central to the Cubist agenda and to Galati's. In his case, by shifting the watcher's perspective on the figure, he caused a small mental jolt that laid bare the eye's willing complicity in the serious business of illusion. He also got a laugh.

On the back side of page one in his binder/script, he made notes on the opening image and the scene that followed.

> The distant figures—the Saltimbanques—grab up the cutout of the seated Pablo and hoist the huge portrait of Gertrude. They bear them both aloft and off—a procession in honor of two saints. Remaining onstage and in the music of the Pastorale—Gertrude in her chair [stage] right of center and the slowly dawning naked male—a Minotaur, blind and lithe. He dances out the last cadences of the Pastorale. At end of music, Gertrude waves a tiny [American] flag at Alice—a bell rings—the earthquake.[28]

Scott Fosdick described Galati's "earthquake" in *American Theatre*: "Steam hisses onto the stage, which suddenly rips in a great gash from up-center downward. Out of the chasm rises Picasso, ripping the earth before him with the point of his umbrella, like canvas with a knife."[29] Russo ripped open the paper "floor" of a raised the dais with the point of his umbrella and emerged from below the stage with the concentrated absorption of a dancer. "I'd tell myself, 'nice and slow, like a mushroom cloud, emerge, roll up, don't move until the umbrella ooo-pens.' Frank wanted me to tilt back, shaded, until the light came up full—lights up—then tilt the umbrella to catch the light full on my face. It had to be timed perfectly." To Russo, the moment remains "the most spectacular and gratifying entrance of my career." Once again, Galati depended on the spectator's complicity to create the scene but this time, there was no red herring, no false lead and no betrayal of the eye as there had been when the famous artist turned into a stage prop. The scene called for willing and playful participation and the naïve pleasure of surrender rather than the sophisticated satisfaction of mastery.

Russo stood and watched as the Saltimbanques danced onto the stage speaking Stein's word portrait of Picasso in unison. "One whom some were certainly following was one who was charming. One whom some were following was completely charming. One whom some were following was one who was certainly completely charming." On the final iteration of the word "charming," Russo stepped off the dais and onto the stage. As the chorus continued, "... one bringing out of himself then something," A distended hand thrust through the slash in the floor and with arm extended high, Ivcich, still in the Minotaur costume, rose up from the pit and stepped onto the stage to confront Picasso. Galati considers Stein to be, "a poet of extraordinary lucidity" and so she was when the cheerful figures of the chorus assured the audience in unison, "Certainly it had been coming out of him, it had meaning, a charming meaning, a solid meaning, a struggling meaning, a clear meaning." Nowhere was that meaning paraphrased, translated, or explained. Meaning was there as it would be throughout the show, in a procession of material things: an umbrella, a red ball, the smoke of a cigarette, and the decisive "click" of a lady's pocketbook closing. Until this point, Galati's staging had been entirely presentational without any attempt to challenge the material reality of the stage. For all its playful invention, the audience had nothing solid to hold on to, nothing that belonged to their world. Then, just when the overall impression was in danger of becoming precious, Alice showed up in sensible shoes.

Alice B. Toklas: An Untroubled Troublemaker

The chorus finished Stein's word portrait and began to disperse as a match flared upstage and a spotlight revealed the figure of an appropriately mustachioed Alice B. Toklas, Stein's lover and life companion played by actor Marji Bank in flat brimmed hat, sturdy shoes, and black cardigan jacket.

She stood with feet slightly splayed, lit a cigarette and inhaled. In her stolid presence, the theatrical trappings of the stage and Picasso's nostalgic circus creatures suddenly seemed insubstantial and egregiously artificial. She snapped her handbag shut, adjusted its strap on her forearm, and said, "Gertrude Stein knocked and Picasso opened the door and we went in." Bank's unhurried pleasure in the cigarette and remarkable likeness to the historic woman fractured the presentational aesthetic Galati had established.

Cigarette in hand, Bank moved downstage to recount the story of "The Studio Visit," a passage from *The Autobiography of Alice B. Toklas* that describes the couple's first encounter with Picasso's work in his studio. Bank turned and stood a little apart to watch Russo and Nussbaum play out the scene as she narrated.

Figure 5 Margi Bank, Goodman Theatre production of *She Always Said, Pablo,* 1987. Courtesy of the photographer. Photo by Mary Griswold.

She appeared to be the elderly woman who outlived Stein while Stein and Picasso were youthful and energetic, as they had been at the time of that visit. Toklas was in her early thirties when she accompanied Stein to Picasso's studio but had already been described as "someone invited to the wedding but not to the wedding feast."[30] The character on stage was authentic, honest, opinionated, down-to-earth and chatty. She belonged to the stage but was also one of us, the wedding guests in the audience who had not been invited to join the feast.

Her description of the artwork piled in the artist's studio was as mundane and precise as her appearance: "an enormous picture, a strange picture of light and dark colours, that is all I can say, of a group, an enormous group...." As she stood back and looked, she said: "I stood back and looked." When she turned to the audience and confided "I cannot say I realized anything," the truth of her admission was our own. Her demeanor was inflected with a quiet triumph as she continued in a clear, strong voice: "but I felt that there was something painful and beautiful there and oppressive but imprisoned." Her account and attitude suggested that at long last, a recognizable plot line was about to emerge. But it was not to be. When she finished, Russo danced away with the chorus and Nussbaum turned from the collection of paintings to face the audience and announce, "One whom some were certainly following was one having something coming out of him something having meaning and this one was certainly working then." Toklas listened attentively, confirmed Stein's last phrase "This one was one who was working" with a nod and stepped back to watch and listen.

Of all the fantastic and familiar creatures on stage, Alice was least what she appeared to be because she alone appeared to be real. Nussbaum brought an impressive verisimilitude to her performance but her "Stein" was real in the way we understand a privileged theatrical character to be real—the distant resident of a reality apart from our own. In contrast, "Toklas" simultaneously validated and troubled the notion of authenticity. Even as Bank seemed to disappear into the character of Alice Toklas, the authenticity of that exotic person—an eccentric lesbian expatriate and notorious minor celebrity of a very different era—depended on the presence of the actor Marji Bank, a popular Chicago actress of a certain age and considerable charm. When she addressed the audience, her words—taken from *The Autobiography of Alice B. Toklas*—were trustworthy and genuine. But Gertrude Stein holds the copyrighted to the "autobiography" and is its acknowledged author. Who then, was speaking? Stein? Toklas? Bank? And how did Galati fit into this labyrinth of origins? The problem of Alice's authenticity is one in which every answer circles back to the same questions of origin and identity, as such questions often do. Stanton B. Garner's suggestion that we think of "theatrical presence as a play of actuality" is helpful in placing Alice on Galati's stage.[31] She was a play of actuality in which absence and presence were cojoined without contest or discord. Better to ask: which is more telling, the truths of our senses or the truths inscribed in art and literature? Our experience of a thing or our memory of it? What I feel or what I know? When Galati managed to render such unresolvable questions compelling—questions about how we perceive and make sense of the world— his production attained the clarity of Stein's writing.

About midway in the ninety-minute show, Bank lit another cigarette and mesmerized the gathered Saltimbanques by blowing a series of impressive smoke rings over their heads and continued to smoke as she watched the circus creatures drift off in pursuit of the decaying circles. She took one last drag, dropped the cigarette, and extinguished the smoldering butt with a decisive twist of her foot, leaving a dark streak on the stage floor. Alight, her cigarette signified many cigarettes smoked long ago and far away. It had meaning. But that dark smudge on the stage floor was a problem. It wasn't art. It wasn't pretty or meaningful. It wasn't a signifier. It was dirt. It didn't belong on Galati's beautiful stage and it worried me. The wardrobe mistress, a petite daemon named Rosalie Piazza, wouldn't like it. Cigarette ash stains are irreparable and forbidden near costumes. Granted, it is highly unlikely that any other theatre patron noted the smudge, much less shared my discomfort. But the play of actuality in that dark streak inundated Galati's entire production. Repeated and unexpected transgressions of the theatrical frame, startling or infinitesimal, created a peculiar tension that compensated for the production's lack of dramatic suspense.

Galati invited his audience to enjoy Cubism rather than explain it to them. He is, however, a professor of literature and happy to delve into Stein's ability to access something he considers to be indisputably genuine. "You're not stalled," he explained, "but you hover there longer than you do in ongoing narrative projects and the word 'project' is very right; it implies projectile, it's more male, more phallic, more dominant—it's more in quest of something whereas Stein is continually hovering and lingering and hovering and returning. There's just a profound authenticity in that mode." Galati ended his production with the question of authenticity in a haunting, final note sung by mezzo-soprano Carmen Pelton. The aria she sang was from Stein's and Virgil Thomson's opera *The Mother of Us All*. It begins "Where is where" and ends with the refrain "Do you know because I tell you so, or do you know, do you know. In my long life my long life." A painted show drop slowly lowered on Pelton's extended and quizzical final note. "'Do you know because I tell you so, or do you know.' To me," says Galati, "that's just an incredible culmination of the whole corpus of her work and of the modern revolution in art. Either you do or you don't." As the final note faded out, it was not what I know but knowing itself that lingered as a perplexing but persistent mystery.

Authorizing Audacity

Pablo was beautiful, even stunning to look at and listen to. The portrayals of Toklas and Stein were admired. The singers and orchestra produced a rich and lyrical sound. The entire cast was handsome, graceful, and confident of what they were doing on stage. There was no political or social polemic, no radical positions taken, no obscene language, no nudity, and it was short, just under ninety minutes. And it was controversial. Throughout the run, patrons continued to walk out or express anger and resentment. Ed Zelnis, the show's composer and musical director, said, "You would not believe the discussion sessions we have with the audience after each performance. They shout at each other—and at us—so strongly do people feel opposed to or in favor of this show. Personally, I enjoy the controversy. What's the fun if you can't be a little provocative?"[32] Disgruntled patrons described it as "meaningless," "silly," and "clownish." The straw that most often broke the camel's proverbial back was the final segment of the first "act" listed in the program as "Portraits." "The spirit of buffoonery," Jean Cocteau famously asserted, "is the only one which authorizes certain audacities." In this scene, Galati established a firm foothold in Cocteau's spirit of buffoonery.

Following the studio visit, Alice began to speak in a series of legible, possibly meaningful, albeit ditzy non-sequiturs of her friend Constance Fletcher, also the name of a character in Stein's opera *The Mother of Us All*. Alice began, "I was fascinated by her fashion of embroidering wreaths of flowers. There was nothing drawn upon her linen, she just held it in her hands, from time to time bringing it closely to one eye, and eventually the wreath took form. She was very fond of ghosts."[33] Galati's binder notes describe the action in the scene that followed: "Shaft of light falls on trap/sparkle rain. Picasso reaches in and helps the Woman in White out of her grave." "Woman in White" is the title of Picasso's 1923 portrait of Olga Koklova, painted in neoclassical style. Galati's Woman in White was costumed in the tight bodice and long bustled skirt of Susan B. Anthony's era, all in white. As she began to sing an aria from the opera, "I do and I do not declare that roses and wreathes, wreathes and roses around and around, blind as a bat . . ." Alice faded from view. The song ended with, "I am a dear, here there everywhere, I bow myself out." Which she did. Gertrude rolled to the lip of the stage and announced, "and so all of a sudden I began to write plays . . ."

Once again, it seemed as if a coherent narrative or perhaps an explanation might be about to unfold. She spoke about plays and writing plays and the difference between plays and stories. She ended, "There is always a story going on. So naturally what I wanted to do in my play was what everybody did not always know or always tell. By everybody I do of course include myself but always I do of course include myself."[34] She pivoted her chair to watch gigantic red rubber balls roll onto the stage, enthusiastically pushed, bounced, or tossed among the Saltimbanques as they declared in unison, "This is the way to play to play, everyone wants them to play all day, to play away, to play all day ..." In the middle ground two larger balls swung across the width of the stage like enormous pendulums, the arc of their path just skirting the stage floor. As the chorus continued to frolic and chant, Russo and Ivcich, still dressed as the Minotaur, hopped on and rode the swinging balls first in parallel then apart and again together. They landed and ran off as the balls were unhooked and rolled off stage. Alice stepped into the light, said "And we all sat down," and sat down at a small, downstage table where she launched into an account of Parisian café habitués. At this point, anyone who was inclined to walk out had probably done so. Those who made it this far were likely to stay the course.

Stein abolished the constraints of narrative structure by creating what she called a landscape, "a new model of meaning whereby making sense is an activity distributed in a text and across successive texts."[35] *Pablo* denied its audience the anticipated and well-rehearsed satisfactions of conventional narrative comprehension. What it offered instead was a cleverly sculpted landscape with a geography of notable landmarks, unexpected turnings, diverse terrains, and meandering paths where one might encounter joy, pain, sadness, or comfort. Steve Scott was with the production from the beginning and traveled to DC for the 1990 remount. He recalled being deeply moved by the show. "What was so staggering was the fact that *Pablo* robbed me of logic and left me in the moment to respond. The emotional impact was for me, overwhelming, particularly in the Washington production. At one point, there was no past or future, only the present which wasn't really safe. It was personal for me and I remember I was in tears. But," he added quickly, "it was emotion, not sentiment. Frank is never sentimental." Nonetheless, in order to keep his audience in the game, Galati needed them to care and care deeply about something that couldn't be expressed in any conventional way. He needed the bond between Stein and Picasso to be an actuality of unique and real value to the spectator, something worth protecting.

Speaking the Unspeakable

In scene six of ten as it appears in the program, Nussbaum positioned herself at the edge of the stage to deliver an extended passage from Stein's 1924, "If I Told Him: A Completed Portrait of Picasso," first published in *Vanity Fair*. This scene initiated a carefully structured series of events that transitioned from the exuberant, early days of their relationship to a subsequent breech and reconciliation. Stein does not name the artist within the poem but "he" is undoubtedly Picasso. Nussbaum noted that this long speech was the most difficult and challenging passage of a difficult and challenging role. The repetitions, variations, alterations, digressions and returns of "If I told Him" had to be precise and its driving energy sustained in order to create the impression of a crushing need to express the inexpressible.

As she spoke, Nussbaum leaned forward, her body slightly torqued with one arm hooked behind and around the wheelchair's handlebar. The position gave her greater vocal control and by happenstance, echoed Stein's forward lunge in Picasso's famous portrait. As the energy of the passage built to a crescendo, the tension in her hooked arm seemed to restrain her even as it helped lift and push her body forward. The multiple circulations and subtle changes of key within the first lines of the passage are relatively ease: "If I told him would he like it. Would he like it if I told him." The level of difficulty builds as the speaker attempts to grasp the complexity and expanse of her subject and the profound bond they share, culminating in an extraordinary aria best spoken out loud for a sense of its inherent challenge and effect: "he and and he and he and he and and as and as he and as he and he. He is and as he is, and as he is and he is, he is and as he and he and as he is and he and he and and he and he."[36]

The speech was a showstopper. In the stutter of Stein's deliberate recurrences, Nussbaum achieved the sense of a strong but suppressed emotion controlled by a formidable will and driven by a passionate desire to speak truth. The repetitions amounted to an incantation that seemed not to describe but to conjure a crushing need to speak, to communicate, to complete a connection between her subject, herself, and her listener. There was no narrative suspense and no anticipation of closure and yet a terrible straining toward it. Peter Amster, the show's choreographer and an ensemble member, felt that her performance had, "a sense of convulsion, as if she needed to stand up. As if she was going to stand." The afterimage that lingers in my memory of Nussbaum's performance is of a tremendous effort to speak what is ultimately unspeakable and a memory of her having somehow succeeded.

Like Stein, Nussbaum was an outsider, an independent artist, and a woman of substance by her own authority. She formed a powerful connection to the role and felt that her performance achieved a rare richness in the Kennedy Center production. "If I Told Him" was the key. She explained,

> Stein's struggle characterized much of how my life felt to me—my life was tangled in the same way as her words. I felt her struggle to describe Picasso was parallel to my own experience. I remember thinking often of Frank and of how

appropriate that speech felt for me. I think we all must have fallen in love with him—we were all so gifted in his eyes. I was so grateful to him.

The search for a symbiotic link between actor and character is a classic acting technique but Nussbaum couldn't depend on the usual tools and methods of psychological realism—a rational and intuitive interpretation of content—to make this connection. Instead, she was profoundly present to Stein's words and her understanding emerged in the sensual, lived experience of speaking the words—for herself as well as her audience.

Nussbaum finished the poem and a spotlight found Bank standing slightly upstage. Alice stepped forward to recount an affectionate anecdote from which the production's title was taken. Her words and demeanor relieved the tension of Nussbaum's aria and confirmed its effect. She described Picasso's naïve pleasure in Stein's curious suggestion that he bore a resemblance to President Abraham Lincoln. Picasso had asked Toklas if she agreed. Alice recalled,

> I had thought a good many things that evening, but I had not thought that. You see, he went on, Gertrude, (I wish I could convey something of the simple affection and confidence with which he always pronounced her name and with which she always said, "Pablo." In their long friendship with all its sometimes troubled moments and its complications this has never changed.) Gertrude showed me a photograph of him and I have been trying to arrange my hair to look like his, I think my forehead does. I did not know whether he meant it or not but I was sympathetic.[37]

Alice confirmed the actuality of the profound bond between the two artists in the unpretentious language of common, everyday gossip. The scene that followed was based on a minor falling-out between Stein and Picasso, an irritant rather than a crisis in their friendship but for Galati's audience, an event that threatened a bond that they had— hopefully—come to value.

After their reconciliation, a tableau came together on stage. Actor Carman Pelton, The Woman in White, sat on an armless chair in the middle ground, facing out toward the audience with an enlarged reproduction of Picasso's *Woman and Child on the Seashore* (1921, Art Institute of Chicago) center stage and slightly behind her. Russo, also in white, reclined on the floor at her side with his head resting against her thigh. Toklas could be seen at a distance, far upstage left watching Stein who sat diagonally downstage right in full profile. Pelton stroked Russo's temple—the only movement in the scene—as she sang a haunting Xavier Montsalvage lullaby. The lighting was romantic and her demeanor serene,

Figure 6 Left to right: Marji Bank, Larry Russo, Carman Pelton, and Susan Nussbaum. Goodman Theatre production of *She Always Said, Pablo*, 1987. Courtesy of the photographer. Photo by Mary Griswold.

neither controlled nor controlling. Her song held the stage in stasis for several minutes.

The stage picture and the beauty and length of the song summoned a sensation of peace, comfort, and reflection. When Galati saw the Kennedy Center production, he reflected on the authenticity of the scene in terms of his own unconscious but deeply felt desire to touch and bring comfort. He explained,

> When we remounted *Pablo* in DC, I could look at what I had done with a slightly more analytical perspective and I realized something about myself and my work in that scene. You see, I had chosen the Woman in White to do this scene—she had sung the part of Susan B. Anthony in *The Mother of Us All* in an earlier scene—and I had chosen the song she sang—a lullaby. I put Picasso sitting at her knees with this huge Amazon mother with the baby in her lap as the background and I had her rubbing his forehead right here [indicating his temple] while she sang to him but I hadn't made any of those connections in my head as I was putting the scene together. I just did it. But you see, this action was my mother doing the same thing to my temple—this particular action is very pleasurable to me. I crave it and my mother could always calm me like this. Well, when I saw what I had done I realized that when you give actors a bit of business, particularly if it's expressive of tenderness and intimacy, you are participating in that tenderness. This sounds strange I know, but it was a way of caressing Larry Russo's head myself, of giving physical comfort to the actor and authenticating

the gesture with the action. I mean it's real, real because one wants to do it and to have it done. So yes, there certainly is that motif of the mother's tenderness—her caring and all that—in this image and throughout my work but there was also the action itself, the action, I suppose, of caring for another person. That action wasn't staged, it happened.

The touch along with the song, the painting, the cool liquid colors, and careful balance of the composition offered a genuine moment of respite. The moment was a present, Galati's gift to the audience as well as the actors.

Shortly after the Chicago production closed, he delivered a speech at the League of Chicago Theatres annual convention and spoke at length on the theme of failure. When he urged his audience "to court, to woo, and to dance with failure," he echoed the Cubist mandate that no matter how doomed the effort, may be, art should seek to make a difference in the world. He quoted the artist Alberto Giacometti to help make his point. "'My success,' says Giacometti, 'will always be less than my failure . . . I have always failed. . . If only I could draw! . . . I can't . . . That's why I keep drawing.'" And finally, he reminded his audience of phenomenologist Martin Heidegger's famous aphorism, "Art, unlike a tool, does not disappear into usefulness.'" *She Always Said, Pablo* continued a journey that began in 1907 and judging by my own experience and that of the many artists and patrons I have interviewed over the years, it did not disappear into usefulness.

Notes

1 Hedy Weiss, "'She Always Said' Speaks to Genius: Pablo and Gertrude Will Lead the Parade at Goodman," *Chicago Sun-Times*, March 6, 1987, 20–22.
2 Frank Galati, handmade binder/script *She Always Said, Pablo*, 1986, Box 33, Folder 2–3, Frank Galati (1943–) Papers, 1948–2914, Northwestern University McCormick Library of Special Collections and University Archives.
3 Hap Erstein, "Modest Master of Stage Adaptations," *Chicago Tribune*, Insight, July 16, 1990.
4 Sam Lesner, "Goodman's 'Pablo' is Stunning Stagecraft," *Skyline Newspaper* (Chicago), March 1, 1987.
5 Lesner.
6 Louise Sweeney, "On stage, a Dreamlike Montage of Gertrude Stein's Circle," *Christian Science Monitor* (Boston MA), July 9, 1990, 9.

7   Richard Christansen, "Frank Galati's 'Pablo' Opens in Washington as 1 More Highlight in a Remarkable Year," *Chicago Tribune*, July 1, 1990.
8   Mira Schor, "The Berger Mystery," *A Year of Positive Thinking* (web log), August 11, 2011. http://ayearofpositivethinking.com/2011/08/11/the-berger-mystery/
9   Richard H. Axsom, *"Parade," Cubism as Theater*, Outstanding Dissertations in the Fine Arts (New York, NY: Garland Publishing, 1979), 194.
10 Linda S. Watts, *Rapture Untold: gender, mysticism, and the "moment of recognition" in works by Gertrude Stein* (New York: P. Lang, 1996), 20.
11 Patricia Dee Leighten, *Re-Ordering the Universe: Picasso and Anarchism, 1897-1914* (Princeton, NJ: Princeton University Press, 1989), 120
12 Leighten, 2.
13 Leighten, 119.
14 Watts, 38.
15 Watts, 18.
16 Taken from a speech by Gertrude Stein at the University of Chicago. Recorded by Thornton Wilder in the introduction to *Four in America* (1947). https://stilleatingoranges.tumblr.com/post/46707637134/now-listen-cant-you-see-that-when-the-language
17 Axsom, 177.
18 Axsom.
19 David E. James, *Power Misses: Essays Across (Un)popular Culture* (London: Verso, 1996), Chapter 3: "Cubism as Revolutionary Realism."
20 Douglas Cooper, *The Cubist Epoch* (London: Phaidon, 1998), 262.
21 Cooper.
22 Gertrude Stein, "Composition as Explanation (1925)," Poetry Foundation, February 15, 2010. www.poetryfoundation.org/resources/learning/essays/detail/69481.
23 Gertrude Stein, "Gertrude Stein on Understanding and Joy: Rare 1934 Radio Interview," interview, PennSound Archives, November 1934. www.brainpickings.org/2012/09/20/gertrude-stein-1934-radio-interview/
24 David Richards, "'Pablo': Gertrude Stein's Colorful Collage," *Washington Post* (DC), June 29, 1990.
25 Jorjet Harper, "Gertrude and Alice 'Always Said, Pablo'" *Windy City Times* (Chicago), March 12, 1987, 15.
26 Hedy Weiss, "'She Always Said' Speaks to Genius: Pablo and Stein Will Lead Parade at the Goodman," *Chicago Sun-Times*, March 8, 1987, Arts sec., 20.
27 Frank Galati correspondence to Sandra, Bob, Roche and Kathy and Kim, "I think we have a cast," January 1986, Box 33, Folder 2, Frank Galati (1943–) Papers, 1948–2914, Northwestern University McCormick Library of Special Collections and University Archives.

28 Frank Galati, unpublished binder/script *She Always Said, Pablo*, 1986, Box 33, Folder 2–3, Frank Galati (1943–) Papers, 1948–2914, Northwestern University McCormick Library of Special Collections and University Archives.
29 Scott Fosdick, "Pablo Loves Gertrude," *American Theatre*, 1985, 4.
30 W. G. Rogers, *When This You See Remember Me: Gertrude Stein in Person* (New York: Discus Books, 1973).
31 Stanton B. Garner, *The Absent Voice: Narrative Comprehension in The Theater* (Urbana: University of Illinois Press, 1989), 43.
32 Howard Reich, "San Francisco's Target is Chicago's Gain," *Chicago Tribune*, March 20, 1987.
33 Galati, *Pablo* binder, 10.
34 Galati, *Pablo* binder, 12.
35 Ulla E. Dydo and William Rice, *Gertrude Stein: The Language That Rises: 1923-1934* (Evanston, IL: Northwestern University Press, 2009), 95.
36 Galati, *Pablo* binder, 97.
37 Galati, *Pablo* binder, 109.

5

The Telling Not the Tale: *The Grapes of Wrath*

In 1990, Frank Galati's adaptation and staging of John Steinbeck's iconic novel *The Grapes of Wrath* played four different cities and received multiple awards, including two Tony Awards for best director and best play of the year. Prior to the New York opening, he explained, "My aim was never to turn *The Grapes of Wrath* into a play per se."[1] Between the 1988 Chicago premiere and the 1990 NYC opening, the Steppenwolf Theatre production was enthusiastically acclaimed in the North American press. Critical acclaim was not universal but pro or con, the critics were in general agreement that Galati had succeeded in not turning Steinbeck's novel into a conventional play. Frank Rich (*New York Times*) observed that "in any ordinary sense there's no 'play' there."[2] Nonetheless, Rich found Galati's "incredibly sophisticated theatrical technique" to be genuinely moving. Linda Winer did not but even so, her summary of the meager plot was not far wrong: "They get on the truck, they get off the truck, someone dies, they settle in a migrant camp in California and get chased away, Tom makes a speech, they settle in another camp, someone dies, Ma makes a speech, it rains."[3] What was "there" for Rich if not for Winer was a theatre event in which the acuity and efficacy of Steinbeck's novel was rejuvenated in some important way, that is to say that its power was in the telling as much as the tale told.

In 1939, John Steinbeck defended the unconventional structure of his novel by declaring to his editor, "I've done my damndest to rip a reader's nerves to rags."[4] Galati's challenge and for many, his achievement in bringing Steinbeck's novel to the stage was to galvanize Steinbeck's resolve for a contemporary audience. "I didn't write this material," he told Hap Erstein in an interview for the *Washington Times*. "I didn't write *The Grapes of Wrath*. I tried, in each case, to give the stage to the text, not my own writing."[5] In giving the stage to Steinbeck's text he transposed the author's social justice agenda to the stage as a lived experience in which the story is always a story and the stage is always a stage. His script lacks dramatic suspense, an individual protagonist, and conventional climatic structure. However, the physical properties and unique resources of the theatre space are embedded in his stagecraft and his script. He provokes an acute awareness of the theatre's material reality and at the same time, occasions a deeply felt emotional investment in the travails of Steinbeck's dispossessed family.

The efficacy of the Steppenwolf production and subsequent success of his widely produced script for *The Grapes of Wrath* is achieved through the carefully crafted multistability of his mise-en-scéne. Multistability is a term used in the sciences in reference to systems that are neither stable nor totally unstable, systems that alternate between two or more mutually exclusive states.[6] The duck/rabbit image is an example of the multistability of perception at its most elementary level. The drawing is stable but the image changes in perception from rabbit to duck according to how it is framed in the mind of the beholder.

It's a trick, writes W. J. T. Mitchell, "a kind of decoy or bait to attract the mind, to flush it out of hiding."[7] The multistability of the three-dimensional theatre space is more complex and challenging than that of a print image. On the printed page, explains Alisa Solomon in *Re-dressing the Canon*,

> One is incapable of seeing the figure simultaneously as both a duck and a rabbit. The mind switches back and forth "maintaining an awareness of the potential duck lurking within the apparent rabbit, and vice versa. In theatre, on the other hand, we see both (or more) layers of fiction and reality at the same time."[8]

Figure 7 From Ludwig Wittgenstein's *Philosophical Investigations* (1953).

The multistability of Galati's staging in *The Grapes of Wrath* was less playful and more worrying than the duck/rabbit image because it attempted to flush out of hiding not the mind but one's construction of self and other. This complex multistability is most apparent when the actualities of the story, the audience, and the actors are perfectly aligned.

Preparing a Theatrical Space for Steinbeck's *The Grapes of Wrath*

In spring of 1985, Galati and Gary Sinise—a founding member of the ensemble and at that time, the company's artistic director—sat on a park bench near Galati's Evanston home. He pointed out the bench as we drove past. "That's where we sat. Right there. It was a sunny afternoon and we were just talking, you know, kicking around ideas. Gary asked me if there was something I wanted to do, something that might be good for the whole ensemble. I said, 'Gary, what about *The Grapes of Wrath*?' Well, his eyes lit up." Steinbeck's widow was approached and gave her approval pending submission of a script. "Once we got permission from Elaine Steinbeck, Gary said he wanted to direct it and I thought, fantastic. I started to work on the adaptation. I didn't get far. I never got a full draft."[9]

In a detailed *American Theatre* account of the production and its making, Jonathan Abarbanel noted that the initial conversations between director and adaptor were exciting but a satisfactory concept failed to emerge. Galati continued wryly:

> I saw this as more a deconstruction of the novel, a postmodern production in which it might be necessary to incorporate contemporary images and to be more didactically Brechtian – even to use portions of the [1940] film in the production in order to get the sting of it off of us by saying to the audience "This is a shared myth and we're exploring it from another angle." We had some ideas about Svoboda-like screens and most definitely a turntable – a huge disc of earth and the truck moved on it. We were very, very smitten by the idea ... it was a terrible idea.[10]

But later that fall, Sinise accepted an offer to direct his first Hollywood film, *Miles from Home*. He agreed to play a role in the Steppenwolf production but withdrew as director and Galati stepped in. "When that happened," he told Abarbanel, "I had sort of a breakthrough. As a director, I had a completely different relationship to the script."[11]

Many of their initial ideas were jettisoned but a few core decisions were retained. John Ford's famous 1940 film ends when Tom leaves the family in Chapter 28 of the novel. However, the novel ends in Chapter 30 as Rosasharn, the Joad daughter who has recently miscarried, gives her breast milk to save a starving man, a stranger encountered by the destitute family when they seek shelter in a barn. The restoration of this passage and its disquieting effect was the primary rationale for the Steppenwolf project.

In January 1936, Steinbeck's friend and editor Pascal Covici sent him a letter expressing reservations about the book's unconventional structure and ending. He acknowledged the powerful symbolism of the novel's final scene but suggested changes. Steinbeck refused. He did not consider the final scene or any other action in the book to be primarily symbolic and replied with some urgency. "I have tried to write this book the way lives are being lived not the way books are written.... Throughout I've tried to make the reader *participate in the actuality*, what he takes from it will be scaled entirely on his own depth or hollowness."[12] Actual things—hand tools, potato peelings, the lament of a singing saw, and the beam of a powerful flashlight—these are not grace notes in Steinbeck's text, nonessential details used to embellish story and purpose. These are the actualities at the heart of his vision and of Galati's. Galati wanted his audience to participate in "the travail of the actor embedded in the narrative. Soaking wet, exhausted, covered with dirt, having hung around a real fire, dug a pit—these things are really endured by the actor. You've been there with them."[13]

The Grapes of Wrath is a book in which fire and water matter, not as symbols but as actualities. Characters are constantly building fires. Fire draws them together to talk, seek warmth, and cook their food. The Joads are invigorated and terrorized by water. The story reaches a crisis when the actuality of unspeakable hardship—the body of a child delivered stillborn in an abandoned boxcar—is placed in a crate and set afloat in a raging river to be carried into the larger community. Metaphor and symbolic meaning cannot match the visceral, gut response triggered by that action.

In 1938 Steinbeck wrote to a friend, "The new book is going well. Too fast. I'm having to hold it down. I don't want it to go so fast for fear the tempo will be fast and this is a plodding, crawling book. So I'm holding it down to approximately six pages a day" (JS to Herbert Sturtz, 1953).[14] To help slow the pace, he inserted alternating inter-chapters with descriptions of landscape and poetic or editorial essays on the causes, conditions, and consequences of the Oklahoma sharecroppers' eviction and forced migration. Susan Shillinglaw explains that the author's interchapters "move from particular to general, from notes of sadness to the thunder of action—from tide pool to the stars, in fact. All of it is important or none of it is."[15] Galati understood that the inter-chapters are critical to the novel's ability to "hit below the belt." He explained, "If I was going to do *Grapes of Wrath*, I didn't want to shirk our responsibility to its full narrative vitality. I didn't want to be shy about these landscape sequences, these more poetic sequences." All of it is important or none of it is.

"I knew I needed a bare stage, a truck, earth, air, fire, and water. Then came the idea that music could drive the story." He recruited Michael Smith, a local musician and composer to set Steinbeck's words to music. Galati identified specific passages from the interchapters and dropped the text down the page like a song lyric. Smith wrote a rhythmic guitar theme that served as the engine of the jalopy. Galati conceived the family's jalopy as "the carriage of time. It moves the Joads and it moves the story—what drives the motor is music and song which is an orchestration of time."[16]

His initial ideas and decisions were made but before he could begin writing, he needed to reconcile the actualities of the novel with the actualities of the stage. He visited the scene shop to discuss the logistics of the physical production with designer Kevin Rigdon. Rigdon recalled that "Out of all the new plays I've ever done, *The Grapes of Wrath* was the most unusual way of working." He explained,

> Frank and I met in my office in the scene shop and looked at pictures and talked about things. I went out into the scene shop and beveled some pieces of plywood and came back in and stuck them in the box in response to Dorthea Lange photographs entitled *The Cultivated Fields*. By the time we were done, we had a plan that Frank could use as he wrote the script.[17]

The horizon and multiple plateaus of the final set design echoed the spatial order of Lang's photograph. With a workable ground plan in hand, Galati was finally ready to begin writing and within three weeks, he had a script. "This," writes Abarbanel, "was the script used by the designers, the composer and the cast. It was the draft that went to the Steinbeck estate for review ... and to the AT&T foundation for funding."[18] Galati's adaptation of Steinbeck's story was told primarily in dialogue, actions and gestures, telling incidents and homely tools as they appear in the novel.

Details, writes Shillinglaw, "matter in *The Grapes of Wrath*. As Steinbeck began the final draft of his novel ... his wife Carol's advice rolled through his mind: 'Stay with the detail' ... Details are ... as essential to his stories as are setting and character."[19] "Thingness" permeates Galati's script but in the profusion of Steinbeck's details, the choice of what of to keep and what to cast aside was crucial. As he began to shape his text, the question he would continue to ask himself and his colleagues was not "What does this thing mean?" but "What does this thing do?" A shovel, the stub of a pencil, a worn and tattered quilt—these are among the unremarkable actualities that Galati deemed necessary. The yellow shoes and the fenny bush were gone. Chapter Three's stoic turtle, so dear to my high school English teacher, was gone. In the first moments of the play, a rough crate and a harmonica establish the rural context of Steinbeck's story. A half pint of "factory liquor" initiates the bond of trust that sets the story in motion, and a chaw of tobacco provides the anticipatory pause before a decisive act. "One of my abiding memories of the performance," wrote *London Sunday Times* reporter John Peter "will be a sense of human activity: people salting meat, lighting fires, digging graves, repairing engines."[20]

Galati's script often provides the actor with more things to use and do than things to say. The things they carry in their pockets or pokes reveal character and purpose. As the family prepare to abandon the homestead, Ma casts every family treasure and nonessential item into the fire. At the last item, Smith hesitated, looked at a small shiny object in her open palm, then pushed it deep into her apron pocket. In Act Two, with no explanation and sparse dialogue, she acknowledged her pregnant teenage daughter's coming of age by withdrawing a pair of golden earrings from the pocket, piercing the girl's ears with a sewing needle, and inserting the small hoops. The gift and the prick of her needle may have symbolic value for the reader but in performance, the earrings, the girl's winch of pain, and the mother's embrace are the actualities of a bond formed between a young woman and her mother.

The fallen preacher Jim Casy is the only central character who does little manual work, talks much, and uses no tools. Words are his tools and Steinbeck's theme of connection and community—the great common soul—is his message. Galati gives him three things to carry in his pocket: a harmonica, a packet of matches, and the stub of a pencil. The sound of his harmonica draws Tom Joad's attention on a lonely road, a meeting that would bring the family together. His match ignites the campfire that draws the men close to tell stories of home, eviction, and loss. And when Grandpa dies and is buried along a lonely country road, Casy's pencil provides the words for a rough marker on the grave—the only physical evidence of the Joad family's otherwise anonymous passage to California.

In his preface to the published script, Galati assures future producers that the elaborate technical effects used in the Steppenwolf production are not necessary to subsequent productions. "We did feel that the actors needed the 'things' that are precious, necessary for survival and also burdensome to the characters they played, just as they needed real clothes, not 'costumes,' to complete the personal environment of each human being in the story."[21] He concludes, "Future productions of this play may not have fire and water and a motorized jalopy, but they may have the power that a bare stage, a few props, and a group of passionate actors can create."[22] The stagecraft of the original production was impressive but the multistable realities of Galati's script are best achieved in small, persistent details rather than grand gestures. Either everything matters or nothing does. As the Steppenwolf ensemble members continued to shape the production prior to the New York opening, they returned time and again to the actualities of the theatre and things that are what they appear to be.

World Premiere, Chicago, 1988

With only a few weeks of rehearsal, the company had a great deal to accomplish in a very short time. Technical problems and blocking issues were resolved but in previews, the show was still nearly four hours long. Too long by half. Between the Thursday and Friday night previews, Galati cut fifty pages of text and made cuts on an additional fifty pages. Decades later, he said with a grin, "They still call it the Friday Night Massacre." The company made the cuts work and the production was much improved on opening night. However, the portentous tone and elaborate staging of the opening sequence remained a problem. "It was driving me absolutely mad," he said with a characteristic eyeroll. "I rehearsed it at least three different ways. I started out asking them to sort of cling to the back wall in, I don't know, desperation. I remember encouraging Rondi Reed to draaaag herself hand over hand along the wall—well, that went. It was all so ponderous."

Abarbanel described the elaborate opening "number" he saw in the 1988 Chicago premiere. The light came up on "a giant shadowbox of weathered wood" with costumed musicians playing acoustic guitar and fiddle. "Other folk instruments ... take up a tune that turns into a chorale as the stage fills with a tableau vivant of laborers and farmers, some are in pools of half-light that dapple the stage; others are back-lit and silhouetted in windows and doors that have opened in the shadowbox's upstage wall."[23] A man and a woman dressed as sharecroppers gazed into a fictive horizon and delivered narrative passages with selections of Steinbeck's prose projected on the walls above and behind them.

The self-conscious artifice of the opening scene was exactly what it appeared to be—costumed actors arranged against an exquisite theatrical backdrop holding symbolic stage props and singing a well-rehearsed song. It was unequivocally another opening of another show and everyone knew it wasn't right. There was much work yet to be done. "But" said Galati, "We were open. We were alive.... The company was willing to continue to rehearse even though they weren't really being paid to rehearse. The project was bigger than all of us and needed all of us to be accomplished. Even the thinking inside the story, 'We're the people—we go on—we survive—we can only do this together.'"

Throughout rehearsals he urged the ensemble to find simple, more direct approaches to the material.

> I said to them, "Everyone comes in here thinking 'My God, this is the great American epic of the Dust Bowl,' and that's how you guys are playing it—as if it were *King Lear*. But you must realize that these people don't know the trouble they're in. They don't see the Dust Bowl as this great American tragedy. It's their problem—a problem that they're trying to solve.

Over the following weeks, he continued to refine and reduce until the opening scene evoked Steinbeck's flat, barren landscape without removing the speaker from the real time and space of the stage and the theatre. It was very close to the scene described in the published script.

> *A frail barbed-wire fence. Two men, some distance from each other, on either side of the fence. One, seated on a wooden crate, plays a rusty wood saw with a violin bow. A simple waltz melody floats up. The other, looking off into the distance, listens and lets the melody conclude. His eyes gleam in the shadow of his broad-brimmed hat.*[24]

A shambling fence line cut a diagonal swath from down left to up right. A single narrator stood upstage left behind the fence. To the right and in front of the fence, L. J. Slavin sat on a wooden crate and played a haunting tune on a saw-harp. Company member Tom Irwin looked directly into the audience as he said "In the morning, the dust hung like fog. Men stood by their fences and looked at the ruined corn, dying fast now . . ." When he finished this short passage from the opening pages of the novel, he looked downstage left. Slavin was gone and Kinney lay sprawled on the raked stage floor at a 45-degree angle to the audience, the worn soles of his shoes facing the audience.

In the revised and final version of the opening scene, every word, gesture, and action fulfilled a purpose. Nothing was extra. Character and action were rendered by things that were exactly what they appeared to be—a man in a battered hat declaimed the famous words of a more famous author and an accomplished musician played a difficult folk instrument. Slavin's absorption as he drew music from the saw was genuine. The sound he produced— "a spectral, beautiful shiver of noise, that gives the tool a kind of feminine personality or unexpected sensitivity"—was real and at the same time, represented a sound heard long ago and far away.[25] The stage directions continue, "*Sunlight through a pattern of leaves reveals Jim Casy sprawled in a pool of dust. He blows into a little harmonica: the reedy opening notes of 'Yes, Sir, That's My Baby.' The man with the saw and the First Narrator are gone. Casy lowers the harmonica and picks up the tune in an easy tenor.*" As Kinney sang, "Yes, sir, that's my Savior, Je-sus is my Savior . . ." his worn shoes marked time like a two-pronged metronome. When he launched into the final refrain, his reedy voice and unfeigned gusto were his own as much as Casy's.

The stage directions describe the scene: "*Tom Joad, in cheap new clothes, walks along the sagging barbed-wire fence. He climbs carefully through, takes off his cap and mops his wet face. A bird whistles nearby.*"[26] When Sinise stepped over the fence, the "wire" showed itself to be a knotted cord connected to wobbly posts set in the stage floor. When he lifted his foot from the "wire," the fence posts popped back into place to reclaim the illusion of a sagging fence. Until the bird whistle, everything on the stage is exactly what it appears to be. But the insertion of this small element of pretending alerts the audience to a subtle shift in perception. Throughout his script, Galati introduces a familiar sound to trigger a perceptual shift. A dog's bark, offstage laughter, and the sound of an approaching automobile signal a subtle but effective spillage toward illusion, drawing the audience into the story.

Character, season, place, and major story points are established in five unhurried lines. Sinise stood at a distance from Kinney, their bodies facing out, toward the audience. The rough, realistic costumes and Oklahoma cadence of the men's speech combined to draw the audience into the story's Depression-era reality.

Tom   Hi. It's hotter'n hell on the road.
Casy Now ain't you young Tom Joad – ol' Tom's boy?
Tom   Yeah. All the way. Goin' home now.
Casy You wouldn't remember me, I guess. Baptized you in the irrigation ditch.
Tom   Why, you're the preacher.[27]

Galati's staging and the unhurried pace of their delivery encouraged the audience to yield to the illusion without denying the physical reality of the stage. He described the scene, played "against the approaching dark clouds of the dust bowl" as "a droll, breezy conversation between two guys—one just out of a four-year spell in the slammer and the other a lecherous ex-preacher."

On opening night in Chicago, the co-presence of actor and character in this exchange was palpable. Sinise and Kinney had achieved considerable local celebrity as the founders with Jeff Perry of the Steppenwolf Theatre and acting ensemble. The story of their determination to establish an innovative and independent theatre company had become part of the city's folklore. The pair faced the audience from opposite sides of the stage, one squatting and tense, the other sprawled on the stage floor. They studied each other for a moment as the audience studied them, two men, still young but worn and wary, taking each other's measure. To Galati, the scene never failed.

> It was great. Gary and Terry were absolutely amazing every time I saw that scene—and they had a great time too, because the last line of the opening sequence is, "My Daddy always said your pecker was too long for a preacher..." When that scene is really clicking, the audience should be saying "Wow! <u>This</u> is *The Grapes of Wrath*?! We'd never have guessed—it's just two guys who are really interesting, talking and having fun! It's really very simple."

And very simply real because while the scene was unquestionably scripted, staged, and acted, what the audience saw on that opening night in 1988 really was two interesting guys talking and having fun.

La Jolla Playhouse, San Diego 1988 and National Theatre, London 1989

Galati continued to make changes during and after the Chicago production. He minimized the role of the narrator, "the boring guy" he explained, "for whom the story is already completed." He cut whole musical sequences and compressed characters and scenes. Company member Randy Arney explained, "Our goal was never to release the audience emotionally but keep them in the game."[28] The company continued to find moments and gestures that increased the pervasive multistability of Galati's conception while keeping the audience in the game.

In the published script the two men in the opening scene confirm a mutual trust when Tom Joad offers Casy a swig from his pint of store-bought liquor. The stage directions read, "*Tom tosses the bottle to Casy. He drinks.*"[29] Galati describes how the actor's unpremeditated impulse in the London production significantly enhanced the impact of the moment by calling attention to the actuality of the stage floor.

> The toss was a kind of virtuoso turn. You'd find yourself thinking, "Is he gonna miss?!"—and of course, he never did. It was great. Then one day, Gary just slid the bottle across the floor. It spun and bounced—the noise of it hitting all the lumps and the cracks of the rough boards was electrifying—and Terry stopped it under the palm of his hand. I remember saying afterwards, "Guys, that's more thrilling than the toss," more thrilling because it acknowledged the surface of the stage. Of course, it's a fictive floor, invested with meaning and illusion, but it's also real, a real floor. In acknowledging the reality of the wood, the Steppenwolf actors were brave enough to acknowledge, with the audience, that it's more exciting to slide the bottle across the weathered boards of a stage than to toss it into the dust filled air of a country road, the "real" environment we see in the movie.

The move stayed in the show because, as Galati says, it was right. Right in that the action confirmed the sense of trust and camaraderie established between Steinbeck's characters and right because it refreshed the connection between the actors, the story, the stage, and its audience.

Jeff Perry did not appear in the Chicago run but took over the role of Noah Joad in London and New York. Noah is described by his family as a "funny kind a fella" and "different," possibly brain damaged by his father's clumsy midwifery. When the Joads reach the Colorado River in Act I, Noah Joad decides to stay behind. His leaving could have been little more than the poignant but un-mourned disappearance from the stage of a mentally impaired minor character. But Noah's departure is essential to Steinbeck's story. If he lacks agency, dignity, and resolve—if he is just giving up—his departure does little more than establish an unfortunate association of "difference" with failure. However, if his leaving is the mindful and decisive act of a self-aware individual, each character's decision to end or to continue the journey is framed as an act of courage and determination rather than desperation or desertion. Perry played the part with ferocious intensity but as with Sinise and Kinney, his performance was compelling because of the multistable actualities of seeming and being, character and actor established in the scene.

When the family arrived at the Colorado River, the downstage floor rolled back to reveal a rectangular water trough about twelve feet long and four feet deep. Jim True, who played the youngest Joad brother Al, let out a whoop, tore off his clothes and cannonballed into the water trough buck naked.

Figure 8 Left to right: Gary Sinise, Jim True, and Jeff Perry. Steppenwolf Theatre production of *The Grapes of Wrath*, 1990. Courtesy of the Steppenwolf Theatre Company. Photo by Paul Cunningham.

Sinise striped to his skivvies and dangled his feet in the water as Perry waded in, shirtless and shoeless but still in his overalls. True dunked Perry's head under, pulled himself out of the trough, grabbed his jeans and sprinted off upstage. When Perry resurfaced, he rested his dripping head against folded arms on the edge of the trough, facing the audience. He gazed into the horizon for a few moments then said: "I ain't a-goin' on." Sinise protested as Perry heaved himself out of the water, retrieved his boots, and walked upstage left. At the highest point of the raked stage, he turned and posed contrapposto against the open expanse of the horizon with his arms hanging at his sides, battered boots dangling from one hand. Water streamed off his body and formed a rivulet on the slanted stage floor. Unfastened at one shoulder and hip, the waterlogged overalls hung across his body in a long diagonal slash that ended in a disconcerting shadow at the crotch—disconcerting because it was unnecessary and inappropriate in that dramatic moment to imagine the body of Noah Joad as sexual or even sexed. But the water-soaked overalls hung on Perry's pale body like a stage role draped across the actor's psyche. It was as much an actor's moment as it was an acting moment.

Perry held the pose, considered for a moment and said "I'm sad, but I can't help it. I got to go." There was not a trace of self-pity or accusation in his voice. "I know how I am. I know they're sorry. But well, I ain't a goin.'"[30] When he turned upstage to make his exit, the weight of the water-logged overalls and the sagging crotch impeded his movement. However, the lumbering determination of the drenched and half-clothed actor skidding on the wet floorboards empowered rather than diminished the resolution of his character's departure. Perry's performance was moving because the actor's passion combined with the actuality of his dripping body gave real gravitas to the moment and nobility to the character.

The brightness Kevin Rigdon designed to illuminate the Steppenwolf production occasionally pretended to be other brightness but never pretended to not be the light on stage. In Act II, Casy delivers a plea for unity among the downtrodden workers, one of the longest monologues in the play. Rigdon framed his speech against the impossibly low horizon of a vast, starry and undeniably theatrical skyscape. As Casy ends his speech, the camp is discovered and attacked by hired thugs. Rigdon's stars disappeared, leaving the stage in near total darkness. The stage directions describe the action. "*Suddenly, dozens of flashlight beams slash through the night. White luminous blades slash moving figures and human voices bark and growl and whisper from the shadows.*"[31] As the shouts of angry men increased, the powerful beams of the attacker's flashlights flailed across the walls, ceiling, and auditorium seating to create an undifferentiated sense of pandemonium in the theatre. "*Suddenly, Tom's face is frozen in a sword point of light.*"[32] Horror registered on his face and then it was gone. As the struggle continued, flashlight beams passed over Casy's fallen body and Tom's violent attack on the assailant. A guard's voice shouted out a warning from the darkness and the men dispersed. The scene ended as described in the text. "*Two or three beams of light remain in the foreground shining out.*" Patrons shielded their eyes from the powerful beams—a real light pretending to be another light—that scanned the auditorium.

In the novel, the film, and in Galati's script, Casy is murdered, Tom attacks the hired thug who killed him, and escapes into the night with a broken nose. In Steinbeck's novel, he hides out for several weeks with Ma's support and aide. Finally, at her urging he leaves the family and the story. Galati compressed the novel's action into a single night and about five minutes of stage time. As Ma said goodbye to her battered child, Galati's staging encouraged the audience to momentarily yield to illusion. He placed the farewell scene upstage left with the two actors seated on a rough bench that extended into the wings. Offstage sounds, the lighting, and stage position suggested a spot of relative privacy in the crowded off-stage migrant camp, all the more realistic for being unseen. A thick layer of stage blood spread across the lower half of Sinise's face. Even those reviewers who had faint praise for the overall production, singled out the performances of Sinise and Smith for praise, particularly in this scene.

Sinise sat hunched on the outside edge of the bench as they talked. When he stood and said "Now, I better go," Smith's action is described in the stage directions: "*Tom stands up and turns to leave. Ma reaches for him but when Tom turns around, she pulls her hands back away.*" Smith explained how the action came about. "We made a lot of changes in the La Jolla run. By the time we finished in Chicago, we knew that things were going to change with the text and the set and I knew that the goodbye, well ... it wasn't there yet. It isn't often that one is informed by a critic, but Frank Rich finally came to see the Chicago production and something he said lodged in my mind." Rich had written,

> Perhaps no moment is more typical of the production's strengths and failings than the one that occurs when Ms Smith, having been left by Mr. Sinise, remains seated in a pool of dim light on a vast, blackened stage. What does Ma Joad think and feel as she contemplates her son's departure? The play is as frustratingly reticent as the novel. But the image of Ma Joad, keeping quiet counsel and strength under the stars, reminds us of what still endures in Steinbeck—an indestructible American mythology that finds its match in Steppenwolf's brawny pioneering vision of American theater.[33]

Late in the La Jolla run, Smith finally found a way to express Ma Joad's unspoken need in a sudden and unbidden release of yearning supplication. As Sinise turned away from her, she leaned forward and reached toward his back with both arms outstretched, fingers distended, then, as he turned to face her, quickly pulled her hands into her lap. Smith explained, "Gary had his back to me and for a long time he didn't know about it. He saw it in a shadow one night and it startled him. Frank had left La Jolla and when he came back, I asked him if it was OK." It was more than OK. "It was brilliant," recalled Galati. London critic Jeremy Lingson described the moment: "Lois Smith's Ma Joad, pulling back her outstretched arms after the departing Tom, making restraint more eloquent than any outburst."[34]

Rich agreed and acknowledged Smith's achievement in his 1990 review of the revised New York production,

> When Ma Joad – in the transcendent form of the flinty, silver-haired Lois Smith – delivers her paean to the people's ability to "go on," it isn't the inspirational

epilogue that won Jane Darwell an Oscar, but a no-nonsense, conversational reiteration of unshakable pragmatism. When Mr. Sinise leaves his already disintegrating family to join a radical underground, his "I'll be all around in the dark" soliloquy is not Fonda's Lincolnesque address, but a plain spoken statement of bedrock conviction.[35]

He also noted that the "the evening's dialogue scenes are few and brief, the lines are reduced to a laconic minimum and the many people are defined by their faces and tones of voice rather than by psychological revelations."[36]

When Tom tells Ma that he has learned to understand and share the Preacher's belief in "one big soul ever'body's a part of," the narrative line established in the first scenes of the play is finished, its promise fulfilled—and the movie ends. But Steinbeck did not write a conventional novel and in Galati's script, as in the book, the family and the story continue toward the all-important final action. His staging of the final scene in which Rosasharn offers her breast milk to save a starving man was powerful on opening night of the original Chicago production and remained essentially unchanged in La Jolla, London, and New York. However, it was clear to the cast and artistic team that the transition between the catastrophic events of the flood and the culminating scene in the barn wasn't working as it should. Not until La Jolla was the company able to deliver the full impact of the novel's final action and once again, the solution they found was in the multistable actualities of the story and the stage.

Gittin' to Higher Groun'

Following Tom's departure, the remaining Joad's find relative safety and shelter among a community of families squatting in twelve abandoned boxcars on the bank of a river. The men have found work and the birth of Rosasharn's baby is imminent. Al Joad and Aggie Wainwright, the daughter of the family who share the Joad's boxcar, announce their intention to marry. There is a promise of new beginnings as the families pull together a meager celebration. But hope for the future is shattered as storm clouds gather and the girl's labor pains commence. The women shelter in the boxcar as the men band together in a desperate battle to save their homes from the rising floodwaters. Shortly before dawn, Rosasharn miscarries and a forty-foot cottonwood crashes into the riverbank, destroying their efforts to keep the rising river at bay. The rain continues as the sodden and defeated family members retreat to the flooding boxcars.

The storm was represented on stage by a spectacular water curtain centered over the downstage water pit with the open boxcar directly upstage. The first thunderclap cued the trough to open and humidity filled the auditorium as the cascade of water was unleashed. The pit teemed with men wielding shovels and shouting to each other over the roar of the falling water. Verbal cues were lost in the din as sopping actors struggled and often failed to keep their footing.

Actors lugged heavy sandbags (added in La Jolla) into place, sloshing water onto the stage floor. Screams from the upstage boxcar indicated Rosasharn's mounting labor pains. Uncle John, played by James Noah, collapsed, and called out as his head slipped beneath the water's surface. The men hauled him to safety at the edge of the pit as the girl's screams subsided. The workers fell momentarily silent, listening for a baby's cry but none came. In the relative stillness of that pause, a blinding flash of light illuminated the stage and the theatre reverberated with the sound of a monumental thunderclap. A warning shout from the men and a sound effect indicated that a gigantic cottonwood was about to crash into the improvised levy. The water continued to fall as the men scattered, taking the sandbags and tools with them. The Joad men retreated into the upstage boxcar behind the water curtain.

Figure 9 Troupe members of the Steppenwolf Theatre Company performing a stage adaptation of John Steinbeck's *The Grapes of Wrath* at the Royal George Theatre. Photo by Steve Kagan/Getty Images.

As the men dispersed, the rain abated slightly. Uncle John emerged from the boxcar carrying a small wooden crate and waded into the water pit. Falling water battered the brim of his hat and streamed onto his face and chest as he set the "coffin" of the stillborn child adrift. "Go down an' tell 'em," he shouted into the rain. "Go down in the street an' rot an' tell 'em that way."[37] The rain softened but continued to fall as he rejoined the family in the flooding boxcar. In the aftermath of the spectacular flood scene, the Chicago audience was confused by the transition from the boxcars to the final action of the play. Abarbanel rightly observed that the audience "found it difficult to follow the through-line of the play's final minutes, as the Joads are flooded out."[38] The company agreed. In La Jolla, scenic elements were added and blocking adjustments were made. Still, the movement into the final scene—and therefore the entire production—was unsatisfactory.

Galati was not in La Jolla when the cast finally found a solution to the problem. Lois Smith recalled the trouble this transition caused and the discovery of a solution:

> We had a terrible time getting from the boxcars to the barn. We were constantly coming up with different answers. We worked on the moment of leaving—we waded through the water pit and got rained on; we tried to turn and back up. We tried everything, but it didn't work—it was just too hard. I remember wracking my brains over and over, and when it came time to play the scene I'd think, "Oh no! Not the boxcars." It was a cruel joke. I got so I dreaded that scene. Then one day in La Jolla somebody's friend saw the show and said something like, "Gee, I don't know why they left the boxcars. They seemed so comfortable." And that began to be the answer. We went back to the book—which was what we always did—and saw that the cars were completely flooded. I started to thinking and got excited again about the trip from the boxcar to the barn. Gary [Sinise] called Frank in Chicago to talk it over and the next day we took away everything of comfort. What we ended up with was an entirely stripped stage—<u>no</u> comfort. No blankets. No lanterns. Nothing. And in the light change [of Uncle John's speech 'Go down an' tell 'em.'], Sally and I snuck off and got ourselves drenched in two child's wading pools we put on the side of the stage. So while we were still in the boxcar, it was clear that we <u>had</u> to leave it. Everyone could see we <u>had</u> to get out of there. There was literally nothing there and we were soaked. After that, there were no more problems with the final scene. We played it, and it just worked.

The stage directions read, "*Al pushes the curtain aside and moves into the Joad's section of the boxcar holding a dim lantern light. Ma and Rose of Sharon, soaking wet, huddle together. Pa and Uncle John, also drenched and raw, are squatting nearby."*[39] Clearly, the family was forced to seek shelter on higher ground.

The boxcar disappeared and the trap closed as Smith herded the actors up left. The lighting was devoid of defining shadow or focal point as they clung to each other, scanning the empty stage for something to mark a departure or an arrival. Twice, Pa asks plaintively, "where we're goin'?" Twice Ma says she doesn't know. Three times, Smith propelled the group in a new direction with a quick turn or a resolute step only to stop short. Neither Ma nor the story had any place to go. Then Smith pointed upstage and said, as if commanding it to be so, "Look there! I bet it's dry in that barn." At her shout, rough wooded doors slid open in the upstage wall. It was a triumphant theatrical turn in which the actor seemed to bring forth a destination by the sheer force of her will. "The actors have lost their way, their place." Galati reflected, "the line 'It's a barn' is the actor's finding their way back. It will be a barn if you make it a barn. They are saving the moment as actors. It gave them back control in the way that the show should empower everyone. That's how these people are gonna get out of this. It will be a barn if you make it a barn."

The group centered themselves in the upstage opening. The men pushed the sliding doors further open and the entire family gathered in its frame as if to enter, then turned out to face the audience in a huddled mass. As they turned, the staged light shifted to suggest a shadowed interior with the brighter light behind them. It was clear that they had entered a vast but dimly lit space in a dull, early morning light. A heavy, hay-strewn beam dropped a few feet from the grid mid-stage—a concession to location added in La Jolla. The six sodden characters had found shelter.

An Action Filled with Ambiguity and Dread

Rosasharn, says Galati, is "the vehicle that delivers the message of the book to the world. I'd say that this young girl, who is pregnant throughout the play, bears in her womb the story itself—of the Joads, the dust bowl. Of their need . . . It's an act of nourishing the moment, the man, the world." True to Steinbeck's purpose, he was intent on doing his damndest to rip the spectator's nerves to rags. But by the late 1980s, the enactment of Steinbeck's controversial scene might amount to little more than a photo opportunity, scandalous to a few patrons and unintentionally titillating to others. Galati described Steinbeck's final scene as an "action filled with ambiguity and dread." What he needed was not a fictive moment of ambiguity and dread but a worrying and ambiguous action within the precincts of the auditorium itself. He explained, "This had to be a moment of tremendous hope and possibility as well as wrenching emotion. We have to believe that the story isn't yet written . . . that we can do better, but only if we will do better—it's a <u>choice</u>." Sympathy or empathy would have begged the question of responsibility and choice and in this final scene. Galati wanted to elicit accountability not sympathy. To achieve this end, he called on the actualities of the theatre event.

The Stranger in Steinbeck's novel is poor, displaced, and white. Galati anachronistically cast African American actor Lex Monson in the part with an African American child as his son. In the Steppenwolf production, as the family entered the barn, the boy emerged from the shadows and pointed toward a prostrate figure laying on the floor slightly off center and very near the edge of the stage. Ma begs the boy for a blanket so she can get Rosasharn out of her wet clothes and is given a ragged comforter by the boy. From this point on, Galati's script follows the novel word for word. Steinbeck writes:

> The boy was at her side again explaining, "I didn't know. He said he et, or he wasn' hungry. Las' night I went an' bust a winda an' stoled some bread. Made 'im chew 'er down. But he puked it all up, an' then he was weaker. Got to have soup or milk. You folks got money to get milk?" / . . . Ma's eyes passed Rosasharn's eyes, and then came back to them. The two women looked deep into each other. The girl's breath came short and gasping. /She said, "Yes."

Sally Murphy, who played Rosasharn, knelt by Monson as Smith corralled the family and herded them toward the opening in the upstage wall. As they exited, the barn doors were pulled shut in a decisive gesture of closure and the lighting shifted to an unsentimental wash without defining edges or obvious focus. There was no stage illusion to palliate Murphy's action as she knelt at the edge of the stage cradling Monson's head in her arms. When she loosened the blanket to bare her breast, he shook his head but she answered, "You got to" and lifted his face toward her exposed breast.

Galati's anachronistic casting and extra-dramatic staging charged the spectator to think beyond race by calling attention to the fact that one was, in fact, thinking about race. It was second nature to frame Murphy as a white, rain-soaked teenager of the depression era but at the same time, Monson was inexorably framed in perception by the color of his skin. If the final scene collapsed into the theatrical frame as illusion, as it did for some critics, the casting of Monson as the stranger was a gratuitous anachronism. But if the multistability of that moment held, when the actuality of Monson's race registered, one's own viewing position was called out and possibly, a cause for concern. Why, for example, am I aware and perhaps uneasy or even offended by Monson at same time I see through Murphy to Rosasaron? In *The Grapes of Wrath*, Galati asked his audience to look again and look more closely, not only at what was represented on the stage but at how one constructs self and other. Perception, he reminds us, "is the secret heart of who we are."

During rehearsal, Cheryl Lynn Bruce, a highly accomplished and respected Chicago director and actor of African descent, was not the only member of the ensemble to express misgivings about the signification of Galati's casting choice but she was the most articulate. In conversations with the director and in her own self-examination over a period of weeks, she came to understand that the purpose and intended consequence of this choice was experiential rather than semiotic. She explains,

> At first, I could only see the typical scenario of the white man or dominant culture possessing all that is good and life-sustaining and the black man, yet again, a powerless and needy victim. But my world view has to allow for the possibility of a white person giving selflessly to a black person—and giving unconditionally—otherwise I'm guilty of perpetuating the same kind of parochial thinking I accuse others of. In my view, white European culture seems unwilling—and perhaps unable—to move beyond the artificially ascribed "otherness" of skin color and the hierarchies that devolve from it. Frank is neither polemical nor propagandistic. He challenges us to live beyond political positions. What makes Frank different is his ability to initiate a serious journey of reflection over a period of weeks and months. In continuing along that path, it's almost impossible not to examine one's own positions.

Bruce added that "the issues I run up against in one way or another tend to be tied to difference—class and gender but firstly to color . . . I think Frank charged us to think beyond skin."

Critic Frank Rich noted Galati's intentional dismantling of the conventional "suspension of disbelief" and judged it to be efficacious. In his review of the 1990 production, he describes the effect of the "living breathing actors" in a final tableau:

> The evening concludes with the coda the movie omitted, in which the Joad daughter, Rose of Sharon (Sally Murphy), her husband gone and her baby just born dead, offers to breast feed a starving black man (Lex Monson) in a deserted barn.... There is no pious sermon—just a humble, selfless act of charity

crystallized into a biblical image, executed by living-and-breathing actors ... The Steppenwolf "Grapes of Wrath" is true to Steinbeck because it leaves one feeling that the generosity of spirit that he saw in a brutal country is not so much lost as waiting once more to be found.[40]

Not every critic praised Galati's casting and staging. Robert Brustein somewhat grudgingly admired the Steppenwolf production for its "authenticity" but considered Galati's casting in the final scene to be a well-meant but wrong-headed gesture toward political correctness. He writes:

> That the unemployed suckler on stage is black ... ignores the fact that segregation was still very much in force in Depression America, even among such virtuous models as the Joads. But historical accuracy is clearly less important in this production than ideals of non-traditional casting and racial togetherness. In any case, the actors perform with such sincerity and conviction that you tend to ignore such anachronisms.[41]

Brustein was true to his own aesthetic inclinations and he was not alone. But he was incorrect when he attributed this anachronism to color-blind casting—a regional theatre trend in the 1980s—motivated by unexamined liberalism. Galati's intentional casting choice contributed to the complex clash of the actualities in the final scenes of the play.

In fact, Galati was surprised that so few critics commented on his flagrant and strategic transgression of conventional verisimilitude. He thought the casting choice was important, even essential to what he hoped to achieve.

> That the starving man was black—and that his son was begging—was a problem for some people in rehearsal and the meaning, culturally, of applying a racial dynamic to that scene was a source of great strain within the cast. It took Cheryl Lynn a long time to absorb and accept the rightness of this choice—this moment in the play. But then, in the end, I was surprised at how seldom this casting choice was mentioned in the critical response, because I think it was all-important to the scene—and really, to the impact of the entire production.

Far from being blind to color and race, Galati hoped that the audience would see the choice made on stage and in doing so, see themselves seeing it. Nonetheless, he gives the company full credit for the powerful impact of the play's final action. "I have to confess, it had nothing to do with me, but coming to that last moment of the play was to a moment of holiness and sanctity, it was always breathtaking to feel that the moment TOOK the stage and it had been earned by the toils and the agony of the characters in the journey that leads to this gesture."

Actor Kevin Chamberlin (Horton in *Seussical the Musical*) had not yet entered the profession when he saw the Steppenwolf production. It was a memorable and important experience for the young actor. He recalled,

> The theatre has moments. If life were only moments, we'd never know we had one. But the final scene in *Grapes*, that was riveting and shocking. I was in college when I saw it and that scene was like a painting that takes you off guard and stops you in your tracks—the Stendhal syndrome, the idea that someone can be in physically changed by a painting, have some sort of visceral reaction, get sick or faint. "Nobody fainted, but I'd never before seen people become enraptured in a play.

Shortly after the New York closing, the production was filmed on the Cort Theatre stage for the PBS American Playhouse series. It is worth noting that every incident of theatrical multistability in Galati's mise-en-scéne was either restaged for the camera or simply doesn't register in the video. Director Kirk Browning, a veteran of televised theatrical performance, rightly judged such stage worthy effects to be irrelevant, even detrimental to the filmed performance. In the opening scene, faces fill the picture frame, dislocated in time and space. Sinise tosses the whiskey bottle to Kinney. Perry's exit speech is filmed in close-up and the sodden women huddled in the boxcar are seen from an oblique angle unavailable to the audience. The stage performance was also taped for the archive of the Billy Rose Theatre Division of the New York Public Library of the Performing Arts. This recording is less polished than Browning's version but is a more accurate record of the stage production. Both videos have value but no recording can capture the phenomenological crisis of the live performance and, therefore, cannot reproduce the powerful effect Galati's final scene achieved in the shared space of the theatre.

Notes

1 Frank Galati, Interview with Jonathan Abarbanel, "Steppenwolf in Steinbeck Country," *American Theatre*, June 23, 1989.
2 Frank Rich, "New Era for 'Grapes of Wrath,'" *New York Times*, March 23, 1990.
3 Linda Winer, "The Joads Hit the Road," *New York Newsday*, March 23, 1990.
4 Steinbeck, John. "To Pascal Covici." 16 January 1939. *Steinbeck: A Life in Letters*, edited by Elaine Steinbeck and Robert Wallsten, (Viking Press, 1975), 178–179.
5 Frank Galati quoted in Hap Erstein, "The Thing's the Play for Frank Galati," *Washington Times* (DC), June 22, 1990, E 22 sec, 58.

6 www.definitions.net/definition/multistability
7 W. J. T. Mitchell, *Picture Theory: Essays on Verbal and Visual Representation* (Chicago, IL: University of Chicago Press, 1995), 50.
8 Alisa Solomon, *Re-dressing the Canon: Essays on Theater and Gender* (London: Routledge, 2005), 16.
9 Frank Galati, Interview with Jonathan Abarbanel, "Steppenwolf in Steinbeck Country." *American Theatre*, August 23, 1989.
10 Galati Interview with Abarbanel.
11 Galati Interview with Abarbanel.
12 John Steinbeck's America: A Life in Letters." http://steinbeck.oucreate.com/exhibits/show/steinbeck-and-oklahoma/a-life-in-letters
13 John Mayer, "An Oral History of Steppenwolf's 'The Grapes of Wrath'" *American Theatre*, December 23, 2016, 8.
14 Quoted on Stanford Institute, *The Grapes of Wrath*; Historical Background and elsewhere. https://steinbeck.stanford.edu/grapeshistorical
15 Susan Shillinglaw, *On Reading the Grapes of Wrath* (New York: Penguin Books, 2014), 181.
16 Galati interview with Abarbanel.
17 Kevin Rigdon in Mayer, "An Oral History," 122.
18 Abarbanel, "Steppenwolf in Steinbeck Country."
19 Shillinglaw, 15.
20 John Peter, "Chicago Shows How to Distill a Potent Brew," *London Sunday Times*, June 25, 1989, Issue 8602.
21 Frank Galati, introduction to *John Steinbeck's The Grapes of Wrath* (New York, NY: Dramatists Play Service, 1991), 8.
22 Galati, *John Steinbeck's The Grapes of Wrath*, introduction.
23 Abarbanel, "Steppenwolf in Steinbeck Country."
24 Galati, *John Steinbeck's The Grapes of Wrath*, 9.
25 David McNamee, "Hey, What's That Sound: Musical Saw," *The Guardian*, June 07, 2010. www.theguardian.com/music/2010/jun/07/musical-saw
26 Galati, *John Steinbeck's The Grapes of Wrath*, 10.
27 Galati, *John Steinbeck's The Grapes of Wrath*, 10.
28 Clifford Terry, "Headin For Broadway; How Steppenwolf Turned 'Grapes Of Wrath' Into An International Hit That Opens This Week In New York," *Chicago Tribune*, March 18, 1990.
29 Galati, *John Steinbeck's The Grapes of Wrath*, 10.
30 Galati, *John Steinbeck's The Grapes of Wrath*, 42.
31 Galati, *John Steinbeck's The Grapes of Wrath*, 76.
32 Galati, *John Steinbeck's The Grapes of Wrath*, 76.
33 Frank Rich, "Chicago's Steppenwolf Group Adapts 'The Grapes of Wrath,'" *New York Times*, October 4, 1988.

34 Jeremy Lingston, "Glorious Ensemble Playing; *The Grapes of Wrath*," *The Times* (London), June 23, 1989.
35 Lingston.
36 Frank Rich, "New Era," 1990.
37 Galati, *John Steinbeck's The Grapes of Wrath*, 84.
38 Abarbanel, 1989.
39 Galati, *John Steinbeck's The Grapes of Wrath*, 85.
40 Rich, "New Era," 1990.
41 Robert Brustein, "What Makes a Play Live," *New Republic*, April 7, 1990.

Part Three

Backstage Process and Onstage Themes: Maternal Projects

Introduction to Part Three

The dominant image of a twentieth-century stage director is that of a paterfamilias, a confident decision maker who may rule as an inspired madman, a disciplined administrator, a benign despot, a visionary artist, or a punishing authoritarian. Galati does not fit any variation of this patriarchal archetype. His attitude, interests, and strengths favor the ethical position and strategies of what psychologist Silvia Vegetti Finzi identifies as the maternal project. Finzi describes such a project in terms that would be familiar to theatre makers and patrons who know Galati's work and working methods firsthand. She writes:

> Freeing oneself of one's own images, keeping possibilities open, trying new approaches, and tolerating not knowing what one will do next are all conditions both of intellectual creativity and of bringing into the world a being who is really "other" but is not alien. In order to express its creative faculty, the maternal experience requires a space of shared silence, a suspension of time in which conceptual (imaginative) forces can converge. Dominance, intentionality, force are only hindrances; what matter are the conditions of distraction, relaxation, and availability.[1]

The creation of something unique but not alien, tolerating not-knowing, a convergence of imaginative forces, letting go of individual force and intention in order to make discoveries in a shared space—all of these aspects characterize Galati's work in the classroom, in pre-production, and rehearsals. They are also thematic in his onstage work.

In the context of our conversation about maternal projects, he was prompted to tell a story about *The Grapes of Wrath* production at the La Jolla Playhouse, prior to the London and Broadway openings.

> I remember thinking to myself what in the hell am I gonna do for five weeks!? What am I going to tell them? What help do they need—for god's sake, they're brilliant. So I told them that I would go in there and sit and watch. And I watched them in the almost complete absorption that I can achieve when I'm working

with actors, when I'm observing a scene being performed. And I realized that I had a million things to do, a million things to say.... I could hear certain things. Just to give them the benefit of a description, what it sort of felt like to me. I was always trusted because they knew that I wasn't pretending. I wasn't trying to make something up and I wasn't trying to pretend that I was directing them. I was just simply there with them, you know. I could do that for the cast and I discovered that I could do it for hundreds of hours and that was my way of interacting with them as a director. It was very much like watching your children play—exactly—and validating the emergence of their personalities in play.

Galati's final product is shaped in the process of its making and by its makers but it also bears the imprint of his unique presence. Jim Corti recalled how in rehearsal for the musical *Ragtime*, Galati "drew the best out of everyone. It never really looks like he's doing anything. He's always conferring, deferring, never taking a domineering position. And yet the final product has Frank Galati's signature all over it."

More than popular, respected, or well liked, Frank Galati is well loved. This mutual admiration society is no hackneyed show business convention. The rapport and openness of ensemble work is the bedrock of his continuing success as a theatre artist. "Is there anyone," asks Libby Appel (Artistic Director Oregon Shakespeare Festival, 1995–2007), "who has ever met or worked with Frank who hasn't fallen immediately in love with him?" Well, yes. Galati is fully aware that a free flow of movement, ideas, and energy that he favors can render the artistic process vulnerable to the slings and arrows of outrageous fortune, obstreperous colleagues, and incompatible methodologies. More than one production has spiraled out of his embrace. Actor Mark Jacoby (*Ragtime, The Visit*) explained, "I've always said that Frank is a poet. If he were an auto mechanic, he'd raise the hood of your car and then he'd write a poem about it. Whether or not he could fix it, well, I guess there have been things he couldn't fix. But," adds Jacoby with conviction, "I'm sure, absolutely sure that those people involved came to work every day feeling like they knew why they decided to become actors. What we're doing here is our life blood and that's the way he makes you feel." The fact that Galati's commitment to ensemble is vulnerable to disruption and failure begs the question of why and how the highly improbable collaboration he seeks works at all.

The central and organizing questions addressed in Chapter 6, Rehearsing Ensemble, are first, how can a director authorize creative collaboration while maintaining a personal voice in the process and quality control over the final product? And second, how is it possible to occasion an actor's strong sense of personal fulfillment and ownership in tandem with a mindful release of ego and individual intention? The answers to these questions lie in Galati's rehearsal room and in the profound respect he has for the contradictions and dualities from which these questions arise.

Throughout his long and varied career, he has given female characters a far greater degree of individuality and subjectivity than is usually allowed to women in dramatic representation, particularly maternal figures. In 1946, Picasso famously advised a friend, "It is not necessary to paint a man with a gun. An apple can be just as revolutionary."[2] In a 1987 interview, Galati said, "my temperament, my outlook is not what you would call strictly political."[3] He does not, in other words, "paint" a man with a gun but his mise-en-scéne is conceived as a form of activism that asks us to see differently. Cultural constructs of gender, race, and identity, and the dramatic conventions connected to such constructs, are consistently put out for interrogation in his work. The enhanced agency he allows maternal characters is no sidebar or condescending nod. Between 1986 and 1996, a period in which his reputation was firmly established and his ability to choose his projects increasingly unfettered, maternal characters, challenges, and interests were everywhere present in his work. He shared a great deal with his peer directors in Chicago, but in this he was unique. For all the vibrance and innovation of the city's theatre in the 1980s, the ratio of male to female dramatic rolls was five to one at best and complex female protagonists were few and far between. Galati was the exception. All but three of over twenty projects he directed between 1986 and 1996 featured female protagonists and there was not a muse or self-sacrificing "good woman" among them. Whether the protagonist's project is ultimately triumphant or disastrous, Galati, his collaborators, and his protagonists are subject to the moral imperative of the maternal project, that is, the necessity of relinquishing control of what one has brought into the world without being, in return, diminished.

Notes

1 Sylvia Vegetti Finzi, *Mothering: Toward a New Psychoanalytic Construction* (New York: Guilford Press, 1996).
2 Alex Danchev, "Picasso's Politics," *The Guardian* (US edition) May 10, 2010. www.theguardian.com/artanddesign/2010/may/08/pablo-picasso-politics-exhibition-tate
3 Colleen Grace, "'She Always Said, Pablo;' A world premiere celebrating the genius of Gertrude Stein," *Nit & Wit*, February 1987, 33.

6

Rehearsing Ensemble: Working All Together All the Time

Ensemble collaboration is a different protocol than cooperation. Cooperation allows a group of individuals to work together to achieve a predetermined goal or product without getting in each other's way. Collaboration requires individual artists to put aside personal intention in order to participate in an unpredictable synthesis of information, talents, ideas, and perspectives. The result of a successful collaboration is something quite different than what each artist could have created on their own. In the theatre, ensemble collaboration begins in preproduction, develops in rehearsals, and matures in performance. Lois Smith felt that the work among the *Grapes of Wrath* ensemble never stopped. "What I recall is working all together, all the time, on the whole thing—the production, not just the part. That's rare in the theatre, but that's Frank."

Galati's collaborations are marked by inclusion and a sense of play. Time and again—in formal interviews and audience talk-backs, backstage chat, casual comments, and personal letters—colleagues and theatre patrons describe the man's uncanny ability to generate a palpable feeling of inclusion. "It is as if you're being physically embraced," says director Norma Saldivar, gesturing with open arms to illustrate an expansive embrace. "You feel as if you are being encircled, pulled in by these huge embracing arms." Saldivar spoke as an audience member and peer director but professional colleagues speak in similar terms of embrace. Doubters as well as enthusiasts characterize Galati's production process by the conditions of play, that is, a freedom of discovery and an uninhibited flow of ideas and energy within clearly defined boundaries. "To really play," says actor Larry Russo, "you don't structure yourself, but equip and empower yourself. This is what Frank works towards and if you can't do that, you aren't going to make it with him." Jim Corti (*Ragtime, The Visit*) points out that "Frank is open to your ideas and inventions and he certainly has plenty of his own, but he gives you really strong boundaries within which to work. He is specific and precise without being autocratic."

Play is essential to human development and Galati's play-based process of discovery was evident in his classroom. He recalled a gathering sponsored by a former student in the late 1990s.

> It was an incredible evening for me. There were 40 or 50 people there. I remembered them all, recognized them all. We reminisced about performances in class, things they remembered. I was really overwhelmed. It was tremendously rewarding and it was a surprise–those years, those classes, those generations of students coming through my watch just as I came through earlier.

He is able to greet his former students as old comrades because he presents himself in the classroom as an expert learner rather than a resident expert. In 2004 I attended his ten-week class in adapting non-dramatic literature for the stage at Northwestern. The only difference I noted between his rehearsal hall and his classroom was that in class, he took attendance. In an Equity company, the stage manager does that. It would be a mistake to undervalue the importance of Galati's academic career to his development and achievements as an artist or to underestimate the impact of his classroom experience on his professional work. Each was informed and shaped by the other and to Galati, they are inseparable.

Prior to an important audition in front of their peers, he delivered an informative and inspirational speech. "Being HONEST, SPONTANEOUS, CONVINCINGLY REAL IS ONLY PART of what must be accomplished in a brief general audition." He continued, "We, out here, are measuring how well you seize the stage, how much you light up when you're in the light, how much you can carry ... We want you to make us active, not passive, because we are charged with the energy you release."[1] A few weeks later, he delivered his notes to the assembled class and found worth and insight in each presentation. He singled out a particular student for praise but ended by musing, "We wanted to applaud. Why didn't we? In part, I think, because you didn't quite let us in. Take us in at the end. Acknowledge your own delight and we'll acknowledge ours." Galati is, at heart, an actor and whether his audience is comprised of students, collaborators, or theatre patrons, he never fails to let them in.

Asked to describe himself as a director, he did not hesitate to characterize himself as an actor cast in a series of three challenging roles.

> As a director, I'm always searching for something that could become a text for performance—a story, an idea, a theme. I'm the first reader and I like to think I'm the servant to the text by picking the orchestra that's going to perform it. I go hunting, shopping for collaborators to share the privilege of getting to know, exploring, and finding the voices in the text. And then they begin their own

independent exploration and I am the first audience for each of these voices. And then I become a critic and try to shape and edit and rethink and fix. And then it is time for a wider public and I try to gage the ways the audience talks back to the performers and the performance can be more sensitive to the audience.

Each of these three characters, First Reader, First Audience, and First Critic, have multiple layers. Galati's First Reader is part literary agent and part group therapist. First Audience is a wide-eyed Everyman and simultaneously, a Periclean first citizen with an acute ear and probing questions. First Critic is an editor who shapes rather than controls the final product and at the same time, acts as a witness whose presence displaces the actor's own inner critic.

Any one of these three "characters" he may slip into the persona of the Poet, a weaver of metaphor, dream, and image. American poet Louis Simpson proposed that "for poets, experience occurs as a *primary* thing, without language in between.... We have visions. We have experiences for which there is not language, and our job is to create that vision into a poem."[2] So it is for Galati but his Poet persona is not so much a creator as a catalyst to creation. Actor Mark Jacoby (*Ragtime, The Visit*) explained, "I've always said that Frank is a poet. If he were an auto mechanic, he'd raise the hood of your car, and then he'd write a poem about it. Whether or not he could fix it, well, I guess there have been things he couldn't fix. But," he added with conviction, "I'm sure, absolutely sure that those people involved came to work every day feeling like they knew why they decided to become actors. What we're doing here is our life blood and that's the way he makes you feel." The Poet can be illusive but is perceived by many of Galati's long-time colleagues as a revelation of his truest self.

First Reader

"He is famous," says Chamberlin, "for his speeches." Galati's speeches on the first day of rehearsal are intended to draw the cast and crew into a circle of active readers. Jacoby recalled such a speech on the first day of rehearsals for the musical *Ragtime*:

> I had never been in a project where we sat down on the first day of rehearsal and the director made a speech. I don't mean he addressed the company. I mean he read a speech like an inaugural address. When he finished, you really felt that you were at the epicenter of what it is to be an artist. He has a tremendous ability

to convey the significance of what we are doing. After one of Frank's speeches, you don't feel like saying, as actors do from time to time, "well it's not brain surgery." You feel that this, what you're doing, is significant. It has importance.

His honesty is disarming. He will speak of personal histories, favorite poems, quotes, stories, and include small confessions and revelations. By sharing something of himself, he tries—and generally succeeds—to establish a work environment that is inhospitable to the enemies of ensemble collaboration: distrust, defensiveness, complacency, and self-censorship.

He takes care to begin by presenting the script as a mystery to be explored rather than a problem to be solved. In 2010, he described the pitfalls of the first day of rehearsal to Jason Loewith:

> You show the cast a model and costume rendering and it's almost like they're looking down a very long corridor at a tiny thing that is way off in the distance, that they're going to approach, like they're supposed to *go* to it. And I feel that's wrong. That's like thinking of a character as being *out there*, like Hamlet is *out there* and I have to go out there and get him and put him on like an overcoat.[3]

Later in the interview, he concludes, "Acting is so internal and it has so much to do with the source being inside that one has to be very careful [as a director] about projecting."[4] To this end, he will extend the company's initial "table work" until easy answers have lost their allure and more interesting questions and possibilities replace conscious or unconscious expectations.

Anne Whitney has had a long and successful career on stage and screen but her first Equity job was a supporting role in Peter Nichol's *Passion Play* (1988) at the Goodman Theatre, directed by Galati. In 1998, she was honored by the Sarah Siddons Society and recalled the experience.

> I'll never forget the first few days of rehearsal . . . We arrived, they said and "now let's read the play," and well, we read the play and at the end Frank said "What do you think it's about?" And well, we thought it's about—well, infidelity, marriage vows, breaking them. It was a terrific conversation. Well, the next day we read the play again, three or four times. And after every reading, Frank would ask the same questions again, "What is it about now?" Well—it's about truth and illusion and reality and fantasy. It's about sexuality and art.[5]

As he continued to draw out new questions and possibilities, Whitney recalled being excited and exhausted by the flow of ideas. "It takes your attention away from the fact that you have to do the play in any particular way . . . it was a way of getting rid of the barriers we build around ourselves."[6] Most directors get actors on their feet immediately after the first reading but Galati often extends table work into multiple days of free form discussion.

On day three of rehearsals for the Steppenwolf production of Don DeLillo's *Valparaiso*, the actors were still at the table. They were deeply engaged in the conversation but several of the company had begun to bounce or sway on their seats. I watched Ensemble member Austin Pendleton kneel on his plastic chair with one foot braced against the floor as if preparing for take-off, only barely able to contain himself. When Galati finally released the cast into the space on day three, they attacked the work with a palpable sense of ownership and a well-established habit of listening to each other and to the text.

Asked how he manages to free his actors from the potential intimidation of the director's surveillance, particularly since his reputation as a director precedes him, he explained, "Well yes. You have to earn it. It's a process that has to begin at the beginning, the very first meeting. If they give themselves over to my eyes once and I don't do them any harm, they are relieved and can do it again." He empowers his collaborators by entering the room as an engaged witness rather than an omniscient adjudicator wielding, however benevolently, the measuring stick of his own expectation and authority. He is an excellent and strategic listener who understands the power of giving silent witness. He explains,

> They, the actors, designers, authors are given the guardianship of your witnessing, the sustaining support of your attention. With the actors especially, you have to take it in from the very beginning, from the first read-through. They absorb it and when they feel you listening, they can dispose of a level of consciousness about themselves. You are there to watch, to become their eyes and see them innocently. You PAY attention lovingly. For an actor, it's exciting to think, "I'm being watched. I'm being heard. What I'm exploring, what I'm doing here and now is being witnessed."

He believes that artists work best from a place of safety and protection and First Reader works to establish and maintain an environment that empowers his collaborators to be vulnerable, take risks and make discoveries.

First Audience

In 2006, journalist Martha Tapp declared that "The best seat in the house for any Frank Galati play is one with a good view of Galati's face."

Rarely is he still. Galati nods as the piece progresses, sometimes mouthing the words—frequently, words that he has adapted himself. Watching him is both exhausting and exhilarating, since his theatrical journey demands so much from himself and everyone else. As he puts it, "Thrill me! Entertain me! Keep me! Hold me! Bring me along!"[7]

As First Audience, Galati performs genuine expressions of delight, doubt, and wonder with the same physicality, exquisite timing, and lack of pretension he brought to the famous stage roles of his youth.

Galati's First Audience is simultaneously his essential self and a performance of self. The effect he achieves in this role is similar to that achieved by the domestic dramatics of a parent who conveys genuine disapproval, admonition, or delight to a child in exaggerated fashion. The real passion of the moment is perfomed and slightly removed, rendered safe and all the more impactful because of that distance. This is no small accomplishment. If the slightest hint of manipulation or condescension is betrayed, the performance of praise or censure collapses on itself. Several actors admitted to a this-guy-can't-be-for-real first impression. But in the rehearsal hall, where emotions are often intense and egos raw, I watched Galati's First Audience render a charged moment safe and slightly removed without losing the real passion and energy of the moment.

He has a genuine ability to laugh at the same joke for the first time many times but when the laugh isn't there, he doesn't laugh. "I can honestly say" he admitted when a laugh line failed to deliver in rehearsal, "that I can't pretend to laugh or to be moved. I seem to be close to the surface of my feelings." Collaborators who are attuned to his First Audience character read the absence of a response as a clear indication that the work is not yet finished. "You never have to guess with Frank," says Barbara Robertson. "There's never that awful feeling of doubt or insecurity in the pit of your stomach, because it's all there on Frank's face and in his body. Yes, I'd say he 'performs' his response—he's a fabulous performer. But it's the performance of a symphony conductor. That's not a metaphor. It's like he's physically conducting and we're the Chicago Symphony Orchestra."

First Audience is an Everyman—naive, loquacious, perpetually open to amazement. As Tapp noted in her article, "As the performance unfolds, he becomes a map, charting the emotions of the action onstage."[8] As rehearsals advance, he underscores scene work with spontaneous and seemingly irrepressible comments like "Oh my!", "I see!" and "Who is this!?" He encountered this technique as an undergraduate at Northwestern University. Though he never took classes with the university's legendary acting teacher Alvina Krause, she directed him in many stage productions on and off campus. He recalled how "she stood on stage with the cast, being there as a side coach, whispering, pushing a shoulder. This could be annoying, but she was wise and calming. We trusted her and took nourishment from her." Later, confronted by the open throttle of undergraduate expectations, he developed a similar practice in his classroom.

> I never liked giving prescriptive instructions but when I did, the students were happy and very grateful. I was critiqued sometimes because they thought I didn't give them enough. The kids would say "I wish he would have told me what I should have done." So I restructured the course and we'd do a rehearsal or rereading of a poem or a piece and I'd be play the listener out there in the audience. I'd say "Oooooooh. Oh, I see," "What? "What was that? "What! Again?" and just that sense that someone is listening actively made a huge difference. In the act of listening there are hills and valleys and things that fall out of focus and are not heard. An exercise like that can underline the fact that the actor needs to hear the audience listening. You need to feel their presence.

As First Audience, he floats muted comments into the air like cartoon thought bubbles. Expressions of amazement, apprehension, delight, surprise, and concern provide the actors with in-the-moment feedback from an engaged audience.

First Audience takes care not to phrase questions as hidden instructions or veiled demands. "Frank's not the kind of director," says Nussbaum, "who says 'Try it this way,' or asks confining questions like 'What's your motivation?' He initiates a discussion." Projection designer Wendall Harrington notes the care with which he chooses his words.

> He's scrupulous in avoiding the kind of language I hear from a lot of directors. Frank never says "I need" or "could you do" whatever, or "show me" this or that. He phrases an idea in a proposition and the question is always, "what would be the consequence if we ...?" With Frank, it really is a question. He takes you forward, not backward.

Susan Nussbaum remembered, "His questions teased a performance out of me—more than I knew I had—as gently as possible. He never forced, never showed impatience." Mark Jacoby, who has an impressive resume of leading roles on Broadway and in national tours, noted that for Galati there are no small roles. "Every single actor has the same significance the way Frank welcomes their questions and discoveries."

Every cast is unique and Galati is sensitive to subtleties that arise in the work and inventive in his response. Sylvia Regan's 1940 drama, *Morning Star* (Steppenwolf, 1999) is a kitchen sink drama—literally—with a relatively large ensemble cast of well-drawn characters. Midway in the rehearsal period, Galati decided to dedicate hours of precious time to a series of private tête-à-têtes with each actor-in-character. I sat outside the rehearsal hall as cast members arrived to wait their turn with him. They had been told not to prepare anything and early arrivals seemed a little self-conscious or apprehensive, unsure what would be expected of them. I wasn't sure either so I stayed to watch the private conversations through a window in the rehearsal room door. I couldn't hear but could see Galati's face and watched him share laughter and serious moments with nodding or concern—just two people chatting. It was playful and each actor left the room pleased but in a more pensive, introspective mood. When the ensemble came together for the next rehearsal, there was a notable change in the way they watched and listened to each other. It was in their eyes, in the beats between or within lines, and how they watched each other from outside an ongoing scene. It occurred to me that Galati serendipitous conversations had encouraged them to make discoveries rather than decisions about their character. Perhaps by allowing each actor a glimpse of the unfathomable nature of their own character, they were more inclined to honor complexity in the others. For whatever reason, it seemed to me that each actor/character was genuinely curious about the inner life of the others, far more so than the days before. Galati managed to create an ensemble ethos by listening to and acknowledging each actor/character as a private and fully formed individual.

Asked if it is possible to fake listening, he laughed, "Well, I guess the only way to perform listening is to do it. So are we back where we started?" Not quite. The only way to drink a glass of water, he continued, is to do it. "We drink glasses of water every day, fully aware of what we're doing so as not to pour water on ourselves but without being the least bit self-conscious. So [*a characteristic pause*] so when someone pretends to listen, they dribble. They look vague, disconnected from the moment. They are not present." Listening requires presence, presence confirms listening, and when Galati performs listening, there is no dribbling. He is fully and profoundly present to the speaker. "I've seen him do it," explained director Michael Maggio, "and felt it myself. When he's talking to you, you are absolutely the most important person in the world. And then he looks away and you feel like an idiot because of course, the play, everything happening in the room is the most important thing in the world." Barbara Robertson explained,

"The way he listens makes you feel important and at the same time, it's hard to <u>not</u> see yourself as a part of something bigger than yourself."

"To be present," explained Galati, "is to listen in a profound way. You have to lower your defenses in order to do that." Recalling his celebrated performance in Tom Stoppard's *Travesties*, he said, "I had one evening where I felt like I was the luckiest person on earth. That I was given the opportunity to be present in a way that very few people can be … to be that quick, that in tune and toned and expressive." But presence is, as Galati is well aware, a troublesome and troubling term:

> Yes, there it is again. Everybody tells you to 'be in the moment.' What does that mean? But there's no better way to say it, not that I know of. To be fully present is to give a riveting performance, whether it's a trapeze act, an aria, or a dramatic scene. The thing is, when you see it and when you're doing it, it seems very clear. Presence is a moment of extra-ordinary clarity.

Presence, he says, propels the audience forward, toward the next moment and into the future. He explains, "cause suggests inevitability—'Ah, I see, I see why this happened.' But by fully understanding and confronting the consequence of our actions we might change our behavior."

When he gives individual acting notes, they are in the form of an action the actor can own and execute, the kind of note he values as an actor himself. In 2001, he returned to the stage to play the role of a brain-damaged farm worker in the Steppenwolf production of Michael Healey's *The Drawer Boy*, directed by Anna Shapiro. He described an incident in rehearsal when he was fidgety and couldn't "settle" into a scene. Shapiro stopped the scene and told him to put his hands on the table and keep them there. He did. They ran the scene again and this time, it worked. He explained, "Anna watched for something that served me not her and it freed me." He continued,

> Actors like to be told what they're supposed to do. I'm obedient. You tell me to put my hands on the table and I do it. But if you're a good director, what you encourage an actor to obey in doing loses its connection to you. You want the actor to own everything. That's what Anna does and it's what makes her such a fine director. If I'm good, it's when I'm able to make those kinds of demands on the actor, demands that create a kind of discipline that frees the actor.

Like Shapiro, he will give an actor something to do, a peripheral action or obstacle that must be played around or through. He recalled providing actor Kenny Ingram with an inspired obstacle in his production of Brecht's, *The Good Person of Setzuan* (Goodman Theatre, 1992).

The only thing I gave him was similar to what Anna gave me in *Drawer Boy*. Actors are really smart but they need something to do. He was always putting his hands on his hips and gesticulating in ways that betrayed him because it was the actor's intention not the character's. So I gave him a pot, a cooking pot with a handle. I said, "Kenny, you just have this pot in your hand the whole time." And he did. He made it his own. It was wonderful what he did with it.

The obstacle encouraged Ingram toward greater discipline and at the same time, gave him a personal sense of control over the moment.

Whether he is working with university students, seasoned professionals, or international opera stars, he is able to establish an extra-ordinary sense of trust and inclusion between the actors and their audience. When his First Audience character steps aside for an actual audience, the actors are primed to give their unconditional trust to the watcher in the house. At that point, he moves into the role of First Critic.

First Critic

Galati's First Critic appears most often in the last week or days of rehearsal and during previews. He links this role to an understanding shared among actors about what it means to be in the moment and believes that the First Critic provides a surrogate for the actor's own internal critic, the watcher within, thus freeing the actor from the insidious inner voice that takes you out of the moment. He explained,

> I like to watch. I'm good at it, and I'm very forthcoming—"this is how the scene felt to me today" or "this is what I saw you do." It's like I've replaced that part of them that wants to watch themselves from the outside, so they don't have to do it in the moment of performance. That's a big part of my job—to watch them so they don't have to watch themselves. I watch them so they won't watch themselves.

Kevin Chamberlin explained, "Frank is an actor himself. He knows that performing is a social situation and to find a spontaneous emotional state in a social situation, you have to lose all self-consciousness." He continued,

> For an actor that means being completely truthful in an imaginary circumstance and in a social situation. I was taught that when I'm asking a person questions about themselves, truly taking attention off myself and giving it to them, I'm in the moment. It is the hardest thing for an actor to do. You're on stage singing a

song and your focus has to be directed entirely outward. It's not a natural thing. It's a skill. It's work. Frank understands this. He's out there in front of you, completely in the moment. No, you never ACT for him, you focus on him, this guy in the audience and you do it as directly and honestly as he listens to you.

Chamberlin believes that "Frank's witness gives you the protection you need to be totally truthful in an imaginary circumstance."

Galati does not approach acting as an unfathomable form of metaphysical channeling but as a series of physical actions to be performed with a combination of precision, passion, and most important, clear articulation in gesture, stance, movement, and pronunciation. In the speech he delivered on the occasion of the first New York run-through of the musical *Ragtime* prior to the Broadway premiere, he acknowledged the difficulty of confronting the exaggerated expectations and anxieties that intrude on a highly touted Broadway opening. He urges the company to focus on what they will do on stage, not on what they will be. This "doing," he explains, is the source of the paradoxical pleasures of repetition and spontaneity in performance. "The thrill of the form is the tension between a pattern which is devised and its accomplishment by an individual soul, one who is absolutely free and spontaneous. In the performance of a great dancer, you cannot tell the dancer from the dance. Isn't it the same for the actor? For the singer?" The actor, he continues, "is the act, that which we, the audience, can see and hear and feel as a human presence in the theatre." Therefore, each infinitesimal action carried out on stage must be clear and pure, the enunciation of each vowel and consonant discrete and distinct. He continues:

> Dramatic singing in opera or musical theatre is not the performance of a song, or a so-called 'number' in a score; it is the pouring forth of feeling, born deep in the character and expressed in sustained vowels that have different sensual colors: aahhh, eeeeee, ooooo, oohh—these emotives have no precise meaning. They are given meaning by consonants. Vowels feel. Consonants make vowels think. That is why the clarity of consonants as they frame vowels is so crucial.

Here as elsewhere, he delivers specific and executable directives—speak clearly and make yourself heard—supported by a panoramic vision, poetic imagery, and spiritual fervor.

In the last days of rehearsal and previews, he prefers to deliver both general and incremental notes to the entire cast in a hand-written and photocopied letter addressed to "all." This practice of shared notes and comments is addressed to each member of the ensemble as an individual and at the same time, supports and reinforces an ensemble ethic. "Trust yourself," he told the *Ragtime* cast,

"Remember to breath. Take the time to inhale as you get the idea ... In the theatre even a whisper must be projected and every word must be heard. Every sentence must land."[9]

The Poet: Mystery, Image, and Metaphor

A great performance is in the end, a great mystery. Galati uses metaphor and imagery to honor that mystery even as he gives executable notes. "Don't step away from the ends of lines. Don't flinch. Good diction and projecting energy is not just technique—it is a passion to be understood."[10] In one of our conversations, he explained that Robert Breen had emphasized "what he called 'coalescence,' whereby the inner form of the poem and the inner form of the performer could somehow coalesce. The performer's 'embodiment' was a result of that commingling of interiorities." In his speech to the *Ragtime* cast, Galati translates Breen's somewhat arcane notion of comingling interiorities into images and language a working actor can understand and use.

> This coming-together isn't the actor and the character but the actor and the act. Sure, there might be a back-story, motivation and all that, but that's for grounding or fun. To become, so to speak, "one with the act" is to commit to what you are doing in the way a dancer commits to the dance. When you do that, consequence, the thing that is going or not going to happen becomes more important than cause.

His comments to actors in his address to the cast on the opening night of *Ragtime* are suffused with references to listening and watching expressed in imagery and actions.

> Really seeing each other is love. Even in the most charged and combative moments, be in each other's eyes. Seek each other's eyes. And hold each other up with your eyes. Go out from yourself—think about reaching each other. Truly. Sometimes, the "other" is the audience. Don't think about them loving you. Love them.

Galati ends his *Ragtime* remarks by urging his cast to listen to the audience and to each to other. "Bend. Give way. Support. Defer, in your hearts as colleagues, so that your characters can clash. True simplicity is gained by bowing and bending."

He speaks from his own experience when he explains that "the actor is so absorbed in reaching and searching and trying to figure things out, they often don't see themselves in the bigger picture. As a director," he continues, "I look for a figure of comparison that is a useful likeness to the moment in order to remind them of where they are, what this is." On opening night of *Ragtime*, he presented lyricist Lynne Aherns with his production notebook, a binder crammed with over two years' worth of clippings, images, diagrams, articles, sketches, doodles, quotes, and notes, details large and small, each linked in some way to the larger context of the story being told. She was honored and described the book as metaphor piled on metaphor.

His big picture metaphors are suited to a theatre maker's sensibility and spirit. Martha Lavey explained, "the images Frank gives you work because they're visceral—they're doable because they involve an action that you can understand as an actor." Lavey played the role of Lemon in *Aunt Dan and Lemon* (Steppenwolf Theatre 1987), a young woman who "'honestly' admires the thoroughness of the Nazi killing machinery."[11] Galati helped her find the character by offering the metaphor of a vulgar physical action. "He suggested an image, drew a picture for me of Lemon pushing these ideas, words—all this vileness—out through her bowels. It was like I was shitting these words out of me. I think I changed my stance and dropped the tension in my body down [*indicating her abdomen*] when I spoke. It changed how I moved. I was very conscious of my bowels. That's where I found the character's energy." Galati's metaphor informed the overall production. Richard Christiansen observed in the *Chicago Tribune* that Galati's "discerning theatrical vision is there in designer Kevin Rigdon's ... lighting ... which seems to be illuminating the action from the bowels of the earth."[12]

In 1980, he directed Lee Hoiby's opera based on Tennessee William's *Summer and Smoke* for Chicago Opera Theatre and worked with the veteran video director Kirk Browning on the televised version for PBS. Browning invited Galati to the filming and encouraged him to work with the actor/singers. The protagonist, a high-strung southern spinster named Alma, was sung by soprano Mary Beth Peal in the stage version as well as the video. In the last scene of the opera, the cerebral Alma is about to give herself over to a tawdry life of physical passion. In the video, Peal gives a truly moving performance infused with confession, longing, surrender, and dread. But Galati recalled that she had a good deal of trouble in the television studio as the taping was about to begin.

> Mary Beth wasn't connecting. She wasn't specific—vague about where she was and what she felt. Well, she was sitting on the wall of a fountain with the statue of an angel above her. The angel's name is "Eternity," and John [the lover who is abandoning her] has just sung, "Eternity and Alma have such cold hands." This

led me to think that the statue has, inside of it, veins that go down to the earth and that the veins of the statue are rusty and the water is cold and metallic because it comes from deep, deep underground. I was just improvising an image to get in touch with this woman and Mary Beth says, "OK, OK," and we do the scene. Well, she told me later that as she sang, she had in her eyes the image of something deep and cold and real. It was all there; I mean the water and the fountain and the stone. I just looked at what was there. I think directors are free to do that in ways that actors aren't.

The image Galati created for Peal helped her to overcome the distractions of the television studio and place herself in the moment of performance.

Affirmation and Reproof

Galati's affirmation and reward are often expressed in physical gestures—applause, laughter, or an enormous eye-popping sigh. Recalling rehearsals for *She Always Said, Pablo*, Larry Russo said "it was like Frank was in love. He'd sit in on dance rehearsals and we knew he was there because you could feel these waves of pleasure coming from him." Maggio described this wordless, full-body expression of physical pleasure as the "Galati glow," often expressed with extended arms and fingers distended as if to grasp something suspended in the air just out of reach. He might suck in a bushel of air to release a long and luxuriant sigh of inexpressible admiration or pause to give a gentle nod of acknowledgment. "It's like you want to serve him succulent sweets," says Harrington, "because you know he likes them, he appreciates them and will be generous and articulate in his description of just how delicious they were."

In rehearsal, Galati will often wander the periphery or into a scene murmuring the word "good," repeating it softly two or three times during an exchange or monologue. His utterance is never tentative—there is no implied approval or hesitation in his inflection and no finality. Corti explains:

He's giving you an affirmation, telling you that you've got hold of something—some feeling, focus, or direction—something you need to keep. When Frank says "good" it means: "where you're at, what you're carrying with you right now—hold that, go there." It will play itself out differently as the scene or the character develops. You can try this or that, but that thing, that thing <u>there</u>, in that moment—you keep it close, carry it with you and let it take you where it will.

Galati's externalized thought is an acknowledgment of the actor's process in the moment of exploration. In a 1980 interview he described an actor's transcendent moment on stage: "When it's really working, there's someone inside you that comes out, someone you can't be any other time. Somehow, it gets down to the real you—it's like being totally naked." When he murmurs the word "good" during scene work, he is most often acknowledging the actor's nascent gesture toward such nakedness. On those fleeting and mysterious moments when an actor achieves a state of naked presence in a rehearsal situation, he is often silent and preternaturally still, as if time has stopped.

He is by all accounts among the most nurturing of directors but "nurturing" is clearly understood to be something other than fretful supervision or uncritical support. Justly known as a "nice guy," he nonetheless demands as good as he gives. He has no patience with excuses or rationalization. Maggio explained, "if you're glib or thoughtless, he goes cold and aloof. He withholds the Frankie-glow of approval and believe me, that can be devastating." Galati expects a certain amount of self-worth, mutual respect, and unflagging commitment to each other. When these standards are betrayed, his critique is articulated with devastating precision and acuity. In comments delivered to the entire New York cast of *Ragtime* on a less than satisfactory afternoon performance well into its New York run he told the cast, "When Younger Brother sings 'The crowd was on its feet,' I feel you're just standing. The call and response is flat. We need more urgency, need, compassion for the suffering. CRY OUT! HOWL! ROAR!"[13] There is no hint of disdain or condescension in his address but the "Frankie glow-of-approval" is clearly withheld. "He gets what he wants from you, that's for sure," says BJ Jones, "but he does it with gentle, unflinching pressure." He is scrupulous in avoiding the first-person singular pronoun in any critique. When he says, "We need to hear ..." or "We don't see ..." this is not the royal "we" of monarchy, but the populist "we," an abstraction of the many who watch and listen from the house.

Chamberlin considers Galati's understanding of the craft of acting to be remarkable. "He's an actor himself and knows the language, so he can give you what you need to be an artist, not what he needs from you. That's rare. I haven't found that ability with any other director—not like Frank does it." He has a rare ability to "read" the actor's body and can spot an evasion, tick, or habitual shortcut with precision. "Sometimes, hands in the pockets," says Galati, "you can see the actor evaluating the choice. It betrays the actor's own deliberation and has nothing to do with the character, crowding too many readings into a line so that the process, the moment becomes a spontaneous diplomatic negotiation."

Chamberlin concluded, "He calls you on the carpet when you're using your tricks. He <u>knows</u> those tricks. When you hear the lie in your voice, you know Frank hears it too."

Not Doing

"The child's design," writes Silvia Vegetti Finzi, "takes shape on its own; it delineates itself in a space between maternal vigilance and inattention."[14] Galati is sensitive to the effect of his own celebrity and the outsized authority implicit in the role of director. To palliate against this, in crucial moments of discovery he takes care to "not do." "Not doing or Wu Wei" explains author and yogi Christina Sarich, "describes the inspired action of a person who is brimming with life energy and has dedicated their actions to a purpose which supports Oneness. This person moves only when the time is right and then, with magnificent acumen."[15] Galati knows the value of not doing, of lingering in the space between vigilance and inattention without comment. "I may have been a director of remarkable performances," he said,

> ... but those are not ever achieved in the same way in any given relationship. I might say nothing to them. I might not ever say "Try this." I may never have said anything like that but I would like to say that performance is as much a result of my not having said anything as having said something. Withholding comment can be more generative than interference. Directors can make matters worse.

Susan Nussbaum depended on his help when she tackled Gertrude Stein's elliptical prose in *She Always Said, Pablo*. "The thing I remember," she says, "is that he said very little. He listened. He was interested, asked questions or told stories, waiting for me to find my own way, my own imagery to lift the words out of the page."

Galati's capacity for not doing is one of the few personal qualities he is willing to speak of with obvious pride. "There are times," he says,

> ... when the actor can feel the director "acting"—sort of doing the work, the part. The director's comment can make the actor flinch or worry. A little alarm goes off in the vicinity of the moment every time it's approached. "What is it I'm not getting???" "Is this what I'm supposed to do?" "Am I doing IT?" The actor becomes distracted and a little vexed just before that moment—it can't be helped or avoided. It's there.

Every actor knows that a director's well-meant intervention can insert an insidious grain of self-consciousness into a line reading. "You have to trust your actors to do their own work. Watch. Be patient. I learned so much about the value of hanging back," he says, "from the Steppenwolf actors, watching them work rather than directing the work." Elia Kazan advised the director, "before you do anything, see what talent does."[16] Galati has been lucky enough to work with great talents and is talented enough to encourage even the most inexperienced actor to find their own way. The actor's art, like that of a child struggling to assert a sense of self, delineates itself in a space between vigilance and inattention.

Doing nothing and knowing when to do it is far more challenging, says Galati, than doing something. "So often, the director—and very often a young director—has the nagging sense that 'I better be doing something or I'm not directing.' And this is dangerous." Dangerous because the young director may not understand or trust the processes of collaboration. He continues, "Few people have any understanding of the collaboration between actor and director. Part of the misunderstanding about what directors do is the fact of what directors don't do." The actor's process, as he knows from his own experience, is private, inarticulate, and uneven. It needs to be protected. "He knows," says Chamberlin, "when to let the actor alone. He lets you flounder but holds your hand as you find your own way, giving hints about which fork in the road to take." He has mentored many epiphanies on stage and in rehearsal but understands that such moments generally arise from repetitive and dogged work. "You don't realize that what you're doing, what is happening is that you are trying to find the way. But the thing is," says Galati, "you have to let the way find you. It takes time. You make thousands of missteps and still it finds you."

He has helped others find the value of doing nothing. When an actor is insecure, unfocused, or troubled in a scene, there is a tendency to rush through lines, to push the scene harder. When this happens, Galati will step forward and murmur softly, "hold ... hold ..." "Hold" does not suggest a pause in the character's speech or action, but prompts the actor to settle in the moment, to find and accept a stillness without intent or decision. By holding oneself in the moment it is possible to hear what is unsaid, to see what has gone unseen, to feel the character searching for a word or a thought and to receive an action rather than initiate one. "He makes you stand there and pause," explained Landis, "because what happens in the pause is life."

Praise for simplicity and repeated reminders to let go, listen, and trust yourself are thematic in his speeches, comments, and letters, particularly when addressing an esteemed and valued colleague. Kingsley Leggs replaced Brian Stokes Mitchell as Coalhouse Walker in the Los Angeles production of *Ragtime*. On the last day of a short put-in rehearsal, Galati wrote Leggs an eight-page letter. He shares personal information about his troubled relationship with his own father and ponders the character's history and cultural context at some length. On page five he writes, "I rehearse all of this here to remind myself, to remind us – why it is so important to simplify. To be grounded in the center of your heart and do less. To remain poised, balanced, suave, and proud. This is Coalhouse—but this is also the actor—making no effort to show, to demonstrate, to prove or to produce emotion. Coalhouse doesn't show, he is."[17] In the final two pages of the letter he lists a series of specific notes on how to achieve greater simplicity and clarity in the role.

> Hold yourself longer in sustained moments ... don't crumble your face or turn your eyes away. Don't rush ... take your time ... don't pose ... take your hand from your pocket and simply be the words you are saying ... when you move downstage in the soliloquy, don't move like a panther, move like a senator ... Don't hold your hands in front of you—it is a sign of weakness.[18]

He describes a crucial scene that was "the best one day upstairs in the rehearsal room with nothing—unadorned, when all you had was Sarah. Play with her, give her the scene and you will get the scene." His letter ends with the refrain "'Tis' a gift to be simple" from the Quaker gift song and a valediction: "A few thoughts with deepest admiration, at the start of this long journey."

Between 1999 and 2003, I was able to observe him work through the entire rehearsal period of three very different productions: the revival of a 1940s domestic drama, the world premiere of a surreal musical tragedy by Kander and Ebb, and a postmodern meditation on loss and being lost.[19] I saw him occasionally double back, overindulge, or be distracted by a too-precious idea. I watched him sculpt a choral segment with his hands and reel in a cynical veteran actor like a canny fisherman. I expected all of these things and watched for them. What caught me off guard was the realization that this man, so widely known for spectacular showmanship and even more spectacular intellect, has the gift of simplicity. It is a gift to be simple, to access the present moment undistracted by past or future and free from the blinders of pretention and intention. After fifty years in show business, Galati's simplicity remains, for him, a portal to essence, to knowing precisely when to do and when to not-do without knowing exactly what it is he knows. Ever the paradoxical professor, this paradox comes closest to explaining his greatest strengths as well as his greatest vulnerability.

Disguise and Revelation

For all his genuine warmth, Galati maintains a self-contained reserve in the role of director. He explained that "as a director you're playing a role" and paused before continuing,

> ...and you know that role doesn't allow for the kind of camaraderie and the openness and the candor that you can have with your friends as an actor. As a director I don't hang out. I don't even go down into the dressing rooms. I give notes at rehearsals. I'm never backstage at a performance, before or after.

Nonetheless, "director" is a role in which he clearly feels himself to be his most authentic self—comfortable, at ease and willing to make himself open and vulnerable to colleagues. In an address to the cast of *Ragtime* delivered a few days before opening night, he confessed, "I am, as most of you know, basically lost—adrift, the only bark I cling to the boards of the stage where we do eight shows a week." This speech—twelve manuscript pages long—is an extended meditation inspired by his visit to a Benedictine monastery in Vermont. To be sure, he has a loving and much-loved family, husband, and close circle of friends but for all his geniality, there is something decidedly monkish about Frank Galati. It is no surprise to longtime associates that outside the role of director he often cloisters himself and is inaccessible to colleagues. Steve Scott has known him professionally for over thirty years and observed, "He's a little awkward and beneath the surface, there's a remove. I don't know how to describe it, but there's always something about Frank that you don't know about—a wariness, a mystery. He protects himself. It's one of the interesting contradictions of Frank."

"Acting itself," he explained, "is not a matter of disguise but of revelation, not a mask but an open face." Galati overcomes his natural reserve with an ability to be in the moment, fully present without history or expectation, past or present—by being where he is when he is there. But as his stature in the theatre world grew, he became increasingly ill at ease in social situations where past and future threaten to overwhelm the present. He is often restless outside the task-oriented intimacy of the work and the easy companionship of long-time friends and family.

> I just don't like pretending and I'm not good at it. I feel so much better when I can hear my own voice and I'm not pretending. It's hard. It's hard. Because some situations are so pretend, so artificial and so temporarily hung out there. The planning, the play—it's just for a few weeks or a few months and we all treat each other as if we were all relatives and we were gonna be together for life. You know,

we love each other. We hug each other. I encourage that affection and intimacy because I think it's vital. It's not pretend but I don't feel comfortable with that kind of intimacy outside the specific task.

It is difficult to escape presumptions of intimacy from associates who unconsciously assume a familiarity based on the man's obvious generosity of spirit and extensive press coverage. But those who know him well, know Galati to be the most private of men.

In the last decades of her life, Martha Lavey, artistic director of the Steppenwolf Theatre (1995–2015), became a close and valued friend to Galati. They shared a rare reciprocity of intellect and interests. Lavey's untimely death in 2017 was a great loss to the theatre community and a personal loss to Galati. Like him, she was a gifted actor, a true intellectual, a bit of a poet, and a deeply spiritual human being. He directed her in the Steppenwolf production of *Valparaiso* and during previews, she shared a unique insight into what it is to play a role on stage or off.

> Frank's an actor and I think we all take refuge in that. I know I do. Acting creates a great solace. You are the one taken care of. One follows the rule of that clock and one submits to the turning of the world. One does not control but releases an unmeasured heart. Acting a role is a super-compressed version of life. The stupid tedium of performance is its instruction and its gift. It presents that challenge—the script already written, you can still love the doing of it with heart wide open to every single predestined moment—be there or die.

The world of the theatre is defined and contained within the boundaries of Equity rules, half hour call, and final curtain. A map of the actor's universe is traced in masking tape on the rehearsal room floor and in the clear delineation of onstage, off stage, and backstage domains. Who you are and what you do—the role you play—is defined by contract and documented in the production's *Playbill*. Acting, explained Lavey, offers an escape from the mask and pose of ordinary life. "Being in this play," she concluded, "lets me be Martha." Performance allows Galati to dispose of the everyday self-consciousness that both protects and inhibits most of us in social situations. And in this work, he strives, reaches for, and surprisingly often achieves a release from self-consciousness and self-protection for his peers and through them, his audience.

In the summer of 2000, he reunited with *Ragtime* composer Stephen Flaherty and lyricist Lynn Ahrens to begin rehearsals for *Seussical the Musical*. The commercial producers anticipated a mega Broadway hit to rival Disney's *Lion King* and the production was much anticipated in the press. *Playbill* reported,

"The Aug. 27 first preview of *Seussical* got a standing ovation and, observers posted on *Playbill On-Line*, the applause was so sustained after the group curtain call that the cast trickled back to the stage for a final makeshift bow."[20] However, as previews continued, it became increasingly clear that ensemble collaboration was not equally valued within the company. In the final days prior to the press opening, Galati and veteran designer Eugene Lee were summarily dismissed. A few days late, the *New York Times* published Robin Pogrebin's feature article and interview with choreographer Kathleen Marshall, who had never warmed to Galati's nonauthoritarian directing style. She told Pogrebin, "'On a big musical like this, you need a daddy.' Or," continued Pogrebin, "a brother. Enter Rob Marshall, Ms. Marshall's sibling. Exit the director Frank Galati."[21] Marshall declared that he intended to "return to the original Seussisan mandate: to take the audience on a fanciful ride to a place populated by familiar, tender, quirky characters." I had always thought of the Dr. Seuss books as decidedly surreal and delightfully creepy. My son liked *The Cat in a Hat* but the character made him a too jumpy for bedtime reading. "He's not pretending," he explained. "He's really naughty—I mean really naughty for real." I agreed. Galati's Cat was played by David Shiner, a brilliant clown with an anarchist grin who appeared on Broadway along with Bill Irwin in *Fool Moon* and *Old Hats*. I thought it was an inspired casting choice. Shiner's Cat was really naughty for real.

A few days after Galati's dismissal, it was decided that Shiner had been misdirected. With Galati no longer in the picture, Shiner was instructed to smile more and to smile "sweeter." I didn't see the revisions but *Seussical* opened in November 2000 to underwhelmed reviews. With shrinking ticket sales, Shiner was replaced by talk show host Rosy O'Donnell but not even her cheery celebrity could save the show. The production closed in May 2001 with what was reported to be one of the highest financial losses on Broadway at that time.

In a speech delivered to the *Seussical* cast on the first day of rehearsal, July 10, 2000, Galati set the stage for the kind of collaborative ensemble work he felt would best serve the project. His speech to the cast begins with a quote from *Always We Begin Again*, the small book he had discovered at the remote Benedictine monastery he visited during *Ragtime* previews. "The book," he says,

> is a contemporary interpretation of the rule of Benedict of Nursia who lived in the sixth century in Italy and, repelled by the vices of Rome, left the city for the solitude of the hills. The gaudy clamor of New York, the hunger and greed of the Broadway marketplace, make the sweet and solitary hills seem remote indeed,

but we can remind ourselves—remind each other by example—of the power of simplicity, good humor and humility in the essential theatre—the poor theatre of the soul—where the true clown lives—where the hero succumbs but the audience survives.

Seussical did not turn out to be the next *Lion King*. However, the staging, text, and score that Galati helped to shape in preproduction, rehearsals, and previews found a different kind of success and possibly a greater one. In the 2020 Educational Theatre Play Survey, *Seussical* was listed as the most produced musical of the twenty-first century.[22] It has had an extraordinary and ongoing journey in the sweet and remote hills of theatre for and performed by a young audience, the poor theatre of the soul where the true clown lives, the hero succumbs, and the audience survives.

Notes

1 Frank Galati, *Presentational Aesthetics, Performance Studies 324-1*, class notes, Northwestern University, Spring 2005. Galati private archives.
2 Hank Lazer, "Reflections on the 25th Anniversary of the What Is a Poet? Symposium," 2009. http://writing.upenn.edu/library/What-Is-a-Poet/index.html
3 Jason Loewith, *The Directors Voice. Vol.* 2 (New York: Theatre Communications Group, 2013), 145.
4 Loewith, 163
5 Anne Whitney and BJ Jones et al., "Salute to Frank Galati: 'Renaissance Man,'" Illinois Theatre Association *Follow Spot*, Vol 10, Issue #4, 1998.
6 Whitney, "Salute to Frank Galati."
7 Mara Tapp, "The Storyteller," *Chicago Magazine*, February 2006, 78.
8 Tapp, 2006.
9 Frank Galati, undated speech to *Ragtime* cast, MS, Box 31, Folder 5, Frank Galati (1943–) Papers, 1948–2914, Northwestern University McCormick Library of Special Collections and University Archives.
10 Galati, undated speech to *Ragtime* cast.
11 Glenna Syse, "'Aunt Dan and Lemon' Better than New York," *Chicago Sun Times*, June 28, 1987.
12 Richard Christiansen, "'Aunt Dan and Lemon' A Magnificent Play," review of Steppenwolf Theater, *Chicago Tribune*, June 15, 1987.
13 Christiansen, "Aunt Dan," 1987.
14 Sylvia Vegetti-Finzi Finzi, *Mothering: toward a New Psychoanalytic Construction* (New York: Guilford Press, 1996), 160.

15 Christina Sarich, "5 Secrets to Wu Wei, the Taoist Principle of Effortless Effort," The Mind Unleashed, November 18, 2016. https://themindunleashed.com/2016/11/5-secrets-wu-wei-taoist-principle-effortless-effort.html
16 Frank Hauser and Russell Reich, *Notes on Directing: 130 Lessons in Leadership from the Director's Chair* (New York: RCR Creative Press, 2018), 12.
17 Frank Galati, *Ragtime* cast notes, MS, Box 31, Folder 5, Frank Galati (1943–) Papers, 1948–2914, Northwestern University McCormick Library of Special Collections and University Archives.
18 Frank Galati to Kingsley Leggs, Dec 1997, Box 31, Folder 5, Frank Galati (1943–) Papers, 1948–2014, Northwestern University McCormick Library of Special Collections and University Archives.
19 I attended rehearsals and previews for Galati's productions of *Morning Star* by Sylvia Regan, Steppenwolf Theatre, May/April 1999; *Valparaiso* by Don DeLillo, Steppenwolf Theatre, December 10, 1999 to January 30, 2000; and *The Visit*, Goodman Theatre, August 2 to Sept 20 2001 (Book by Terrence McNally, music by John Kander, lyrics by Fred Ebb, based on the Play *The Visit* by Friedrich Dürrenmatt, translation by Maurice Valency, Choreographed by Ann Reinking,),
20 Kenneth Jones, "Costume Designer Catherine Zuber Exits Seussical," *Playbill*, Aug 30, 2000. www.playbill.com/article/costume-designer-catherine-zuber-exits-seussical-com-91562
21 Robin Pogrebin, "Is There a Dr. In the House for 'Seussical'?; Some Rays of Sunshine Upon a Troubled Production," *The New York Times*, November 14, 2000,
22 Education Theatre Association, 2020 Play Survey, www.schooltheatre.org/blogs/edta-news/2020/07/30/2020-play-survey

7

Mise-en-scène as Activism: Galati's Dangerous Women

Throughout his long and varied career, Galati has given female characters a far greater degree of individuality and subjectivity than is usually allowed to women in dramatic representation, particularly mothers. The enhanced agency he allows maternal characters is no sidebar or condescending nod. His mise-en-scène has consistently positioned a significant female role as the story's central character. He has returned time and again to maternal protagonists, challenges, and interests. However, mothers and mother figures were everywhere present in the productions he initiated between 1986 and 1996, a period in which his reputation was firmly established and his ability to choose his projects increasingly unfettered. Mothers who fulfill their social role without sacrificing full personhood for themselves or those they care for, new metaphors for maternity as a model for creative and intellectual "labor," and the negotiation of competing responsibilities to self and to community were thematic in his work throughout this period.

Whether their project ends in triumph or disaster, Galati's characters are subject to the moral imperative of the maternal project, that is, the necessity of relinquishing control of what one has brought into the world without being in return, diminished. In a dysfunctional or unhealthy stage world, female protagonists will trouble the status quo by insisting on a renewal of the values on which the community is supposedly founded (*Born Yesterday, Grapes of Wrath*). A mother's initiative may renew the social bond within the fictive world or reveal it to be a fraud *(Good Person of Setzuan, The Winter's Tale)*. Whether a corrupt society crumbles or endures, the female protagonist denied full personhood must withdraw or perish (*Earthly Possessions*). A formidable female character may be empowered by what she has herself released into the world (*She Always Said, Pablo; Grapes of Wrath*) or riddled with spiritual rot, desperation, or betrayal, do harm to herself or others (*Aunt Dan and Lemon, As I Lay Dying, The Glass Menagerie*).

In 1992, he directed Northwestern students in his adaption of material recently published by Marguerite Duras. At that time, he wrote, "It has been my personal goal as a university professor to focus attention on women writers and to bring to the stage (so long impoverished by the relative absence of female voices) a number of non-dramatic texts by women whose genius provides a vital insight into the human experience."[1] This statement is taken from his response to a theatre patron who wrote to express outrage at the sexual content of the Duras production, particularly in a university setting. Decades later, Galati recalled the incident:

> The show turned out to be so controversial that our department held a public forum to discuss the production and Duras's work. At the time I had the flu and Carol Simpson Stern, our Chair at the time, read [my] letter out loud to the audience. Carol reported that the consensus was enthusiastic support for the project. I also received numerous letters from non-university patrons who were moved by the eloquence and courage of Marguerite Duras. It may be interesting to note that Mary Zimmerman and Jessica Thebus, grad students at that time, were both in the production. Mary "played" Duras with a luminous candor. It was one of the high points of my teaching life.

Galati's letter is a personal manifesto of profound and abiding commitment to female voices, including those of his students. Mary Zimmerman now holds the Jaharis Family Foundation Chair in Performance Studies at Northwestern and is a recipient of a prestigious Guggenheim Fellowship. Jessica Thebus is an accomplished director, author, and head of the MFA program in directing at Northwestern. Both women are prominent American theatre artists and both credit Galati as a mentor and a friend.

His letter begins with a gracious acknowledgment that many people might find it difficult to listen "to a writer of the stature of Marguerite Duras on the subject of our common mortality." But, he continues, "many of us in the final chapter of our own stories may, like Duras, be looking back over lives that are bruised and battered, injured deeply by the wounds that some kinds of love may cause, by the kind of wounds that love causes." He points out the international respect Duras commands, the literary accolades her work has received, and her advanced age, 78, at the time she wrote the work he had staged. That said, he proceeds to repudiate the writer's accusation of pornography. "Obviously," he writes,

> this material is the work of a very mature, I might even say profoundly wise and visionary writer, who believes that writing opens every door; it doesn't close

doors it opens them. What Ms Duras finds on the other side of the doors she opens may be painful or disturbing, all the more so because she is confronting the truth in herself and not fashioning a narrative to beguile or excite the reader and may arrest us on our own journey because we prefer to keep those doors closed. But the history of art is the history of opening doors, and in my opinion, Marguerite Duras is one of the most important artists of this century. She has dared to send messages back from a strange, erotic, and feverish land, the land of her own soul. Critics agree that her mastery of French prose and her uncanny insight into human character and relationships make her an inheritor of the literary mantles of Jane Austen, Flaubert, and Proust. To suggest that Ms Duras deals in pornography is to degrade the mission of a woman who's very being and collected life's work condemned the obscene, the banal, and the simple-minded. Pornography is a product manufactured to arouse and stimulate the customer for the purposes of autoeroticism. Few would argue that an artist of the philosophical depth and maturity of Marguerite Duras is a purveyor of pornography or is interested in ambushing the vulnerable reader or listener and attacking her or him with tasteless images. One of the most powerful and moving images in her 1991 text, *Man Sitting in the Corridor*, is a phallic image, one that resonates with countless such images in art from the ancient Greeks and the Incas to the paintings of Picasso. It reveals the ways in which the male weapon wounds, and the language in which this image is cast has undeniable grace and discipline: "... it's a shape from the earliest ages of the world, undifferentiated from stones and lichens, immemorial. It's planted in him and around it he struggles ..." This is not pornography. It is poetry, and as a teacher I feel it is my duty to acquaint both my students and our public with the highest level of poetic art.

Why are women who, like Duras, tell the truth of their own bodies open to the charge of pornography? Author and activist Andre Lorde offers an answer. She writes, "The erotic offers a well of replenishing and provocative force to the woman who does not fear its revelation, nor succumb to the belief that sensation is enough ... Of course," she adds, "women so empowered are dangerous."[2] The productions included in this chapter helped to rectify the unconscionable loss to the American theatre of such empowered and dangerous women.

Born Yesterday (Steppenwolf Theatre, 1987)

The second production Galati directed for the Steppenwolf company after joining the Ensemble was Garson Kanin's 1946 comedy *Born Yesterday*. It was the theatre's 1987 holiday selection and starred company members Glenne Headly (1955–2017) as Billy Dawn and John Mahoney (1940–2018) as Harry Brock, a thuggish scrap-metal tycoon with a ready bribe and the political pull to keep Billie in furs, champagne, and expensive hotels. The plot thickens when Brock hires a young journalist to help educate the streetwise Billy in the social niceties of DC society. In many ways Billie Dawn is Galati's ideal comic protagonist: smart, vulnerable, tough, honest, and unapologetically sexual. After the first meeting with her new tutor, Billy unselfconsciously expresses her appreciation of the young man as sexual desire—"I got a yen for ya." Headly's delivery wasn't a come-on. It was frank statement of fact, perhaps a cautionary warning delivered as a compliment. This being a romantic comedy, there is little doubt that her yen will be satisfied by the final curtain but along the way, she troubles the status quo by insisting on a renewal of the values on which the country was founded.

Glenne Headly died far too young and may be best remembered for her role in the 1988 film *Dirty Rotten Scoundrels*. Her film character, Janet Colgate, is introduced as a gawky and unsophisticated ingénue and revealed in the final

Figure 10 Glenne Headly, 1987. Courtesy of the Headly Estate.

scenes to be a consummate hustler who has conned a pair of old pros as well as the audience. The character was in many ways a reprise of Headly's 1987 star turn in *Born Yesterday*. *Scoundrels* was her first feature film and she more than held her own with the film's stars, Steve Martin and Michael Caine.

She also held her own in comparison to Judy Holiday's acclaimed performance in the 1946 Broadway production and 1950 film of *Born Yesterday*. But where Holiday was excitable in the role, Headly's character was measured. Where Holiday was impulsive and quick, Headly was inclined to let the wheels be seen turning. Holiday's Billy had a definite edge but in the first half of the film, the joke could be at her expense. Headly's character was never the butt of her own laugh lines. In the first act, she tells the male love interest played by Randall Arney, "I'm stupid and I like it ... I got everything I want. Two mink coats. Everything." She paused before delivering the tag line, "and if he don't come across, I don't come across." It was Arney not Headly who landed the laugh. Caught off guard by her blunt honesty and unapologetic sexuality, he was surprised, a little intimidated, and clearly interested. And so was the audience.

Eugene Kennedy described the play in the *New York Times* as "a tale about a junk tycoon's efforts to buy a United States Senator."[3] Galati didn't see it that way. Billy was clearly the central figure in his production. "The story," he explained, "is about Billie Dawn, a woman who is born again through her education, who becomes her full self though her education, fulfilling the great ideal of every immigrant group. She symbolizes the importance of each citizen's contribution to democracy." It was impossible to look away from Headly's savvy and undeniably adorable portrayal of Billie Dawn and the stage felt bereft when she was absent. Arney played the role of her tutor as a bourgeoning fan, in awe of a pupil turned instructor.

Commercial and dated without being outdated, the play's themes struck Galati as timely and relevant. But since the 1960s, author Garson Kanin had allowed very few professional productions. "When the play was written," he explained, "it was a fable, but after Watergate it became a documentary."[4] Galati pulled off the script's corny romantic plot without losing the underlying critique of power by deliberately framing the action as a theatrical fable. A bevy of choreographed chamber maids and bellhops set the stage for dramatic scenes in mini musical "numbers" and whisked props and people off stage with theatrical flourishes. The production opened with Aaron Copland's "Fanfare for the Common Man" and ended in a toast to the audience. He encouraged ensemble members to play character rather than caricature. Arney explained that the acting company hadn't "treated this as a broad farce but as a serious play. We all grew up with Watergate. That we touch the dark side and emphasize the ambivalence of the characters makes them real personalities and lets the humor emerge in a more ironic way."[5] Kanin was delighted with the result and called the show "extraordinary." Kennedy noted that Galati's inventive staging allowed the play's "sardonic humor to emerge naturally from protagonists with complex destinies rather than from characters with thin talents for one-liners."[6] I felt that Headly's anti-ingénue suggested an alternative destiny for women on stage.

She Always Said, Pablo (Goodman Theatre 1987, Kennedy Center 1990)

The "she" of *She Always Said, Pablo* is the expatriate author Gertrude Stein. In her life, her work, and on Galati's stage, Stein modeled the excitement of a radical new vison, the autonomy of an iconoclast, and the freedom of an artistic innovator. She claimed a woman's right to be seen and heard with honor and to love and be loved as she chose. The "Stein" Galati put on his stage was the originator of intellectual and artistic innovations that changed the way in which we perceive and function in the world.

Susan Nussbaum was a commanding, splendid, and endearing Stein. With the help of costume and lighting, the perpetually seated Nussbaum, who requires a wheelchair, managed to look more like Picasso's famous portrait of Stein than Stein did herself. The portrait's distinctive seated pose is described by art historian Judith Rodenbeck as an angle of attack. Picasso's Stein, writes Rodenbeck, "is all body, spilling off the canvas and threatening to take [the artist's] place."[7] The portrait marks Picasso's initial breakthrough to what would later be called Cubism and had given him considerable trouble until he finished it suddenly and without Stein's presence. Rodenbeck explains, "After three months of painting her figure daily, going over the lines, filling in the mass, insisting (to use Stein's word) on her presence, he suddenly senses not her absence, but his own."[8] Galati's staging and Nussbaum's authority as an actor enhanced the impression that the portrait's female subject eclipsed its famous maker.

"Except for the writer, Apollinaire," explained Galati, "she was the only person [Picasso] felt fully understood him. I don't know what he was to her except an equal. And perhaps the confirmation of her own genius."[9] In modern parlance,

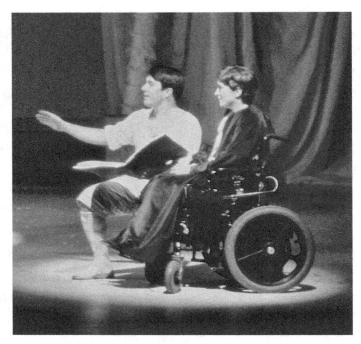

Figure 11 Larry Russo and Susan Nussbaum, Goodman Theatre of *She Always Said, Pablo*, 1987. Courtesy of the photographer. Photo by Mary Griswold.

they totally "got" each other. Picasso and Stein "were phenomenal together," wrote the painter Gerald Murphy. "Each stimulated the other to such an extent that everyone felt recharged witnessing it."[10] The production did not have a plot in a true Aristotelian sense but it did have an emotional arc with a crisis and resolution occasioned by a temporary rift between Stein and Picasso. Galati's staging of their reconciliation was redolent of maternity, visually serene, and intellectually dynamic. A reproduction of Picasso's monumental *Woman and Child on the Seashore* (1921, Art Institute of Chicago) dominated center stage (see figure 6 in Chapter 4). The Woman in White, Carmen Pelton was seated downstage left of the painting. As she sang a haunting lullaby, Picasso (Larry Russo) also dressed in white, sat on the floor with his head resting on her thigh, echoing the pose of the mother and child in Picasso's painting. Stein sat in full profile down stage right under a warm pool of light that illuminated her face. Toklas gazed at Stein from the shadows far upstage left. Each of the women in Galati's collage were deeply interconnected and at the same time, isolated as an independent presence defined by her own unique gifts. Galati held this tableau in stasis for the full length of Pelton's song, allowing his audience to enter and explore the complex maternal landscape. In doing so, he unsettled the perception of maternity as the passive acceptance of natural function and virtuous self-sacrifice. Galati's mise-en-scène equated maternity and nurturing with creativity, independence, and connection.

The Grapes of Wrath (Steppenwolf Theatre, 1988–1990)

The agent of the action in Steinbeck's novel is Ma Joad. "We loved the movie deeply," Elaine Steinbeck told *New York Times* feature writer Glenn Collins. "But everyone knew the film was kind of a vehicle for the emerging star Hank Fonda.... In the book, the key character is really Ma Joad. And Frank has restored that emphasis."[11] Galati rejected the worrying sentimentality and doughty asexual goodness of Jane Darwell's Ma Joad in John Ford's film of *The Grapes of Wrath* (1940) and cast Lois Smith, a stunning woman whose stage presence resulted in no small part from a palpable sense of inner life and physical vitality.

With a small child in tow, obviously mature and physically weathered, she was believably still in her childbearing years and well equipped to confront the physical and psychological demands of the Joad's odyssey. Smith's Ma Joad was not an iconic figure with a literary function to fulfill. She was a complex person with work to do and decisions to make.

Figure 12 Gary Sinise and Lois Smith, Steppenwolf Theatre production of *The Grapes of Wrath*, 1990. Photo by Paul Cunningham.

In the final pages of the novel, her daughter, Roasharn has suffered a miscarriage and attempts to save—or at least prolong the life of—a starving man by suckling him at her breast. In his final scene, an unsentimental wash of light spilled into the audience where Sally Murphy (Rosasharn) knelt beside the Stranger, actor Lex Monson, who lay prone at the edge of the stage. Smith stood slightly upstage and looked down at her daughter. When she caught Murphy's eyes, the girl nodded once and turned back toward Monson whose head lay in her lap. Smith's line, "I knowed you would. I knowed," quoted directly from Steinbeck's novel, is troublesome. It could have been, and perhaps was, intended by Steinbeck to indicate acceptance rather than decision, as if to say, "I knew that in the end, you would fulfill the natural role of your female body." However, the choices made by Murphy and Smith, supported by Galati's staging, affirmed courage and compassion rather than an acceptance of manifest destiny. The two actors were profoundly present to each other, their characters connected as equals for the first time in the play. As Murphy loosened the blanket draped around her shoulders, Smith turned upstage to exit with the rest of the family. They were just two strong women in grave circumstances getting on with work that needed to be done.

Draped in a ragged quilt, Murphy looked fragile, wan, and bedraggled, but her presence as a living and self-directed woman of flesh and blood was palpable and unsettling. The fact that Galati had anachronistically cast a Black actor as the stranger, the unadorned stage, the actor's proximity to the audience, and the unfocused light that spilled into the house combined to blur the separation of actor and audience. Murphy's manner was calm and rational and her final line, "You got to," was without pathos or pleading. She offered nurture where it was needed because it was needed and not because she needed to do it. Sylvia Vegetti Finzi proposes that glimpsing "an ethical paradigm in the mother/child relationship can significantly alter the role of women in our society."[12] With Galati's support, Lois Smith and Sally Murphy offered such a glimpse in the Steppenwolf production of *The Grapes of Wrath*.

The Winter's Tale (Goodman Theatre, 1990)

The impossibly sprawling story and epic scope of Shakespeare's *The Winter's Tale* includes two kingdoms from opposite sides of an ocean, jealousy, infanticide, remorse, a man chased and eaten by a bear, and miraculous reunions with tragedy, pastoral, and comedy in equal measure. In most tellings, the play is about a powerful king who wrongly condemns his queen and their child to death, repents, and sixteen years later is redeemed. However, Galati's *Winter's Tale* was very much the story of a mother and daughter who transcend the violence of a cruel and reckless authoritarian father whose redemption is far from certain.

Frank Rich compared Galati's work on this problematic text to contemporary productions of the same play staged by directors Andre Serban and JoAnne Akalaitis, adding that Galati "goes them one better by holding his entire cast to a consistent, serious standard of acting even as he takes all kinds of idiosyncratic chances with his staging."[13] The performances were consistently strong but Martha Lavey's Hermione, the wronged and stately Queen of Sicilia, and Linda Emond's Paulina, Hermione's take-no-prisoners ally, were consistently singled out for praise. Emond was statuesque and unbending in a purple robe, literally a pillar of strength. She was the voice of reason and decency and when she spoke, male attendants were driven into the margins of her space. Rich noted that the first act—and perhaps the entire production—belonged to Martha Lavey. "If there is one performance that dominates the production, it is Ms Lavey's tremendously affecting Hermione—despite the fact that the queen is absent for much of the play."[14] With few lines and surprisingly little stage time, Lavey's performance was nonetheless central to Galati's conception of the play. He explained, "*Winter's Tale* is in part the story of a child who dies because of his parents' dismantled marriage caused by his father's passion and jealousy."[15]

The production began as an ominous beat shook the auditorium then morphed into the tinny clash of a toy bear's symbols as the stage lights revealed an aristocratic child seated on the forestage playing with the mechanical bear. Far upstage, a company of adults circulated an elegant world of fine art, high fashion, and politics behind the massive pillars of a set designed by John Conklin. Galati's staging immediately established the fate of this lonely child as central to the story about to unfold. The upstage performance of Verdi's opera *Othello* came to an end and as the adults dispersed, the young prince extended his arms to greet his mother, the queen, with an embrace. Galati's staging placed the king in the queen's physical sphere rather than she in his and the action of the scene revolved around the axis of the woman and her child. Lavey was extravagantly pregnant under a widespread satin skirt and train designed by Virgil Johnson. Her bodice was cinched tight with a provocative neckline that plunged into the swell of her belly. She caressed her son and held him near while the king looked on from a distance.

Shakespeare shatters this idyll within a few pages of the text when the king is suddenly and inexplicably overtaken by a fit of jealous rage. In Galati's production, Leontes's suppressed insecurities and irrational jealousy were antagonized by the queen's unselfconscious sensuality, her easy assumption of independence, and by the bond of affection between herself and her child. Convinced without reason that he is a cuckold and his son and unborn daughter are another man's bastards, Leontes accuses his wife of treason and orders her immediate imprisonment and trial. In every other production of this play that I have seen—and I have seen several—Leontes appeared to fall victim to his own "natural" masculine passions and outsized power. But the murdered child was the key to Galati's story and from the first scenes, his staging short-circuited any rationalization for the father's arrogance and brutality.

The Queen is quickly brought to trial. Stripped of regal trappings and exhausted by the recent birth of her child while imprisoned, Lavey's Hermione dominated the stage. Rich described the scene,

> To testify in the trial scene, she rises from her prison through a trapdoor in a gray smock and bare feet, then argues against her husband's false accusations. As she does so, Ms Lavey stands completely still, her arms dangling at her side, her raven hair streaming down her back, her eyes glassy with grief but never pleading. She offers the simple dignity of a true martyr, not the melodramatic piety of the self-martyred.[16]

Leontes, played by John Hutton, was dressed in elaborate military regalia that seemed to engulf him and sat enthroned in full profile on a shallow platform. His features and coloring were flattened by a harsh light and when he rose to sentence the queen to death, his rigid figure was weirdly disconnected from the metallic voice that blasted his words through an imperfect public address system.

Critic Joel Henning felt that the production was "above all Frank Galati's triumph," and his staging was "full of inspired touches."[17] One of those touches was his interpretation of Shakespeare's most famous stage direction, "Exit, pursued by a bear." The first section of the play ends when the courtier Antigonus, who had secretly brought Hermione's newborn daughter to safety in a far-off land, is pursued and eaten by a bear. The silhouette of a rampant bear flailed and roared in the tumultuous shadows of a raging storm and the aged Antigonus fled from the stage in deadly terror, "pursued by a bear"—in Galati's version, an actor in a ratty bear costume. Designer Virgil Johnson explained, "Frank wanted people to laugh ... nervously." The following scene opened at what appeared be dawn. A strong sidelight cast the shadow of a rampant bear across the stage but as the light lifted, the "monster" was revealed to be a shadow cast by the child's toy, abandoned now at the side of the stage and exaggerated by a trick of the light. The tragedy had come to an end but Galati opened Shakespeare's Elizabethan pastoral with an unsettling reminder of the murdered child at the heart of the play.

Hermione returns in the final scene of the play. Her daughter Perdita has returned to the court as a young bride and is happily reunited with her repentant and welcoming father. Shakespeare's opening dialogue places the scene in a public room where Paulina announces that she intends to reveal a remarkable statue of the dead queen. Galati opened the final act with Hermione alone on stage, seated on a small downstage dais with monumental male nude torsos seen in silhouette against an upstage drape. Paulina and the king were heard off stage as they approached the small, curtained chamber where the queen sat in repose, one hand resting on the arm of the chair, the other supporting her temple in quiet contemplation. "Dominance, intentionality, force are only hindrances," writes Finzi of the maternal experience, "what matter are the conditions of distraction, relaxation and availability."[18] Her pose embodied these qualities. On Paulina's signal, the "statue" came to life. Hermione looked up, acknowledged her husband, and rose to gather her daughter and son-in-law into her embrace. With the family reunited, the upstage drapery was pulled aside to reveal a convivial

Figure 13 Left to right: Martha Lavey, Linda Emond, Sally Murphy, and John Hutton in the Goodman Theatre production of *The Winter's Tale*, 1990. Courtesy of Virgil Johnson. Photo by Steve Leonard.

backstage after-party in full swing with the entire cast and crew. There was music and toasts to the audience, laughter, and dancing.

Galati found a moral and emotional through line in Shakespeare's sprawling tale by following the consequences of an act of violence committed by a powerful man against a woman, an action that devastated their world until three women—a mother, her daughter, and their loyal friend—put the pieces of the shattered family back together again.

Earthly Possessions (Steppenwolf Theatre, 1991)

"Anne Tyler's subject," writes Lisa Allardice, "has been the everyday lives of middle-class women ... her writing an attempt, to borrow Updike's phrase, 'to give the mundane its beautiful due.'"[19] Anne Tyler is an artist of the act that goes unnoticed. She is also one of very few contemporary novelists to put mothers centerstage in her books. In 1989, Galati shared screenplay credit and an Oscar nomination with director Lawrence Kasdan for his adaptation of Tyler's novel *Accidental Tourist*. In 1990, he was commissioned to write a screenplay for her Pulitzer Prize-winning novel *Breathing Lessons* (1988) and in 1991, the Steppenwolf's newly constructed purpose-built theatre on Halsted Street opened with his adaptation of her seventh novel, *Earthly Possessions* (1977). He described the novel as the "portrait of a woman of intelligence and courage, and there are not many such characters created for the stage today."

Earthly Possessions is a fractured backward look at the life of a middle-aged woman. As the play begins, Charlotte Emory, a mother, housewife, and talented photographer, approaches a bank teller in Clarion, Maryland to make a withdrawal. For as long as she can remember, Charlotte has longed to escape her lackluster marriage and the burden of earthly possessions that have needlessly accumulated in her life. This is not the first time she's considered escape but this time, the decision to leave is made for her when she is taken hostage by a would-be bank robber played by Kevin Anderson. Her inept kidnapper flees with his hostage to liberate his pregnant teenage girlfriend from a home for unwed mothers. The reunited couple set off to start a new life in Florida with their hostage in tow. As they travel, Charlotte relives mundane incidents and encounters with the people who shaped her life.

Galati told an interviewer, "I can't think of another modern American writer who so brings to the forefront the problems of maternity. It's glib to say, but *Earthly Possessions* is really the portrait of the artist as a 35-year-old housewife and mother."[20] He double cast the central character as two separate aspects of his protagonist. Ensemble member Joan Allen played Mrs. Emory, the thirty-five-year-old housewife and mother who is taken hostage. Molly Regan, also an Ensemble member, appeared as the story's first-person narrator Charlotte, the artist who lives within Mrs. Emory. Allen's Mrs. Emory was humorous, adaptable, and occasionally bemused. Regan, the artist persona, was observant and detached. In his review, Frank Rich wrote, "Charlotte is so inward a personality that her two selves are indistinguishable, no matter how her thoughts, lines and actions are divided up, no matter how many distinctions the actresses try to draw."[21] He wasn't wrong but I saw a real woman in Galati's split protagonist. She—the amalgamated personae of Charlotte Emory—was illusive and untethered in ways I know real women to be.

There are three mothers in the book: Charlotte, her own disaster of a mother, and her abductor's waif-like mother-to-be played by Sally Murphy. Charlotte's mother appeared in Galati's production as an obese, controlling harridan played by Rondi Reed in a fat suit and garish makeup. It was impossible to feel a connection or sympathy for this gross cartoon mother but Reed's insatiable monster was the embodiment of Charlotte's confrontation with a life of self-imposed servitude. A middle-aged woman's abnegation of self to a grossly unworthy person or cause is not the stuff of classic tragedy but it is the stuff of a woman's life. The mother's death is, as critic Sid Smith wrote in his review, the "fulcrum of the play as well as the book." But, continued Smith, "even in the end her survivors remain confused, at once suffocated and sustained by that pile of earthly possessions they call home."[22] Galati's protagonist had none of the epiphanies, reversals, or shocking revelations of conventional drama. But his portrait of the artist as a 35-year-old housewife and mother made it clear that in the end, the choice we face is not whether to leave or to stay but how to live the life we have.

I was close to Charlotte's age at the time and like her, a mother and an artist. I would like to think that many, perhaps most middle-aged mothers who grew up in the sixties and matured in the seventies fanaticized about hitting the road in the eighties. I know I did. *Earthly Possessions* made a surprising and surprisingly indelible impression on me. I didn't know why at the time but in retrospect, I think I saw my story and my own mundane world reflected and refracted through eyes of the protagonist on stage, a woman's eyes and that was a rarity in Chicago's off-Loop theatre.

Galati's interest in Tyler's work is spurred by a deeply felt connection to her female protagonists. "They're private," he says of the author's fictive mothers, "inscrutable, not very revelatory about themselves. They're also whimsical and a little eccentric, gifted with an ability to drift off and observe their own lives as if from afar." He described his own mother in similar terms a few days before her death in hospice care. "There was always a sense of mystery about my mother. She was <u>always</u> there for us—watching us, listening, thoughtful or interested, but she seemed to have this huge interior life. I always felt her presence very profoundly, but also some sadness ... something. I don't know." Virginia Galati was a familiar figure in her son's social circle. "She had a wacky sense of humor," explained designer Mary Griswold, who has known the family since the 1970s. "Her conversation was full of non sequiturs and odd juxtapositions. She could be quiet, withdrawn—then all of a sudden she'd come up with a real zinger—some wicked, insightful comment." Galati shared his mother's love of stories, games, and books. "She read," he says. "She smoked cigarettes. She played cards. Stories and her children were her great loves."

His parents divorced when he and his sister were still children. He never saw his father again and seldom spoke of him even though the man lived within an hour's drive. Virginia supported her children as a department store clerk. In the 1980s, she suffered encroaching dementia and was eventually confined to a wheelchair. She lived in Evanston with Frank and his partner Peter or close by with his sister Franny and her two children. Fair weather or foul, Galati took Virginia out for vigorous outings in the neighborhood. I caught sight of him one day, pushing her wheelchair near the rocky Lake Michigan breakwater south of Northwestern University. The day was cold, overcast, and windy. The sight of the two long bodies hunched into the lake wind and silhouetted against a horizonless sky bore an uncanny resemblance to the self-absorbed figures of the promenades that appear in many of his productions. In Galati's staging, life is often presented as a parade, an endless line of eccentric and isolated figures dancing toward nowhere-in-particular with enthusiastic delight or stoic resolve. Virginia died in April 1991 and actor/director B. J. Jones, a long-time friend, recalled the funeral: "At the end of the mass the violinist tore into a rendition of the Edith Piaf tune *La Vie en Rose* as the casket traveled down the aisle. It was his mother's favorite. Upbeat, resilient, earthy and proud, it embodied for me the spirit of this remarkable family."[23]

The Good Person of Setzuan (Goodman Theatre, 1992)

In spring of 1992, Galati returned to the Goodman's big stage with a big cast—thirty actors and musicians according to the press release—and a big play, Bertolt

Figure 14 Cherry Jones, Goodman Theatre production of *The Good Person of Setzuan*, 1992. Courtesy of the Goodman Theatre. Photo by Charles Osgood.

Brecht's *Good Person of Setzuan*. Shen Teh, a poor woman and a whore, happily offers to share what little she has with three gods in search of a good person. They reward her generosity with a gift of money and admonish her to thrive and to be a good person. This, she tells the audience, "tore me in two like lightning." The open-hearted Shen Teh survives the prosperity bestowed on her—a small tobacco shop—by adopting the guise of Shui Ta, a ruthless morally corrupt businessman and opium dealer who puts Shen Teh's interests above all others.

Galati cast Cherry Jones in the role of Shen Teh. Jones is now an award-winning performer with extensive credits and major awards in film and television as well as on Broadway. However, in 1991, she was a young and upcoming actor in New York, known as a generous ensemble player with tremendous range. Galati explained that it was Jones' idea to use the emblems of archetypical masculine privilege to define her character's evil alternative persona, Shui Ta.

> The elegant oily façade of Shui Ta, the moustache, top hat, and tails were all her idea, and they were great because she could play the suavity of the character in the icon of the dandy. The hat also gave her access to the authority of the tycoon. As Shen Teh she was very much herself, very athletic and alive, open and curious. She was very accepting of the fact that this open-hearted, open-faced girl was a

whore. Really, as a woman, Shen Teh wasn't at all split or fragmented—she was the mother, the whore and the innocent all at once. She split herself into two out of necessity. It wasn't a <u>natural</u> thing to do. Cherry definitely played it as a choice.

Jones' Shen Teh was complex, not conflicted. She was a pragmatic idealist who survived by splitting the pragmatist and the idealist into two separate and conflicting entities.

Tribune critic Richard Christensen admitted to liking the production better than the play. He was as usual, openhanded in his praise of the actors, the design, and Galati's work but uncomfortable with the director's more extravagant flourishes of theatricality. "This is," he writes, "very much a Galati vision of Brecht, filled with the director's ever-strong pictorial sense and awash in the impassioned good will (and occasional nervous tic) that exemplify his work in the theater."[24] The "nervous tic" Christiansen most objected to was the casting of dancer/actor Kenny Ingram as Mrs. Shinn, Shen Teh's mouthy but loyal shop assistant. Ingram is an African American bantam weight dancer who toured in *A Chorus Line* as the height-challenged wanna-be basketball player, "Gimmie the Ball" Ritchie. He auditioned for Galati with a shaved head and on an impulse, Galati asked him to read the part of Mrs. Shinn. He did and was cast in the role. On stage, Ingram wore a series of shabby or upscale dresses and answered to the name Mrs. Shinn but nothing else about him—bald head, cocky attitude, and exposed limbs—was gender specific. "The great thing was," says Galati, "that we never talked about the fact that he was Mrs. Shinn. We never asked questions like, 'Why am I playing a woman – am I in drag? Am I what I am or am I her?' He never felt he had to ask—he was Mrs. Shinn. That was his character."

Christiansen didn't buy it. He wrote, "Though played well, the bitchy drag act doesn't do anything for the production except load it with a lot of cheap laughs."[25] Ingram was certainly funny, his line delivery caustic and biting, and his exaggerated gestures reminiscent of the posturing ironies of drag. But Galati felt that this casting choice was linked to important questions about gender identification that were central to his understanding of the play. He explained,

> The casting of Mrs. Shinn as a male is a way for me of italicizing the gender reversal that is in Shen Teh's appropriation of the male character. It's complex and interesting for the audience to be watching a scene in which there's a woman who's playing a man and there's a man playing a woman. In the scene they're playing with each other, the man who's playing the woman is a woman interacting

with a man who's being played by a woman. So, in other words, what I'm trying to do is put up two mirrors and having them face each other so that there a kind of infinite regression into a hall of mirrors that keeps multiplying the question of gender identification.[26]

The alliance between a small bald man in a bias-cut gown and a statuesque woman in top hat, tailcoat, and moustache, both intent on protecting the life of Shen Teh and her unborn child, may have been funny but it was no joke. Without tedious intellectualizing or abstraction, the pairing unsettled socially determined gender roles and at the same time, called attention to more troublesome and pressing issues about the difficulty of survival in a world that has no place for generosity, compassion, and ambiguous gender.

As a graduate student at Northwestern, Galati had studied Brecht's theories, essays, and playscripts with Robert Breen. Breen understood Brecht's famous "alienation" or V-effect to be a technical device. Galati recalled, "He used to say that alienation was a way to get further in. You rear back in order to dive deeper in." Draped in the costume of Mrs. Shinn, Ingram's body countered the habitual suspension of disbelief, causing one to "rear back" from the emotional draw of the story without losing interest in the plight of the protagonist and the injustice of her world.

At a turning point in Act I, Jones grabbed hold of a small child and strode out of the fictive environment to confront the audience directly. In that moment, she was both herself and the woman she represented, a woman empowered by and committed to a maternal project. She swung the boy out to face the audience in front of her and leaned over him, holding his head with both hands for the audience to see. She spoke with a hard-edged conviction. "Look at this filthy mouth." She demanded. "Is this how you treat your fellow creatures? Have you no compassion for the fruit of your wombs? No pity for yourselves?" She sneered, "Un-happy people. Know that I will fight for my own even if I have to turn into a tiger." She released the boy and held her ground for a fierce moment as he fled. In that moment, Jones' action and that of her character merged as a powerful warning delivered with physical daring and absolute commitment.

The Glass Menagerie (Roundabout Theatre, 1994)

In 1994, Galati directed Tennessee Williams's *The Glass Menagerie* (1944) for the Roundabout Theatre, "a production company that can make a familiar play

Figure 15 Poster for the Roundabout Theatre production of *The Glass Menagerie*, 1994. Courtesy of the artist, Scott McKowen.

new again, by pairing actors and directors with a strong commitment to Broadway as it once was."[27] The production marked the fiftieth anniversary of the play's premiere. Scott McKowen's evocative poster design captured the complexity and emotion of Galati's conception. A child, nearly a woman, with her back to us accepts the embrace of an apprehensive and possibly overprotective woman. It is a mother's embrace and whatever else she is, the girl's carefully brushed hair and the neatly tied bow at the back of her dress speak of loving care and attention. In the script, Williams mentions a portrait of the absent father displayed on the living room wall. In most productions, it is placed in a prominently position but for Galati's production, media and video designer John Boesche created a washed-out sepia image that waivered in the background like a ghostly apparition no longer able to assert itself.

Julie Harris played Amanda Wingfield, a single mother living in reduced circumstances in the late 1930s. The character is based in part on Williams' own mother who is described by his biographers as domineering and ineffectual. Amanda is both. However, Harris's Amanda, wrote reviewer Jeremy Gerard, "is less the Southern belle who once entertained 17 gentleman callers on a single sultry afternoon a lifetime ago in a Dixie that no longer exists, than the stern, meddling and desperate single mother of two grown children whose prospects are marginal at best."[28]

In Act I, Amanda is determined to make a good impression on a young man invited to dinner as a marriage prospect for her daughter Laura. Desperate to raise money for the event, she makes a series of phone calls in the early morning hours in a futile attempt to renew or sell magazine subscriptions. In Galati's production, the kitchen area floated like a small pageant wagon on the Roundabout's thrust stage. The area was framed by a kitchen counter with a sink cabinet on one end and an icebox at the other. A wall phone was mounted on the righthand end of the counter. Harris was alone on stage. She curled her right hand into a fist around the handset and consulted a thin telephone directory on the counter. She dialed, simpered, made her pitch, paced, bullied, and wielded. Each time she was rebuffed she found and dialed another number. And then another. Tethered by the phone cord, she careened between the icebox and sink like a caged tiger. As she talked, her free hand traced hope, disappointment, and frustration in the air. She was fierce, fawning, pushy, too obviously desperate, and undeterred by rejection.

A fan letter addressed to Harris is preserved in Galati's personal archives. In it, the theatre patron writes,

Surrounded by such truly fine talent, you seemed freed to deliver your completely well-rounded Amanda instead of what too often, in other less total productions, amount merely to rather flamboyant, self-serving star turns. Your generous portrayal was shaded so as to reveal the often-overlooked paradoxes of Mrs. Wingfield in all her humanity—spontaneous/exhausted, strong/giddy, devoted/overbearing, determined/bored, charming/empty, admirable/frustrated, tragic/comic. You managed to show all sides, both good and bad, of this fascinating woman whose moonlit wish of 'success and happiness' for her children could be believed.[29]

The mother in Galati's production of *The Glass Menagerie* tried and failed to keep possibilities open. She struggled to find new approaches to survival for herself and her children and in this too, she failed. No matter how fierce her dreams for her children might have been, she could not bring them into the world as truly "other." Amanda Wingfield failed her children but she did not fail to love them. In Galati's production, there was no maternal monster and no subliminal justification for the father who had deserted her and her children. Harris's performance acknowledged the fortitude and fallibility of real mothers coping with real distress in the real world.

As I Lay Dying (Steppenwolf Theatre, 1995)

Galati's adaption of William Faulkner's Southern Gothic Novel *As I Lay Dying* opened at the Steppenwolf Theatre in April, 1995. Set in 1928, the primary action of the novel is a tragic/comic nine-day funeral march to a cemetery "on the other side" of Yoknapatawpha County in rural Mississippi. In accordance with her dying wish, the rotting body of Addie Bundren is being transported by her husband and children to the cemetery where her parents are buried. Each of the living characters has a secret agenda for making the trek—an abortion, new teeth, revenge, escape.

Galati was attracted to Faulkner's novel as an unsentimental and darkly comic counterpart to Steinbeck's *Grapes of Wrath*. Both novels feature a road trip with a significant river crossing midway. Both families are dirt poor and both endure fire and flood. Both families have multiple sons and one pregnant daughter. In both books, the mother is central to the story. And both are major twentieth-century works of American literature. But unlike *The Grapes of Wrath*, Faulkner's story is about the dystopian failures of communication and community and Addie Bundren, the mother at the center of the story, is resentful, complex, unfaithful, and for most of the story, dead. Galati explained, "Faulkner's story is almost a mock epic because the characters do not have the stature of real tragedy. They're actually comic characters."[30]

In his speech to the cast on the first day of rehearsals, Galati quoted Harold Bloom's assessment that: "the Bundrens manifestly constitute one of the most terrifying visions of the family romance in the history of literature." He also posed a question to the cast that would direct their work together, asking "Is the weird quest of the Bundrens a violation of the natural, or is it what Blake would have called a terrible triumph of the selfish virtues of the natural heart?" Neither saint nor harridan, Faulkner's matriarch is no conventional stage mother. She is a failed and ultimately absent mother but in Galati's conception, both her failure and her absence are framed as the extraordinary triumph of the selfish virtues of a natural heart. Galati explained to the cast that Falkner's conception of the "mother, dead or undead, is uncannier even than these children when she confesses the truth of her existence: her rejecting vision of her own children." Addie speaks only once and her speech is the fulcrum of Faulkner's story and the center of Galati's script. Everything in the production led the audience either toward or away from this speech.

Sun-Times critic Hedy Weiss was taken with the show's triumphant theatricality and the singular performance of Cynthia Baker as Addie Bundren. In the previous theatrical season, Robert Falls had cast Baker as Maxine Faulk in Tennessee Willliams's *Night of the Iguana*, a character played by an aging but still vibrant and frankly carnal Eva Gardner in the 1964 film. As Addie Bundren, Baker projected the same earthy sensuality she brought to the character of Maxine but with an equally earthy and fierce intelligence. Hedy Weiss described her performance in *As I Lay Dying* as "enthralling—ferocious and grippingly intense in her pivotal soul-searching monologue and insanely laughable."[31] Galati was aware that "to overstress how funny the characters are, how quirky and grotesque, is to miss its terrible depths, the darkness, the poetry, the windy dread. It's full of pain and suffering and loss—and deep, deep, longing." Baker found the right balance.

Galati's second act opened as the deceased Addie, who had been a schoolteacher before her marriage, watched from a distance as her male children struggled to haul her coffin and its rotting body from the rain-swollen river it had fallen into then turned out to the audience and began a spoken aria of wrenching honesty and insight. She began, "In the afternoon when school was out and the last one had left with his little dirty snuffling nose, instead of going home I would go down the hill to the spring where I could be quiet and hate them." Her uninflected manner and unexpected turn got a reaction from the audience. Not exactly a laugh, but something like it. As she moved into one of Faulkner's most famous passages, her delivery was dry, undecorated and despite the peculiar syntax, completely natural. She spoke of isolation, motherhood, adultery—which she did not regret—and passion—which she did or at least knew to be a punishable sin. She was tormented, erotic, and tragic but even in her most revealing confessions, Baker never lost the comic tragedy of Falkner's language.

Near the end of her speech, she acknowledges death in a line I had heard before, "My father said that the reason for living is getting ready to stay dead." The sentence that follows circles back to the mundane and I had never heard it before: "I knew at last what he meant and that he could not have known what he meant himself, because a man cannot know anything about cleaning up the house." Baker let the woman's serrated perception hang in the air for a moment and once again, earned herself an audible stir in the audience. It was, for me, a rare moment of clarity in the theatre. I knew—and in that moment knew that I knew—that getting ready to stay dead has more to do with chores than metaphysics. I didn't think my companion would know what the second line meant and asked him. He said it was a throw-away, a pause to let the first line sink in and maybe reinforce Addie's contempt for men. He had fought to stay alive too hard and for too long to be ready to stay dead or, for that matter, to know anything about cleaning up the house.

Galati had the passion, courage, and rare insight to take on Falkner's challenging text with its troubled and troubling mother. The production was uneven, but intentionally so—more like life than art with lulls and storms, tedious plodding, and flashes of unexpected truth. Baker's Addie was audacious and irredeemable. She suffered and was the cause of suffering, isolation, and betrayal but she was too big, too knowing, and too honest to deny her faults and her failures. Her husband, her children, and life in general had failed her without even noticing. Falkner is a hard read for me. I always feel like I deserve a reward when I finish one of his books, like coffee ice cream or new shoes. But after seeing Galati's production, I returned to the novel and this time it was its own reward. This time, I found in it "the terrible triumph of the selfish virtues of a natural heart" and for once, that heart belonged to a flawed, mundane, and glorious woman.

Ragtime 1996–1998

In 1996 and for the two years following, Galati was entirely engaged by work on the new Broadway musical *Ragtime*, based on E. L. Doctorow's novel. Stephen

Flaherty wrote the music with lyrics by Lynn Ahrens. Terrence McNally wrote the adaptation. Galati directed. I cannot think of a director better suited to stage Doctorow's novel. The story, an American fable set in the Ragtime era of the early twentieth century, is centered on music, the American experience, and three mothers, absent and present. Mother—the character's name—is a young, white, upper-class woman increasingly uncomfortable with the entitlement and inflexible bias of her class. Sarah is a homeless unwed mother of color. Mameh, a poor Jewish immigrant cast out by her husband Tateh for submitting to the sexual demands of her employer, is never seen in the novel or the musical. Mameh's story is referred to in the novel but never told. She could have easily been omitted from the musical all together but Galati and McNally did not allow her absence to go unmarked, unquestioned, or unmourned.

Since the mid-nineties, a legion of twenty-first-century characters have joined the pantheon of Galati's dangerous women. He returned to Chicago in 1999 and in 2002, brought Lois Smith back to the Steppenwolf Theatre as the feisty *grande dame* of a showbusiness dynasty in the 1927 comedy of theatrical manners, *The Royal Family* by George S. Kaufman and Edna Ferber. With company members Amy Morton in the pivotal role of Broadway's ruling diva and Rondi Reed in a small star turn of her own, the comedy celebrated a woman's life in the theatre. In 2003, he worked with Tony Kushner on the author's last revision of *Hombody/Kabul* staged at the Brooklyn Academy of Music. Galati described the play as an "explosive drama" in which "a father and estranged daughter go to Afghanistan in search of the Homebody, the wife and mother drawn away from her deeply neurotic family to the world of Islam and the grave of Cain, the slain brother in that primal biblical family."[32]

In 2006, he returned to Gertrude Stein and Alice Toklas with *Loving Repeating*, a biographical musical that celebrated their life together as partners and lovers. Their enduring relationship began in 1907 and ended with Stein's death in 1946. Galati approached Stephen Flaherty to set Stein's words to music. He agreed with some trepidation but warmed to the challenge as he began to love Stein's language as Galati did. I saw the production at Northwestern University. Sung to Flaherty's music, the deep understanding, pleasure, and loving appreciation expressed in Stein's words had a visceral authenticity that wasn't available to me in reading. When I heard a young woman sing "My wife is my life is my life is my wife," I wanted to hear the words sung again and of course, this being Stein, I did. The play ends with Alice's account of her last hours with Gertrude, spoken in a time when the music of their life together seemed to be fading.

By that time Gertrude Stein was in a sad state of indecision and worry. I sat next to her and she said to me early in the afternoon, what is the answer? I was silent. In that case, she said, what is the question? Then the whole afternoon was troubled, confused and very uncertain, and later they took her away on a wheeled stretcher to the operating room and I never saw her again. (*Alice turns and walks slowly away, lighting a cigarette as she goes.*)

As she walked away, the musicians took up a familiar tune and the chorus joined in to sing one of the first and often repeated musical lines of the play: "YOU ARE MY HONEY HONEY SUCKLE./I AM YOUR BEE." Galati and Flaherty quickened the erotic, sweetly domestic, loving and repeating life these two unlikely and unconventional women created, each without diminishing the other or being herself diminished. Dangerous women indeed.

Notes

1 Frank Galati to J. W., "Thank You for Your Memo," February 20, 1993, Box 3, Folder 1. Frank Galat (1943–) Papers, 1948–2914, Northwestern University McCormick Library of Special Collections and University Archives.
2 Andre Lorde, "Uses of the Erotic: The Erotic as Power by Audre Lorde," by Melody Godfred, Fred and Far Blog, https://fredandfar.com/blogs/ff-blog/the-erotic-as-power-by-audre-lorde
3 Kennedy, "Born Yesterday," 1988.
4 Richard Christianson, "'Born Yesterday' Remains a Classic Today," *Chicago Tribune*, December 14, 1987, 3.
5 Randall Arney interview with Eugene Kennedy, "'Born Yesterday' Is Reborn in Chicago," *New York Times*, February 21, 1988. www.nytimes.com/1988/02/21/theater/theater-born-yesterday-is-reborn-in-chicago.html
6 Kennedy, "Born Yesterday," 1988.
7 Judith Rodenbeck, "Insistent Presence in Picasso's Portrait of Gertrude Stein," Columbia University, Fall 1995. http://theatreonthesquare.com/picasso'picstein.html.
8 Rodenbeck.
9 Hedy Weiss, "'She Always Said' Speaks to Genius: Pablo and Stein Will Lead Parade at the Goodman," *Chicago Sun-Times*, March 8, 1987, Arts sec.
10 Weiss, "She Always Said," 1987.
11 Frank Galati interview with Glenn Collins, "Staging a 'Grapes' of Dust, Fog, Fire and Blood," *The New York Times*, April 3, 1990, Culture Desk ed., sec. C.
12 Sylvia Vegetti Finzi, *Mothering: Toward a New Psychoanalytic Construction* (New York: Guilford Press, 1996), 52.

13 Frank Rich, "New Interpretation of Shakespeare's 'Winter's Tale,'" *New York Times*, January 31, 1990.
14 Rich, "New Interpretation," 1990.
15 Qtd in Weiss, 1990.
16 Rich, "New Interpretation," 1990.
17 Joel Henning, "Frank Galati's 'Winter's Tale,'" *Wall Street Journal*, February 1, 1990.
18 Vegetti-Finzi, 160.
19 Lisa Allardice, "Anne Tyler: A Life's Work." *The Guardian,* April 13, 2012. www.theguardian.com/books/2012/apr/13/anne-tyler-interview
20 Sid Smith, "The Galati-Tyler Connection Has a Secret for Success," *Chicago Tribune*, August 2, 1991.
21 Frank Rich, "Adapting an Anne Tyler Novel," *New York Times*, September 4, 1991,
22 Smith, "Galati-Tyler Connection," 1991.
23 BJ Jones et al., "Salute to Frank Galati: 'Renaissance Man,'" *Follow Spot*, Illinois Theatre Association, November 1998.
24 Richard Christiansen, "A Model 'Good Person'; Best of Brecht Is Brought Out," *Chicago Tribune*, May 6, 1992.
25 Christiansen, "Best of Brecht," 1992.
26 "Backstage at the Goodman: 'The Good Person of Setzuan 1992,'" Richard Pettengill director. Vimeo, posted November 13, 2018. https://vimeo.com/11116874.
27 Malcom Johnson, "Julie Harris Moving in 'Menagerie,'" *Hartford Courant*, Hartford, CT, November 20, 1994.
28 Johnson, "Julie Harris," 1994.
29 W.W.S. to Julie Harris, "Amanda Wingfield, Roundabout Theatre, December 28, 1994," Box 8, Folder 1, Frank Galati (1943–) Papers, 1948–2914, Northwestern University McCormick Library of Special Collections and University Archives.
30 Frank Galati, "Fiddling with Faulkner Q&A," *Stagebill,* Steppenwolf Theatre, July 1994,
31 Hedy Weiss, "Falkner Churns with Subversive Life," *Chicago Sun-Times*, July 10, 1995.
32 "A Conversation with Frank Galati." *Stay Thirsty Magazine*, Spring, 2014. www.staythirstymedia.com/201404-084/html/201404-thirsty-galati.html

Epilogue

Among Galati's papers is a handwritten note dated December 12, 1966. It was sent by a Florida State University colleague in response to a student production of "Santa Claus Is Really the Gasman," an adaptation of selections from *The Tin Drum* by Günter Grass, written and directed by Galati. The selection he staged speaks of the grim realities of Hiroshima after the atomic bomb. The note, signed only SH, begins "I have deliberately delayed writing this, hoping that I might view the performances more objectively. Until the boy in the red jacket came forward for his part, I was so moved by the picture presented of our fraud and hypocrisy that I just wanted out of there."[1] Throughout his career, the emotional and intellectual demands of Galati's productions have discomfited many theatre patrons. He is a storyteller and an entertainer but his presentation of human failings, struggle, and injustice is constructed to engender a catharsis of accountability and a sense of shared responsibility. "The boy in the red jacket," continues the author of the note, "is you Mr. Galati—nearly every tone, move, and gesture." As a director, a teacher, an artist, and a citizen, Frank Galati is still the "boy in the red jacket." He is, as SH describes an artist "whose vision is not cynical and whose spirit is not exhausted." He is also an astute and penetrating reader who finds hope and the possibility of forgiveness, even redemption in literature. Admitting that she does not entirely understand every word this peculiar boy has to say—not an uncommon response to his mature work—the author concludes with a stammering expression of appreciation: "... never, never, never have I been so caught up in a performance."

When SH wrote this note, Galati was a twenty-four-year-old, under-paid, overworked MA stranded on a south Florida plain. In June 2021, he addressed a virtual meeting of the American Association of Community Theatres as a celebrated elder of the American theatre but his voice was still that of the boy in the red jacket. He looked to the past as he and his audience contemplated an uncertain future. "Only now, at seventy-seven, am I somewhat able to look back and decipher patterns, to pull back for a wider shot and see the landscape. In these sequestered days I've been inclined to reflect on fundamentals, not certainties, but verities of the heart. Why" he asked, "do we do it?" He answered, as he often does, by telling a personal and self-reflective story. "Most aspiring theatre artists of my generation," he began,

> ... truly wanted to change the world. The theatre was the site of public discourse. Working in theatre was a commitment to work for social change. We were twenty-somethings in temp jobs, unconsciously white frat boys and show girls with liberal arts degrees—autodidacts and stowaways drawn to the side-show— we were also critics obsessed by the mystery of "representation." MOST OF ALL We were enthralled by the act of performance and we perceived that there was some sorcery in it. It was magic, yes, but to perform was to accomplish something.

He spoke of "radical theatre groups and artists who framed the discourse in the English language in the 1960s and 70s," of Viet Nam and the Living Theatre, of Dr. Martin Luther King Jr., and the grotesque farce of Watergate. "But now?" he asked. "What about Now?"

> Where are we in this threshold moment? Does fiction matter? As much as Black Lives Matter? I think not. How do we serve our fellow human beings in the middle of such turbulence? How, after the murder of George Floyd, how, after the insurrection on January 6th, and how after seemingly endless mass-shootings, do we dare compete when the mirror we hold up to nature has been smashed to pieces by political history.[2]

He spoke at length of the deep humanity of his revered teacher and mentor, Robert Bacon who was white and of Bacon's partner Robert Love who was black, of his Northwestern colleague Dwight Conquergood, a pioneer ethnographer in the field of Performance Studies. He spoke of learning to play and of plays, of ritual and of his own origin-story, the cultural narrative "adhering in my bones. I didn't know it, but the developing story of my own identity was being invisibly molded by my tribe's values." None of us grows up unscathed or uncompromised and yet "one upheaval after another we go forward." But how? His answer is, as usual, a challenge rather than a resolution.

> We try to meet the moment with our work. We try to reach those verities Faulkner talked about in his Nobel address. The "verities of the heart." But this suspended moment in time must be the moment when we as theatre artists reject the old ways, the systemic racism, sexism, ageism, homophobia, transphobia and rid ourselves of cruel stereotypical depictions of character. I believe in the power of story, I believe in the benediction of great literature, I

believe poetry can heal and I believe you, the artists who create a truly living theatre, will answer the 'call.' You will transform our theatre for the future in ways I can't even imagine but meanwhile never forget what so vexed Ferdinand and with what infinite sagacity Prospero calms him down.

> Be not bent out of shape, my boy … "OUR REVELS NOW ARE ENDED.
> THESE OUR ACTORS, AS I FORTOLD YOU, WERE ALL SPIRITS
> AND ARE MELTED INTO AIR. THIN AIR.
> AND LIKE THE BASELESS FABRIC OF THIS VISION
> THE CLOUD-CAPPED TOWERS, THE GORGEOUS PALACES
> THE SOLEMN TEMPLES, THE GREAT GLOBE ITSELF
> YEA, AND ALL THAT IT INHERIT SHALL DISSOLVE
> AND LIKE THIS INSUBSTANTIAL PAGEANT FADED
> LEAVE NOT A WRACK BEHIND.
> WE ARE SUCH STUFF AS DREAMS ARE MADE ON …

In this speech, Galati, along with Prospero and his maker William Shakespeare, acknowledge that their own revels—spectacular as they may be—will end sooner than later, leaving not a wrack behind. Ever the Paradoxical Professor, he finds a life affirming solace in this melancholy truth. How to go forward and at the same time end my story? I defer to the boy in a red jacket, whose vision is not cynical, whose spirit is not yet exhausted, and who knows far better than I how to end a good story.

> And you, artists and guardians of our American theatre,
> you must, in this defining moment of our history,
> Answer Shakespeare's call … To dream on.

Notes

1 SH, "Letter to Frank Galati, December 6, 1966." Frank Galati (1943–) Papers, 20/68. Box 3, folder 3. Northwestern University Archives. Evanston, Il.
2 Frank Galati, "Why Do We Do It?" (manuscript), American Association for Community Theatres Virtual Conference. Keynote Speech, June 19, 2021. https://whova.com/portal/aacte_202106/videos/1YTNzYTO1IDN/

Bibliography

Abarbanal, Jonathan. "Steppenwolf in Steinbeck Country." *American Theatre*, June 23, 1989.

Axsom, Richard H. *"Parade," Cubism as Theater*. Outstanding Dissertations in the Fine Arts. New York: Garland Publishing, 1979.

Banes, Sally. *Greenwich Village 1963: Avant-Garde Performance and the Effervescent Body*. Durham: Duke University Press, 2007.

Bartow, Arthur. *The Director's Voice: Twenty-One Interviews*. New York: Theatre Communications Group, 1999.

Beckerman, Bernard. *Theatrical Presentation: Performer, Audience and Act*. New York and London: Routledge, 1990.

Berger, John. *The Success and Failure of Picasso*. New York: Pantheon Books, 1989.

Berger, John. *Ways of Seeing*. London: British Broadcasting Corporation, 1977.

Breen, Robert S. *Chamber Theatre*. Englewood Cliffs, NJ: Prentice-Hall, 1978.

Christiansen, Richard. *A Theater of Our Own: A History and a Memoir of 1,001 Nights in Chicago*. Evanston, IL: Northwestern University Press, 2004.

Coleman, Janet. *The Compass: The Improvisational Theatre That Revolutionized American Comedy*. Chicago: University of Chicago Press, 1991.

Crowther, Paul. *The Language of Twentieth Century Art: a Conceptual History*. New Haven: Yale University Press, 1998.

Davis, Tracy C. and Thomas Postlewait. *Theatricality*. Cambridge: Cambridge University Press, 2003.

Fensch, Thomas. *Steinbeck and Covici: The Story of a Friendship*. Cork: BookBaby, 2014.

Garner, Stanton B. *Bodied Spaces: Phenomenology and Performance in Contemporary Drama*. Ithaca: Cornell University Press, 1995.

Galati, Frank and John Steinbeck. *John Steinbeck's The Grapes of Wrath*. New York: Dramatists Play Service Inc, 1991.

Galati, Frank and Mikhail Bulgakov. *Heart of a Dog*. New York: Dramatists Play Service Inc, 1988.

Galati, Frank, Stephen Flaherty, and Gertrude Stein. *Loving Repeating: A Musical Adapted from the Writings of Gertrude Stein*. Evanston, IL: Northwestern University Press, 2009.

Goodall, Jane R. *Stage Presence*. London: Routledge, 2008.

Hauser, Frank, and Russell Reich. *Notes on Directing: 130 Lessons in Leadership from the Directors Chair*. New York: RCR Creative Press, 2018.

Larson, Mark. *Ensemble: An Oral History of Chicago Theater*. Chicago: Midway, an Agate Imprint, 2019.
Lee, Charlotte, and Frank Galati. *Oral Interpretation*. 5th ed. Boston: Houghton Mifflin Company, 1977.
Leep, Jeanne. *Theatrical Improvisation: Short Form, Long Form, and Sketch-Based Improv*. New York: Palgrave Macmillan, 2008.
Lehmann, Hans-Thies, and Jürs-Munby Karen. *Postdramatic Theatre*. London: Routledge, 2006.
Leighten, Patricia Dee. *Re-Ordering the Universe: Picasso and Anarchism, 1897–1914*. Princeton, NJ: Princeton University Press, 1989.
Loewith, Jason. *The Directors Voice. Vol. 2*. New York: Theatre Communications Group Inc., 2013.
Mayer, John. *Steppenwolf Theatre Company of Chicago: in Their Own Words*. London: Bloomsbury Methuen Drama, 2016.
McMillin, Scott. *The Musical as Drama: A Study of the Principles and Conventions behind Musical Shows from Kern to Sondheim*. Princeton, NJ: Princeton University Press, 2014.
Mitchell, W. J. T. *Picture Theory: Essays on Verbal and Visual Representation*. Chicago, IL: University of Chicago Press, 1995.
North, Michael. *The Dialect of Modernism: Race, Language, and Twentieth-Century Literature*. New York: Oxford University Press, 1998.
Patinkin, Sheldon, Robert Klein, and Alan Arkin. *The Second City: Backstage at the World's Greatest Comedy Theater*. Naperville, IL: Sourcebooks, 2000.
Pearce, Howard D. *Human Shadows Bright as Glass: Drama as Speculation and Transformation*. Lewisburg, PA: Bucknell University Press, 1997.
Roach, Joseph R. *It*. Ann Arbor: University of Michigan Press, 2007.
Roach, Joseph R. *The Players Passion: Studies in the Science of Acting*. Ann Arbor: University of Michigan Press, 2011.
Shapiro, Mel. *The Director's Companion*. Belmont, CA: Wadsworth/Thomson Learning, 1998.
Shillinglaw, Susan. *On Reading the Grapes of Wrath*. New York: Penguin Books, 2014.
Solomon, Alisa. *Re-Dressing the Canon: Essays on Theater and Gender*. London: Routledge, 2005.
States, Bert O. *Great Reckonings in Little Rooms: On the Phenomenology of Theatre*. Berkeley: University of California Press, 1985.
Stein, Gertrude. "Composition as Explanation (1925)." Poetry Foundation. Poetry Foundation, February 15, 2010. www.poetryfoundation.org/resources/learning/essays/detail/69481.
Stein, Gertrude, and John L. Sweeney. *Geography and Plays: by Gertrude Stein*. Boston: Four Seas Co., 1922.
Stein, Gertrude. "Gertrude Stein on Understanding and Joy: Rare 1934 Radio Interview." New York: PennSound Archives, November 1934. www.*brainpickings.org/2012/09/20/Gertrude-Stein-1934-Radio-Interview/*.

Sutcliffe, Tom. *Believing in Opera*. Princeton, NJ: Princeton Univ Press, 2016.
Thomas, Mike. *The Second City Unscripted: Revolution and Revelation at the World-Famous Comedy Theater*. Evanston, IL: Northwestern University Press, 2012.
Vegetti-Finzi, Sylvia. *Mothering: toward a New Psychoanalytic Construction*. New York: Guilford Press, 1996.
Young, Harvey, and Queen Meccasia Zabriskie. *Black Theater Is Black Life: An Oral History of Chicago Theater and Dance, 1970-2010*. Evanston, IL: Northwestern University Press, 2014.

Index

Dates of performances are shown in brackets after titles. Illustrations are shown in *italic* figures.

Abarbanel, Jonathan 19, 120, 122, 124, 134
Abbot, Jack, *In the Belly of the Beast: Letters from Prison* (1985) 29
Accidental Tourist, The (1989) 54, 184
acting 3, 35, 36, 152, 159, 163–4, 167, 168
   see also Chicago style; improvisation; naturalism
acting notes 51, 150, 157, 159–60, 166
action(s) 26, 28–9, 70, 114–15, 134
activism 97
   see also female characters
Actor's Co-Op 43
actualities 121, 123, 128, 136–7
Addams, Jane 21
Ahrens, Lynn 161
   see also Flaherty, Stephen and Lynn Ahrens
Albert Herring (1979) 53
Alceste (1990) 79
Algren, Nelson, *Devil's Stocking, The* 77
Allardice, Lisa 184
Allen, Joan 185
American Buffalo (1975–76) 48–9
American theatre 15
Amster, Peter 57, 112
Andries, Dorothy 49, 79
Apollinaire, Guillaume 100
Appel, Libby 146
Appel, Paul 43
Argento, Dominick
   Postcard from Morocco 78–9
   Voyage of Edgar Allan Poe, The 79–80
Aristotle 2
Arney, Randall 36, 127, 176–7
Artaud, Antonin 91
Artist-in-Residence program 48
As I Lay Dying (1995) 192–4
attention 99
Aunt Dan and Lemon (1987) 74–5, *75*, 161

awards and nominations 43, 45, 46, 54
Axsom, Richard 6–7, 97

back acting 35
Bacon, Wallace 5, 24–5
Baitz, Jon Robin 15
Baker, Cynthia 193–4
Balcome, William, *View from the Bridge* 82–3
Balm in Gilead (1980) 71–2
Bank, Marji 106, *107*, 108, 113, *114*
Beaufort, John 72
Beckerman, Bernard 5
Beckett, Samuel, *Endgame* 61
Bernstein, Leonard, *Candide* (1977) 49
Bethune, Robert 2–3
bicentennial celebrations 47–8
Bilandic, Michael A. 48
Blue Eyes Black Hair (2003) 27
Body Politic 21, 23, 24
Boesche, John 191
Bommer, Larry 69
Born Yesterday (1987) 174–7, *175*
Boss (1973) 45–6
Bragan, Douglas 19–20
Brantley, Ben 42
Braque, Georges 100
Brecht, Bertolt
   Good Person of Setzuan, The 157–8, 186–9, *187*
   Mother Courage and Her Children 31–2, 61
Breen, Robert
   and Brecht 189
   chamber theatre 6, 25, 26, 27
   coalescence 160
   distancing effects 44
   economy in style 30
   and Galati 5, 24–5

Britten, Benjamin, *Albert Herring* 53
Browning, Kirk 139, 161
Bruce, Cheryl Lynn 137
Brustein, Robert 138
Bulgakov, Mikhail, *Heart of a Dog* 61–2

Cambridge, Godfrey 46
Candide (1977) 49
Cassidy, Claudia 46
casting 136–8, 188
Chalfant, Kathleen 32–3
chamber theatre 5, 6, 25–8
Chamberlin, Kevin 139, 151, 158–9, 163–4, 165
Chekhov, Anton, *Cherry Orchard* 67
Cherry Orchard (1985) 67
Chicago
  as a liability 16
  off-Loop theatre 23
  origins of theatre 19–20, 20–1
  rise of theatre in 22–4
  risk taking 36
  status of 65
  work, opportunities for 49
Chicago Opera Studio/Theatre 50, 52–3
Chicago style 1–2, 4–5, 16–17, 21, 29, 35–6
Christiansen, Richard 21, 47, 59, 70, 84, 96
  on *Aunt Dan and Lemon* 74, 161
  on *Division Street* 60–1
  on *The Good Person of Setzuan* 188
  on *The Government Inspector* 68
  on *The National Health* 43
  on *Strider* 57
  on *Who'll Save the Ploughboy* 22–3
Christmas Carol, A (1984) 61, 66–7
cliff of disbelief 30
Close, Del 36
codeswitching 57–8
Coleman, Janet 25
collaboration 149, 165
  see also directing
Collins, Glenn 179
community-based theatre 21, 22
Compass Theatre 24, 25
Comprehensive Employment and Training Act (CETA) 48
connection 28, 33, 112–13, 185–6
Coons, Nancy 66
Corti, Jim 146, 149, 162

Covici, Pascal 121
critics 25–6, 46–7
Cubism 6–7, 93, 96–7, 98–100, 102, 105

Daley, Richard J. 45
Day in the Life of Joe Egg, A (2001) 42
Debussy, Claude, *Pelleas and Melisande* 80–1
DeLillo, Don, *Valparaiso* 153
Dettmer, Roger 49
Devil's Stocking, The (1984) 77
DeVries, Hilary 4, 7, 16
Dick Gibson Show, The (1977) 53
Dickens, Charles, *A Christmas Carol* 61, 66–7
Dillon, John 8, 41
directing 7–8, 145–7, 149–70
  affirmation and reproof 162–4
  First Audience 153–8
  First Critic 158–60
  First Reader 151–3
  imagery and metaphor 160–2
  not doing 164–6
  reservation of Galati 167–8
  Seussical the Musical 168–70
Dirty Rotten Scoundrels (film, 1988) 175–6
disbelief, cliff of 30
distancing effects 44–5
Division Street (1982) 60, 60–1
Doctorow, E. L., *Ragtime* 81–2 *see also* *Ragtime* (1998)
doing nothing 164–6
Drabinsky, Garth 81–2
Drawer Boy, The (2001) 157
Duras, Marguerite 173–4
  Blue Eyes Black Hair 27
  Man Sitting in the Corridor 174

Earthly Possessions (1991) 184–6
Eckert, Thor Jr. 81
Edson, Margaret, *Wit* 32–3
Elkin, Stanley
  Dick Gibson Show, The 53
  Living End, The 53–4
Emond, Linda 181, *183*
empathy 28
enjoyment 101
ensemble acting 36
ensemble collaboration 149

Epstein, Matthew 83
equation, opening of 5
Erstein, Hap 118
Everyman (1995) 82
extra-ordinary attention 99

failure 36, 115
Falls, Robert 17, 34, 48, 49–50, 70
   In the Belly of the Beast: Letters from Prison (1985) 29–30
   Moonchildren (1975–76) 48
   Mother Courage and Her Children (1981) 31–2, 61
   Night of the Iguana (1994) 193
Faulkner, William, *As I Lay Dying* (1995) 192–4
female characters 147, 172–96
   As I Lay Dying 192–4
   Born Yesterday 174–7, *175*
   Earthly Possessions 184–6
   Glass Menagerie, The 189–92
   Good Person of Setzuan, The 186–9
   Grapes of Wrath, The 179–80
   Marguerite Duras 173–4
   Ragtime 194–5
   She Always Said, Pablo 177–9
   Winter's Tale, The 180–4
   other shows 195–6
Ferber, Edna *see* Kaufman, George S. and Moss Hart
First Audience 153–8
First Critic 158–60
First Reader 151–3
Flaherty, Stephen, *Loving Repeating* 195
Flaherty, Stephen and Lynn Ahrens
   Knoxville (2022) 9–10
   Ragtime (1998) *see Ragtime* (1998)
   Seussical the Musical (2000) 168–70
Forum Theatre 42
Fosdick, Scott 57, 105
framing, theatrical 3, 55, 91–2, 109
Freedman, Samuel G. 67
funding 48

Galati, Frank
   on action 28–9
   the "boy in the red jacket" 199
   career, development of 2, 4, 17, 20, 41, 49–50, 59, 62, 65, 73–4, 84

   chamber theatre 25–8
   and Chicago theatre 1, 4–5, 65
   Cubism and 93, 97, 98, 100, 105
   directing 7–8, 145–7, 149–70
   education and training 5, 19, 24–5, 41, 50, 189
   on failure 115
   on Krause 155
   on landscapes 97
   on Marguerite Duras 173–4
   mother, relationship with 186
   musicals *see* musicals; *Ragtime* (1998)
   opera 50–1, 52–3, 55–6, 77–81, 82–3
   paradoxical qualities 8–9
   perception 3–4
   performances 31, 42–3, 54, 55, 61
   on the person in sentences 26
   on presence 32–3
   reflections on theatre 199–201
   rehearsals 151–60
   reservation of 167–8
   screenplays 53–4
   simplicity of 32, 166
   space, use of 91, 92
   speech at auditions 150
   speeches at rehearsals 151–2, 159, 160, 167, 169–70
   on Stein 100, 101, 109
   on Steppenwolf 73
   teaching 37–8, 150, 155
   theatricality 3, 21, 59
Galati, Frank - productions and works
   Accidental Tourist, The (1989) 54, 184
   Albert Herring (1979) 53
   As I Lay Dying (1995) 192–4
   Aunt Dan and Lemon (1987) 74–5, *75*, 161
   Blue Eyes Black Hair (2003) 27
   Born Yesterday (1987) 174–7, *175*
   Boss (1973) 45–6
   Devil's Stocking, The (1984) 77
   Dick Gibson Show, The (1977) 53
   Division Street (1982) *60*, 60–1
   Drawer Boy, The (2001) 157
   Earthly Possessions (1991) 184–6
   Everyman (1995) 82
   Gertrude Stein: Each One as She May (1995) 82

210 Index

Glass Menagerie, The (1994) 189–92, *190*
Good Person of Setzuan, The (1992) 157–8, 186–9, *187*
Good Soldier Schweik (1979) 53, 55–6
Government Inspector, The (1985) 68, 69–70
Grapes of Wrath, The (1988) *see* Grapes of Wrath, The (1988)
Guilt of Lillian Sloan, The (1986) 77, 78
Heart of a Dog (1985) 61–2
Homebody/Kabul (2003) 195
Knoxville (2022) 9–10
La Traviata (1993) 81
Ladies' Voices (1974) 51–2
Living End, The 53–4
Loving Repeating (2006) 195
M Company 38
Merry Wives of Windsor, The (1978) 52–3
Miss Lonelyhearts (1973) 43–5
Morning Star (1999) 156
Mother of Us All, The (1976) 52
Pale Fire 41
Passion Play (1988) 152
Pelleas and Melisande (1992) 80–1
Postcard from Morocco (1987) 78–9
Ragtime (1998) *see* Ragtime (1998)
Royal Family, The (1999/2002) 195
"Santa Claus Is Really the Gasman" 199
Seussical the Musical (2000) 168–70
She Always Said, Pablo (1987) *see* She Always Said, Pablo (1987)
Strider (1981) 56–9, *58*
Summer and Smoke (1977) 52
Summer and Smoke (1980) 161–2
Three Cuckolds, The (1975) 46
Tosca (1993) 81
Travesties (1981) 54–5
Valparaiso 153
View from the Bridge (1999) 82–3
Visit, The (2001) 9
Voyage of Edgar Allan Poe, The (1990) 79–80
Winter's Tale, The (1990) 180–4
You Can't Take It with You (1986) 71
Galati, Virginia 186
games 24
Garner, Dwight 53

Garner, Stanton B. 108
gender reversal 187–9
Genovese, Mike 58–9
Gerard, Jeremy 191
Gertrude Stein: Each One as She May (1995) 82
Gilroy, Frank D., *Who'll Save the Ploughboy* (1963) 22–3
Glass Menagerie, The (1994) 189–92, *190*
Glengarry Glen Ross (1984) 66
Gluck, Christopher, *Alceste* 79
Gogol, Nikolai, *Government Inspector, The* 68, 69–70
Good Person of Setzuan, The (1992) 157–8, 186–9, *187*
Good Soldier Schweik (1979) 53, 55–6
Goodman Theatre 65–71
    bicentennial season 48–9
    FG at 4, 9, 68
    history 19, 49–50, 65–6, 70–1
    New Theater Company 67
    stage and auditorium 68–9
Goodman Theatre productions
    Christmas Carol, A (1984) 61, 66–7
    Good Person of Setzuan, The (1992) 186–9, *187*
    Government Inspector, The (1985) 68, 69–70
    She Always Said, Pablo (1987) *see* She Always Said, Pablo (1987)
    Winter's Tale, The (1990) 180–4
Gordon, Stuart, *Warp!* (1971) 23
Government Inspector, The (1985) 68, 69–70
Graham, Jory 22
grants 48
Grapes of Wrath, The (1988) 118–39, 179–80
    actualities 121, 123, 128, 136–7
    casting 136–8
    changes 127–8, 131–2
    Cubism and 7, 91, 92, 93
    female characters *179*, 179–80
    final scene 135–9, 180
    flood scene 132–5, *133*
    inter-chapters 121–2
    Jim Casy, murder of 130
    lighting 130, 135
    maternal project 146

multistabilities 119–20, 136–7
music 122, 125, 126
Noah Joad, leaving of 128–30, *129*
opening scene 124–7, 127–8
perceptual shifts 126
script 120–1, 122, 123
sets 32, 122, 126, 128, *129*
things (props) 123–4
Tom Joad, leaving of 130–2
video recordings 139
Grass, George 81
Grass, Günter, *Tin Drum, The* 199
Griswold, Mary 16, 52, 55, 82, 97, 178, 186
Guilt of Lillian Sloan, The (1986) 77, 78

Hall, Peter 30
Harrington, Wendall 155, 162
Harris, Julie 191–2
Harris, Sydney J. 43, 46
Hart, Moss *see* Kaufman, George S. and Moss Hart
Harwood, Ronald, *Dresser, The* 61
Hasek, Jaroslav, *Good Soldier Schweik* 53
Headly, Glenne 31, *175*, 175–6
Healey, Michael, *Drawer Boy, The* 157
Heart of a Dog (1985) 61–2
Henning, Joel 182
Heston, Lila 51
Hill, Holly 30
Hoiby, Richard, *Summer and Smoke* 52, 161–2
Holiday, Judy 176
Holten, Kasper 76
Homebody/Kabul (2003) 195
Hull House 21, 22, 23
Hurlyburly (1984) 15

illusion 92, 100
imagery 160, 161, 162
improvisation 24, 34, 35, 36
In the Belly of the Beast: Letters from Prison (1985) 29–30
Ingram, Kenny 157–8, 188, 189
inter-chapters 121–2
interpretation 5, 25, 37
Iveich, Steve 101

Jacoby, Mark 146, 151–2, 155
Jeff award *see* Joseph Jefferson Award

Johnson, Virgil 49, 79, 181, 182
Jones, B. J. 55, *60*, 70, 163, 186
Jones, Cherry *187*, 187–8, 189
Joseph Jefferson Award 43, 45, 46
journalists 46–7
juxtaposition 97

Kanin, Garson, *Born Yesterday* 174–7, *175*
Kart, Larry 49
Kasden, Lawrence 54
Katz, Leon, *Three Cuckolds, The* 46
Kaufman, George S. and Edna Ferber, *Royal Family, The* 195
Kaufman, George S. and Moss Hart
  Man Who Came to Dinner, The 35
  You Can't Take It with You 71
Kazan, Elia 165
Kennedy, Eugene 176, 177
Kerr, Walter 3
Kinney, Terry 15, 72, 126, 127
Kleinfeld, Lenny, *Warp!* (1971) 23
Knoxville (2022) 9–10
Kogan, Rick 57
Koopman, Constantijn 36
Krainik, Ardis 77, 79, 82
Krause, Alvina 154–5
Kurka, Robert, *Good Soldier Schweik* 53, 55–6
Kushner, Tony, *Homebody/Kabul* 195

La Traviata (1993) 81
Ladies' Voices (1974) 51–2
Landis, Ruth 165
landscapes 97, 111
Lane, Ralph 19–20
Lanzener, Sonja 31
Lavey, Martha
  Aunt Dan and Lemon 74–5, *75*, 161
  and Galati 168
  on risk-taking 36
  Winter's Tale, The 181, 182, *183*
Lee, Charlotte 24
Leggs, Kingsley 166
Leighten, Patricia 98
Lesner, Sam 95–6
Lingson, Jeremy 131
listening 155, 156–7
Living End, The 53–4

Loewith, Jason 4, 152
looking 105
Lorde, Andre 174
Loving Repeating (2006) 195
Lyric Opera 77, 79–83

M Company 38
Macy, William H. 48, 49
Maggio, Michael
    Candide (1977) 49
    career 50, 56, 60, 70–1
    on Galati 156, 162, 163
    Heart of a Dog (1985) 61–2
    Travesties (1981) 54
Mahoney, John 73, 175
Malkovich, John 16, 72
Mamet, David 23, 48, 66
    American Buffalo (1975–76) 48–9
    Cherry Orchard (1985) 67
    Glengarry Glen Ross (1984) 66
Man Who Came to Dinner, The 35
Marsh, Robert C. 53, 78–9
Marshall, Kathleen 169
Marshall, Rob 169
Mason, William 82, 83
maternal projects 8, 145–7, 172, 189
Mays, Bruce 54, 55
McKowen, Scott *190*, 191
McNally, Terence 82
Mencken, H. L. 25–6
Merritt, Michael 16, 31, 53, 66, 96
Merry Wives of Windsor, The (1978) 52–3
metaphors 161
metapicture 91–2
Metcalf, Laurie 35
Meyerhold, Vsevolod 62
Miller, Arthur, *View from the Bridge* 82–3
Miss Lonelyhearts (1973) 43–5
Mitchell, W. J. T. 91, 119
Mohrlein, John 43
Monson, Lex 136
moon-booting 32
Moonchildren (1975–76) 48
Morgan, Heather 48
Morning Star (1999) 156
Morton, Amy 195
Mosher, Gregory 48–9, 61, 65–7
Mother Courage and Her Children (1981) 31–2, 61

Mother of Us All, The (1976) 52
mothers 172, 179–80, 184–6, 191–4
multistabilities 119–20, 136–7
Murphy, Gerald 178
Murphy, Sally 136, 180
Museum of Contemporary Art (MCA) 51
music 38, 113–14, 122, 125, 126
musicals 9–10, 84
    Boss 45
    Candide 49
    Loving Repeating 195
    Ragtime see Ragtime (1998)
    Seussical the Musical 168–70
    Strider 56–9

Nabokov, Vladimir, *Pale Fire* 41
narrative voices 26
National Health, The (1972) 42–3
naturalism 21, 28–30
Neil, William 77–8
    Devil's Stocking, The 77
    Guilt of Lillian Sloan, The 77, 78
New Theater Company 67
New York City 15, 16, 22
Nichols, Peter
    Day in the Life of Joe Egg, A (2001) 42
    National Health, The (1972) 42–3
    Passion Play (1988) 152
Nicolai, Otto, *Merry Wives of Windsor, The* 52–3
Night of the Iguana (1994) 193
Northwestern University 5, 24–5, 37, 41, 50
not doing 164–6
notebooks 68, 110, 161
notes *see* acting notes
Novel Ventures 53
Nussbaum, Susan
    on Galati 155, 164
    She Always Said, Pablo (1987) 103–4, 108, 111–13, *114*, 177, *178*

O'Donnell, Rosy 169
"open the equation" 5
opera 50–1, 52–3, 55–6, 76–81, 82–3
    Alceste 79
    Devil's Stocking, The 77
    Guilt of Lillian Sloan, The 77, 78
    La Traviata 81

Pelleas and Melisande 80–1
Postcard from Morocco 78–9
Tosca 81
View from the Bridge 82–3
Voyage of Edgar Allan Poe, The 79–80
oral interpretation 5, 25, 37
Orphans (1984) 31
Ortmann, Jeff 54
Oscar nominations 54, 184
Ostrander, John 43
Overton, Marcus 52

Page, Tim 78
Pale Fire 41
Paoletti, John 102–3
Passion Play (1988) 152
Patinkin, Sheldon 52
Peal, Mary Beth 161–2
Pearce, Howard 7, 93
Pelleas and Melisande (1992) 80–1
Pelton, Carman 109, 113, *114*, 178
Pendleton, Austin 153
perception 3–4
performance 5, 160
Perry, Jeff 71–2, 128–30, *129*
Petersen, William 29–30
Phillips, Sharon 48
Picasso, Pablo 6, 96, 97, 98, 99, 147
 and Gertrude Stein 177–8
 Gertrude Stein, portrait 177
 She Always Said, Pablo 102, 103, 104, 105–6, *178*, 178
 Woman and Child on the Seashore 113, *114*, 178
Piper's Alley 33–4
play 95, 102
play of actuality 108–9
playful subversion 99
Pogrebin, Robin 169
"popera" 84
pornography 173–4
Postcard from Morocco (1987) 78–9
presence 32–3, 101, 156, 157, 162
production style 30–2
pronunciation 159
props 123–4, 157–8
Puccini, Giacomo, *Tosca* 81
Pullinsi, William 41–2, 43, 45–6

Rabe, David, *Hurlyburly* (1984) 15
Ragtime (1998)
 critique of 163
 Galati address 167
 Galati joins team 82
 notes for 166
 production notebook 161
 rehearsals 146, 159–60
 women in 194–5
realism 28
 see also naturalism
reality 92, 100
Reddin, Keith 70
Reed, Rondi 73, 74, 185, 195
Regan, Molly 185
Regan, Sylvia, *Morning Star* 156
regional theatre 15
rehearsals 146, 151–60
Reinking, Ann 9
Rich, Frank
 on *Aunt Dan and Lemon* (1987) 74
 on *In the Belly of the Beast: Letters from Prison* (1985) 29
 on *Earthly Possessions* (1991) 185
 on *The Grapes of Wrath* (1988) 118, 131, 137–8
 on Steppenwolf 73
 on *The Winter's Tale* (1990) 181, 182
Richards, David 29, 102
Rigdon, Kevin 30–1, 32, 33, 122, 130
risk taking 36
Roach, Joseph 3
Robertson, Barbara *58*, 58, 154, 156–7
Rodenbeck, Judith 177
Roven, Bob 46
Royal Family, The (1999/2002) 195
Royko, Mike, *Boss* 45
Russo, Larry
 on Galati 149, 162
 She Always Said, Pablo (1987) 101, 104, 105–6, *114*, 178, *178*

Sahlins, Bernard 36, 47
Saldivar, Norma 149
"Santa Claus Is Really the Gasman" 199
Sarich, Christina 164
Schneider, Alan 22
Schor, Mira 96
Scott, Steve 95, 96, 111, 167

screenplays 53–4
scripts 6, 123
Second City 19, 24, 34–5
Sellars, Peter 65
Selznick, Daniel 1, 81
sentences, person in 26
sets 32, 43, 57, 102–3, 122
Seussical the Musical (2000) 168–70
Shakespeare, William, *Winter's Tale, The* 180–4
Shapiro, Anna 157
Shawn, Wallace, *Aunt Dan and Lemon* 74–5, *75*, 161
She Always Said, Pablo (1987) 6, 7, 91, 92, 95–7, 100, 101–15, 177–9
   Alice B. Toklas, character in 106–9, *107*, 113, *114*
   buffoonery, spirit of 110–11
   controversy 110
   Cubism and 96–7
   female characters 177–9, *178*
   Gertrude Stein, character in 102, 103–4, 108, 110, 111–13, 177
   landscapes 111
   Pablo Picasso, character in 102, 103, 104, 105–6, 113
   rehearsals 162, 164
   staging 101–6
   Woman in White tableau 113–15, *114*, 178
Shepard, Sam, *True West* (1983) 16
Shepherd, David 25
Shiflett, Rev. Jim 23–4
Shillinglaw, Susan 121–2, 122–3
Shiner, David 169
Sickinger, Robert 22–3
Sills, Paul 23, 24
simplicity 30–2, 166
Simpson, Louis 151
Singer, Sandra 51
Sinise, Gary
   Balm in Gilead 72
   Grapes of Wrath, The 120, 126–7, *129*, 131
   and Steppenwolf 71
   True West 16
Slavin, L. J. 125, 126
Sloan, Larry 66–7
Sloan, Lillian 77

Smith, Lois 131–2, 134, 149, *179*, 179–80, 195
Smith, Michael 122
Smith, Sid 29, 61, 185
Solari, Fred 56
Solomon, Alisa 119
songs 113–14
space 91–3
spectacle 2–3
Spolin, Viola 21, 24
St. Nicholas Theatre 48
stage position 35
stagecraft 6
Stahl, Les 57
States, Bert O. 2, 3–4
Stein, Gertrude
   language of 51–2, 98, 99, 100, 101, 109
   Loving Repeating 195–6
   Mother of Us All, The 52, 109
   and Picasso 177–8
   plays as landscapes 97, 111
   portrait by Picasso 177
   She Always Said, Pablo 6, 102, 103–4, 108, 110, 111–13, 177, 178, *178*
   Three Lives 82
Steinbeck, Elaine 179
Steinbeck, John, *Grapes of Wrath, The see Grapes of Wrath, The* (1988)
Steppenwolf 71–5
   and the audience 15–16
   early work 49
   ensemble 71, 72–3
   Halsted Street theatre 33
   and New York City 16
   production style 30–1
Steppenwolf productions
   As I Lay Dying (1995) 192–4
   Aunt Dan and Lemon (1987) 74–5, *75*, 161
   Balm in Gilead (1980) 71–2
   Born Yesterday (1987) 174–7, *175*
   Drawer Boy, The (2001) 157
   Earthly Possessions (1991) 184–6
   Everyman (1995) 82
   Grapes of Wrath, The (1988) 118–39, 179–80
   Royal Family, The (1999/2002) 195
   You Can't Take It with You (1986) 71

Stone, Alan 52
Stoppard, Tom, *Travesties* 54–5
Strider (1981) 56–9, *58*
student projects 27
subversion 99
Summer and Smoke (1977) 52
Summer and Smoke (1980) 161–2
Summer Comedy Theatre 49
Sutcliffe, Tom 76–7
Sweeney, Louise 96
Syse, Glenna 47, 68, 69, 74

table work 152–3
Tapp, Martha 153–4
Tesich, Steven, *Division Street 60*, 60–1
theatre games 24
theatre space 91–3
theatres 33–4, 68–9
theatrical framing *see* framing, theatrical
theatricality 2–3, 21, 59
Thebus, Jessica 27, 173
Thomson, Virgil and Gertrude Stein,
    Mother of Us All, The 52
Three Cuckolds, The (1975) 46
Tillman, Helen 54
Toklas, Alice B. 106–9, *107*, 110, 111, 113,
    114, 178, 195–6
Tolstoy, Leo, *Strider* 56–9
Tosca (1993) 81
Travesties (1981) 54–5
Traviata (1993) 81
True West (1983) 16
Tyler, Anne 184, 185–6
    Accidental Tourist, The 54, 184
    Earthly Possessions 184–6

understanding 101
University of South Florida (USF)
    37–8

Valparaiso 153
Vegetti Finzi, Silvia 145, 164, 180, 183

Velázquez, Diego, *Las Meninas* 92
Verdi, Giuseppe, *La Traviata* 81
View from the Bridge (1999) 82–3
Visit, The (2001) 9
visual codeswitching 57–8
Von Rhein, John 55–6, 78, 79, 80, 81
Voyage of Edgar Allan Poe, The (1990)
    79–80

Wardle, Irving 29
Warp! (1971) 23
watching 158–60
Watergate 176–7
Watts, Linda 97–8, 99
Weiss, Hedy 74, 193
Weller, Michael, *Moonchildren* 48
West, Nathaniel, *Miss Lonelyhearts* (1973)
    43–5
Wetzsteon, Ross 20, 34
Whitney, Anne 152
Who'll Save the Ploughboy (1963) 22–3
Williams, Albert 19, 22
Williams, Tennessee
    Glass Menagerie, The 189–92, *190*
    Night of the Iguana 193
    Summer and Smoke 52, 161–2
Willis, Thomas 52
Wilson, Langford, *Balm in Gilead* 71–2
Winer, Linda 16, 24, 43, 44, 118
Winter's Tale, The (1990) 180–4
Wisdom Bridge Theatre 29, 54–5
Wit (1998) 32–3
women *see* female characters
Woodman, William 65
Woodstock, Illinois 56

You Can't Take It with You (1986) 71
Youhn, Xenia 57, 61

Zacek, Dennis 47
Zelnis, Ed 110
Zimmerman, Mary 173